Hot Topics for MRCGP
and
General Practitioners
3rd Edition

Louise R Newson
BSc (Hons) MBChB (Hons) MRCP MRCGP
General Practitioner
West Midlands

Ash M Patel
MBChB MRCGP DRCOG DFFP
General Practitioner
Cheshire

Rupal Shah
MBBS (Hons) MRCGP DRCOG
General Practitioner
London

PASTEST
Dedicated to your success

© 2004 PASTEST Ltd
Egerton Court
Parkgate Estate
Knutsford
Cheshire
WA16 8DX
Telephone: 01565 752000

First edition 2001
Second edition 2002
Third edition 2004

ISBN 1 904627 18 8

A catalogue record for this book is available from the British Library. The information contained within this book was obtained by the authors from reliable sources. However, while every effort has been made to ensure its accuracy, no responsibilty for loss, damage or injury occasioned to any person acting or refraining from action as a result of information contained herein can be accepted by the publishers or authors.

PasTest Revision Books and Intensive Courses

PasTest has been established in the field of postgraduate medical education since 1972, providing revision books and intensive study courses for doctors preparing for their professional examinations.
Books and courses are available for the following specialties:
MRCGP, MRCP Part 1 and Part 2, MRCPCH Part 1 and Part 2, MRCS, MRCOG, DRCOG, MRCPsych, DCH, FRCA and PLAB.

For further details contact:
**PasTest, Knutsford, Cheshire WA16 8DX
Tel: 01565 752000   Fax: 01565 650264
Email: enquiries@pastest.co.uk
Web site: www.pastest.co.uk**

Typeset by Breeze Ltd, Manchester.
Printed and bound in the UK by MPG Books Ltd, Bodmin, Cornwall

Contents

The Polypill
Hypertension
Hyperlipidaemia
Diabetes mellitus
Obesity
Coronary heart disease – other risk factors
The Coronary Heart Disease National Service Framework
Heart failure
Atrial fibrillation
Risk of stroke in non-rheumatic atrial fibrillation
Stroke

Asthma
Chronic obstructive pulmonary disease (COPD)
Smoking cessation
Influenza

Mental Health National Service Framework
Depression
Postnatal depression
Schizophrenia
The new antipsychotic drugs
Eating disorders
Alcohol
Drug misuse
Counselling

Foreword

Awareness of the current best evidence is essential for providing effective clinical care. However, the ever-increasing volume of studies makes it impossible to keep abreast without some form of summary. This excellent book provides clear and concise summaries of the present state of knowledge for a variety of areas that are of importance and relevance to primary care.

It is essential reading for registrars who wish to prepare for the MRCGP examination, and it will also appeal to all doctors who want to quickly get to grips with the evidence base of primary care.

I am delighted to recommend this book by Louise, Ash and Rupal. Can you manage without it?

John Sandars
General Practitioner, MRCGP Examiner and Lecturer, School of Primary Care and Evidence for Population Health Unit, The University of Manchester.

February 2004

Acknowledgements

We would like to thank our families, especially Paul, Priti and Alistair, for all their patience, support and tolerance over the past months. We would also like to thank John Sandars for all his advice and encouragement in developing this book. Finally, we thank the PasTest Publishing Department, as without their help and guidance we would have never been able to create it.

The chapter on Prostate Cancer is written by Paul CB Anderson BSc(Hons) MBChB(Hons) MRCS, Specialist Registrar in Urology, West Midlands.

The section on Osteoarthritis is written by AJ Tindall MRCS (Eng.) Specialist Registrar in Orthopaedics, SE Thames.

Introduction

Following the success of the first and second editions of the book, we have updated and revised it to produce this edition. We have also added some new chapters on important and topical subjects.

The MRCGP exam seems a long way off at the beginning of the Registrar year, but unfortunately it soon comes round! The amount of information required to work as a general practitioner and to pass the exam can appear to be completely daunting and overwhelming.

When Ash and Louise were preparing for the MRCGP exam in Summer 2000, they were disappointed to find a relative paucity of books and courses to help with 'hot topic' revision. They and other members of their VTS group spent numerous laborious hours trawling through and summarising back issues of the *BMJ* and *Br J Gen Pract*, hoping it would help with their revision, but they found it quite a fruitless exercise. It is also sometimes difficult to prioritise and become familiar with the more important, well-researched papers on a topic.

This book has been designed to help you improve your breadth and depth of knowledge of various important clinical and non-clinical subjects. Medicine is a dynamic specialty and information is constantly being updated and theories altered as more research is performed and attitudes of both doctors and patients change.

It is impossible to predict topics for future exams successfully, and for that reason the subjects covered in this book will be as relevant as possible to present and future general practice. This book is not meant to be a comprehensive revision course for the exam; it is written to provide some guidance and ideas upon which to base your revision. It will also hopefully save you some time by reducing the need for reading and summarising all the journals.

Each of the hot topics is presented as a broad overview with reference to recent literature. References, useful reading material and relevant websites are also included for each topic.

The reviews of various key 'hot topics' are important for both the exam and future careers in general practice. The book is also very useful for established GPs who would like a review of the current literature on a wide variety of topics.

Why bother with Hot Topics?

There are questions in Paper 1 (the written paper) specifically designed to test candidates' knowledge and interpretation of general practice literature. Candidates are expected to be familiar with items in the medical literature that have influenced current thinking in general practice. Paper 2 (the MCQs) has questions based on articles and reviews printed over the last eighteen months. The viva also concentrates on topics that require an awareness of the recent literature.

In addition, good GPs use evidence-based medicine as a starting point and are able to apply it to meet the needs and circumstances of an individual patient, and to reach a joint decision with the patient. A 'patient-centred' approach is a highly desirable quality for the MRCGP exam and for future practice.

Myths about Hot Topics for the exam

You need to know everything
Although the amount of information you are expected to know may feel insurmountable, it is important to remember that it is impossible to know everything, the examiners certainly don't! There is no shame, and indeed much credit, in knowing your own and your professional limitations. Too much pride or arrogance can actually be off-putting to the examiners.

You need to be able to quote papers to pass the exam
Candidates are not expected to be able to quote individual references of articles. It is more important, for example, to know that there are many papers with different results regarding the antibiotic treatment of sore throats rather than to know only one paper and its design faults in detail.

If you know a key paper was printed recently in the *BMJ*, for example, then it is worth stating. However, it is worse to misquote a reference or quote a reference in the wrong context than to not quote at all! The College states that inaccurate or incomplete references will not be penalised but misleading ones will.

Hot Topics are the most important part of revision for the exam

Recently, more emphasis has been placed on candidates' awareness of current issues for the exam, especially as evidence-based medicine is becoming a very important part of clinical practice.

However, the examiners are actually more interested in ensuring that candidates are broad-minded, patient-centred and can consider problems in general practice from many different perspectives and be able to think about social, ethical, political and cultural factors. It is the application of any knowledge obtained rather than the knowledge itself which is important for both the exam and working in general practice.

Although $3^1/_2$ hours seems a long time for the written paper, the exam passes quickly with very little spare time. If candidates spend too much time on Hot Topics or current literature in their answers this may be detrimental because it leaves less time to spend on other very relevant issues. For example, when considering an answer about the optimal management of a newly diagnosed diabetic patient, the impact this diagnosis may have on both the patient and their family is equally as important as discussing various trials regarding target glycosylated haemoglobin levels.

Useful reading material for 'Hot Topics' revision

There are a large number of revision books for the exam and a huge number of books about general practice. Your trainer and VTS scheme will be able to advise you about these.

It is generally advised that candidates should be up-to-date with the past 18 months of the literature. However, it is worth bearing in mind that there are many older studies which still influence general practice. The main journals to read are the *British Medical Journal* and the *British Journal of General Practice*, as exam questions are usually set from these and also they are the journals that examiners usually read! The *Drug and Therapeutics Bulletin* is a useful journal as it provides unbiased reviews. The new *Clinical Evidence* book, produced every six months by the *BMJ* is a useful reference source for evidence-based medicine.

The free weekly newspapers – *GP*, *Pulse* and *Doctor* – contain very useful relevant discussion material, both clinical and non-clinical. *Update* also produces some very relevant articles and includes self-assessment exercises every month, which consist of MCQs, Modified Essay Questions, Short Answer Questions and a Critical Reading Exercise. These can be very useful for discussing with your trainer or in your study groups.

It is preferable to try to read some journals on a regular basis rather than trying to cram everything in the month before the exam. This not only makes last-minute revision less stressful but it also means that some of the knowledge can be used during your clinical practice.

KEY POINTS

✓ Do not panic!
✓ You do not have to know everything
✓ Try to read journals regularly
✓ Use evidence-based medicine in your practice

 ## USEFUL JOURNALS/PUBLICATIONS

✓ *British Medical Journal (BMJ)*
✓ *British Journal of General Practice (Br J Gen Pract)*: evidence-based medicine
✓ *GP/Doctor/Pulse*
✓ *Update*
✓ *Drug and Therapeutics Bulletin (Drug Ther Bull)*

Chapter 1:

Cardiovascular Diseases

Chapter 1: Cardiovascular Disease

The prevention of coronary heart disease (CHD) is one of the most important tasks for general practice. CHD remains the principal cause of death in the UK (half the population of the UK will be killed or disabled by an MI, CVA or other cardiovascular event) and one-fifth of these deaths occur below retirement age. The main risk factors are smoking, hypertension, hyperlipidaemia, diabetes, obesity and social deprivation. These will all be discussed within this chapter.

The medical priority is to focus on those who are at highest risk of CHD. The first priority is secondary prevention for patients with established CHD. The second priority is primary prevention for people at high risk of developing CHD: ie those with an absolute CHD risk ≥15% over 10 years, as calculated using the Joint British Society's coronary risk-prediction charts.

The Polypill

It has recently been proposed by professors of epidemiology from the University of London that a pill with six ingredients could prevent 80% of heart attacks (or other events caused by IHD) and strokes (*BMJ 2003;326:1419–22*). They suggest that everyone over 55, or younger if they have established cardiovascular disease, would benefit from taking the pill; whose ingredients would include a thiazide, a statin, an ACE inhibitor, aspirin, folic acid and a β-blocker (the blood pressure lowering agents would be at half the standard dose). The authors derived their evidence from analysing over 750 trials, with 400,000 participants. They conclude that routine screening and follow-up would be unnecessary, due to the excellent safety profile of these drugs, and that cost would not be prohibitive since these drugs are either already or about to be off-patent.

Of course, there has been much controversy generated by the polypill. There have been arguments about whether we as doctors are trying to medicalise the whole population, and about the ethics of treating well people. There have also been concerns about whether these drugs are actually as safe as the authors claim; it is well known for example, that ACE inhibitors can cause renal impairment in patients with renal artery stenosis, that aspirin causes gastric bleeds and that β-blockers are contraindicated in asthma.

The polypill is mentioned at the beginning of the cardiovascular chapter because if it was to be introduced much of what follows will become redundant!

Hypertension

Hypertension has been defined by the World Health Organisation (in 1993) as the blood pressure above which intervention has been shown to reduce risk. Hypertension is a very common but poorly managed condition. Some 50% of hypertensives are undetected, 50% of those detected are not treated and 50% of those treated are not adequately controlled! Up to 20% of the adult population in the Western world is hypertensive.

Hypertension treatment decreases the risk of fatal and non-fatal stroke, cardiac events and death. It may also actually improve quality of life. People at a greater cardiovascular risk when they start treatment, such as elderly patients with other risk factors, derive the most absolute benefit from drug treatment.

How much should BP be lowered by?

A very large, randomised controlled trial, the Hypertension Optimal Treatment Trial (HOT), looked at outcomes in terms of major cardio-vascular disease (CVD) events (*Lancet 1998;351:1755–62*). The British Hypertension Society (BHS) guidelines (see later) are based on this study. This study showed that the lowest incidence of CVD events occurred at a mean diastolic blood pressure of 82.6 mmHg and the lowest CVD mortality at 86.5 mmHg. An even lower diastolic blood pressure was found to be beneficial in diabetics (optimal 80 mmHg).

The HOT study is the only study that has set out to evaluate optimal target BP levels and they reported an optimal pressure of 139/83 mmHg. This study also showed a 15% reduction in major CVD events and a 36% reduction in non-fatal myocardial infarction (MI) for patients on aspirin. The benefit of aspirin for primary prevention had been controversial before this study.

What is the best drug regime to treat hypertension?

It is still unclear whether the benefits of specific antihypertensive drugs come from their direct effects on raised blood pressure or from various other indirect actions.

The LIFE (Lorsartan Intervention For Endpoint reduction in hypertension) study (*Lancet 2002;359:1004*) looked at 10,000 patients with hypertension and LVH. It concluded that there was less cardiovascular morbidity (ie MIs) and mortality, fewer strokes and fewer new-onset diabetes in patients treated with losartan compared with atenolol, despite BP being lowered by the same amount; however, the differences were small (the absolute risk reduction was 2%, with an NNT of 56 over 4.5 years).

The recent ALLHAT (Antihypertensive and Lipid Lowering to prevent Heart Attack Trial) study (*JAMA 2002;288:281*) is the largest ever hypertension trial, involving 42,000 patients, one-third of whom were Afro-Caribbean. All participants were over 55 with hypertension and one other risk factor. They were randomised to treatment with an ACE inhibitor (lisinopril), an alpha blocker (doxazosin), a Ca-channel blocker (amlodipine) or a thiazide (chlortalidone). Interestingly, the doxazosin arm of the trial was stopped early, due to an excessive number of deaths from cardiac failure. The primary outcome was death or non-fatal MI and there no difference was seen in the three arms of the trial over 10 years of follow-up. Chlortalidone was more effective at lowering blood pressure and at preventing CVA and heart failure than the other drugs. There was no evidence of impaired glucose tolerance with its use and it was equally effective in diabetics. Critics of the trial have complained that it is well known that Afro-Caribbeans do not respond well to ACE inhibition and that this was not taken into account when interpreting the results. However, there is mounting evidence in favour of using diuretics. The *BMJ* was certainly very clear in a filler published in 2003 (327:7413): it concluded that 'Diuretics – the least expensive and most effective agents – should be the first-line treatment for almost everyone with hypertension, including people with diabetes and asymptomatic LVH'.

In the HOPE study (Heart Outcomes Prevention Evaluation), patients at high risk of cardiovascular events were given the ACE inhibitor ramipril (*New Engl J Med 2000;342:145–53*). This resulted in a 22% reduction in the combined endpoint of cardiovascular death, non-fatal myocardial infarction and stroke. These benefits were similar in normotensive and hypertensive patients. From this it could therefore be argued that all patients at a high risk of CHD should receive ramipril! The HOPE study is mentioned again, in the diabetes and CVA chapters.

Several large, multicentre trials have established the value of angiotensin-II receptor blockers (ARBs) in renoprotection in type 2 diabetes (*New Engl J Med 2001;345:851, 861, 870*). It therefore seems logical that the treatment of patients with type 2 diabetes, hypertension and nephropathy should begin with ARBs or angiotensin-converting enzyme inhibitors (ACEIs).

It is generally accepted that best practice is to choose therapeutic agents likely to do more good than harm, given each patient's social circumstances, preferences, coexisting medical conditions and risk factors. This is also likely to improve compliance. The evidence is that giving low-dose anti-hypertensives in combination is more effective and produces fewer side-effects than a single drug at high dose (meta-analysis of 354 trials. *BMJ 2003;326:1427–31*).

A recent draft ruling from NICE has concluded that there is no evidence to support the first-line use of ACE inhibitors or calcium channel blockers. This opposes the advice from the British Hypertension Society, who recommend an ABCD approach, whereby to select the first-line anti-hypertensive acording to the pateint's age and ethnic group. The ABCD rules recommend an ACE inhibitor, ARB or β-blocker first-line in non-black pateints under 55 years and a calcium channel blocker or diuretic as the first-line choice in non-black over 55s and black patients of any age.

What is the evidence for treating hypertension in the elderly?

In the past decade, several landmark trials have helped to firmly establish the value and importance of treating hypertension in the elderly. The STOP-2 (Swedish Trial in Old Patients-2) study compared treatment with beta-blockers or thiazide diuretics with ACE inhibitors or calcium-channel blockers in patients aged 70-84 years (*Lancet 1999;354:1751*). The findings were that blood pressure was decreased similarly in all treatment groups and that old and new drugs were similar in preventing cardiovascular mortality or major events.

Isolated systolic hypertension affects about half of people aged over 60, and 75% of those aged over 75. It confers a significant cardiovascular risk; pulse pressure is a better predictor of risk than systolic or diastolic blood pressure alone in patients over 50 (*Hypertension 1999; 34:372–4*). It is therefore important to treat isolated systolic hypertension, although GP's have traditionally been reluctant to do so.

 British Hypertension Society (BHS) Guidelines
(*BMJ 1999;319:630*)

These are evidence-based guidelines, which aim to present the best currently available evidence on hypertension management. They recommend starting treatment on the basis of risk rather than blood pressure for patients with borderline hypertension. They are largely based on the HOT trial and may need to be updated soon.

Important points

- All adults should have their BP checked every five years, or every year if it's borderline
- All patients should receive non-pharmacological advice
- Initiate treatment if SBP > 160 or DBP > 100 mmHg
- Consider treatment in borderline patients (SBP 140–160, DBP 90–100) if target organ damage/diabetes/10-year coronary risk > 15%
- Choice of drug should be tailored to patient, eg ACEI for LVF, ß-blockers for ischaemic heart disease (IHD)
- Aspirin should be considered if 10-year CVD risk > 15%
- Statins should be considered if 10-year CVD risk > 30%
- Drug treatment is of proven value until age 80 years; over this, the decision to treat should be based on biological age

Note:

The 10-year coronary heart disease risk is estimated using the risk chart issued by the Joint British Societies in their recommendations for coronary heart disease prevention (*Heart 1998;119:329–35*).

Good points of guidelines

They are clear, concise and based on good evidence. They aim to address the incomplete detection, treatment and control of hypertension prevalent across all sections of the community. The emphasis on the assessment and reduction of cardiovascular risk rather than just the maintenance of an optimal blood pressure is to be welcomed.

Problems with these guidelines

Some of the treatment recommendations are based on consensus rather than evidence.

The resource implications are huge for GPs as the guidelines will result in a far greater proportion of patients needing treatment, monitoring and close follow-up.

It has been estimated that an average GP will have 272 patients under 75 years of age who would be eligible for treatment, which could mean a potential extra four hours of work a week to devote to their ongoing management!

It is worth noting that new guidelines were recently proposed at the European Society of Cardiology Annual Congress in September 2003. These guidelines have introduced a new multifactorial risk model – the SCORE model, based on European data as opposed to the Framingham data. They aim to cover atherosclerotic disease as a whole, rather than just focusing on CHD. Blood pressure targets have been tightened to < 130/80 for patients with cardiovascular disease or diabetes.

What are the risk tables – and are they any good?

They are based on the Framingham data, which came from a 10-year follow-up of 5000 patients in North America. The risk equations from the Framingham data have been shown to be reasonably accurate when applied to other populations in northern Europe and the USA – but they have been criticised for not including other cardiovascular risk factors (such as family history, sedentary lifestyle and obesity). They can underestimate risk in:

✓ Ethnic minorities such as South Asians and Afro-Caribbeans who have a high incidence of end-organ damage

✓ People with a family history of cardiovascular disease

✓ People with impaired glucose tolerance, and probably in diabetics

✓ Obese, sedentary patients

✓ Patients who come from socially deprived backgrounds; deprivation appears to be an independent risk factor for CHD

With the exception of these particular groups, it may be that in general, use of the Framington data actually leads to an overestimation of risk of death from CHD and risk of fatal and non-fatal events (*BMJ 2003; 327:1238–9*)

Note:
Patients should still be considered to be smokers for five years after giving up. If a patient's BP has been well controlled on anti-hypertensives for 5 years, the BP on treatment can be used in risk calculation. Otherwise, the pre-treatment value should be used.

These tables can only be used in primary prevention; patients who have already suffered from a cardiovascular event are automatically at high risk, as are patients with familial hyperlipidaemia.

There are three main tables: The New Zealand, Sheffield and Joint British Societies. These take absolute rather than relative risk into consideration, which is far more relevant to individual patients. In addition, a simple new scoring system for calculating a patient's risk of death from CVD is now available which can help clinicians decide whether to start patients on antihypertensive treatment (*BMJ 2001;323:75–81*). There are likely to be alternatives to the Framingham data in the future, such as the Score model mentioned above, based on European data.

How do the different risk tables compare?

Both the Joint British Societies chart and the Sheffield table are compatible with UK guidelines. However, a study in primary care found that although the Sheffield table correctly identified slightly more people who were at high risk compared with the Joint British Societies chart, it also falsely labelled more low-risk people as being at high risk. Overall, this study concluded that the Joint British Societies chart has the best balance of accuracy (*Heart 2001;85:37–43*). A study in the BMJ showed that GPs and nurses both find the Joint British chart easier to use than the Sheffield table (*BMJ 2000;320:690–1*).

How easy is it to measure cardiovascular risk for patients?

Accurate estimation of cardiovascular risk without the use of explicit risk charts or computer-based clinical decision support systems is not easy. Health professionals find it difficult to assimilate multiple risk factors into an accurate assessment of cardiovascular risk (*BMJ 2000;320:686–90*).

How can risk information be given to patients?

Results of a study from a surgery in London have shown that patient decisions regarding medication are strongly affected by the way information is explained to them (*Br J Gen Pract 2001;51:276–9*). A questionnaire was sent to patients asking their likelihood of accepting treatment for a chronic condition on the basis of relative-risk reduction, absolute-risk reduction, number needed to treat and personal probability of benefit. The results varied from 44% stating they would accept treatment with a personal probability of benefit model, to 92% stating they would accept treatment using a relative-risk reduction model. In general, absolute risk reductions should be used rather than relative risk when discussing treatment options with patients.

What should we use to measure blood pressure?

GPs should not make decisions about treating patients with hypertension based solely on high readings of blood pressure taken by doctors, according to a recent study (*BMJ 2002; 325:254–7*). This study concluded that measurements taken by the patient or a nurse helped to counteract the negative 'white coat' effect, as measurements taken by a GP were considerably higher. However, we should remember that all the major trials that influence our practice today have used BP measurements from the clinic setting.

Accurate measurement of blood pressure in patients is of paramount importance. For example, consistently underestimating the diastolic pressure by 5 mmHg could result in almost two-thirds of hypertensive individuals being denied potentially life-saving and certainly morbidity-preventing treatment (*Can Med Assoc J 1999;161:277–8*). Consistently overestimating it by 5 mmHg could more than double the number of individuals diagnosed as hypertensive (half of whom would be inappropriately labelled and treated).

In Sweden and The Netherlands the use of mercury is no longer permitted in hospitals. In the United Kingdom the move to ban mercury has not been received with enthusiasm because we do not have an accurate alternative to the mercury sphygmomanometer (*BMJ 2000;320:815*). Aneroid devices can be extremely inaccurate and automated devices vary enormously.

Another problem is one highlighted in a survey of 1500 sphygmomanometers, which revealed that 20% were 'appreciably inaccurate' and 2% were 'very seriously inaccurate' (*J Hum Hypertens 2001;15:587–91*). None of the 240 general practices surveyed had arrangements for regular checks and calibrations of their sphygmomanometers.

Are patients being overtreated?

An old study by Fry in 1979 demonstrated that one in three patients with hypertension became normotensive with time. This has been confirmed in a study that found 20% of well-controlled hypertensives could have their medication reduced without problems (*Br J Gen Pract 1999; 49:977–80*).

One recent study has managed to identify simple long-term predictors of maintenance of normal blood pressure after withdrawal of anti-hypertensive medication (*BMJ 2002; 325:815–17*). Patients who were younger (65–74 years), had relatively low on-treatment systolic pressures and minimal drug treatment were more likely to respond well to a trial of withdrawal of treatment; 40% remained normotensive a year after stopping.

The overall conclusion regarding treatment choice is that it is the level of blood pressure that counts, not the drug used to treat it. It is sensible to prescribe the medication most likely to suit the patient's past medical history and, probably more importantly, to choose a medication that is less likely to cause side-effects, so improving compliance.

USEFUL WEBSITES

www.hyp.ac.uk/bhs – British Hypertension Society
(Includes copies of CVD risk charts)
www.bhf.org.uk – British Heart Foundation
www.eshonline.org – European Society of Hypertension

ROUTINE INVESTIGATIONS FOR HYPERTENSION

✓ Urine dipstix for blood/protein
✓ Urea and creatinine
✓ Blood glucose
✓ Serum total:HDL cholesterol ratio
✓ 12-lead ECG

SUMMARY POINTS FOR HYPERTENSION

✓ Hypertension is underdiagnosed
✓ BHS guidelines have huge resource implications
✓ Familiarise yourself with risk tables
✓ Risk is very difficult to explain to patients
✓ Consider statins and aspirin
✓ BP targets are lower for diabetics
✓ Some patients are actually overtreated

Hyperlipidaemia

What are the benefits of lowering cholesterol?

There is overwhelming evidence that statins are highly beneficial in both the primary and secondary prevention of CHD.

There is no longer any doubt that treatment benefits those who are at substantial coronary risk. An updated meta-analysis (*BMJ 2000; 321:971–2*) shows that drugs which lower lipid concentrations prevent nearly one-third of myocardial infarctions and coronary deaths. However, many people who could substantially benefit from statins are not receiving them, perhaps due to a lack of understanding by physicians or to poor organisation (*BMJ 2000;321:971–2*). A recent study has found that patients with established CHD were much less likely to be on statins if they were older, smoked or had a history of angina (*Heart 2002;88:15–19*).

Not enough patients at high risk of CHD are receiving statins. In addition, target cholesterol concentrations are achieved in less than 50% of patients receiving treatment. Treating all patients with a 10-year CHD risk of 15% would, in effect, mean statin treatment for about one-quarter of the UK's adult population – which is clearly not achievable with current NHS funding!

Certain groups of people are at higher risk of developing CHD and need to be given special consideration. These include:

✓ Patients with diabetes mellitus (risk of developing and dying from CHD is 2–5 times higher than non-diabetics)

✓ Patients of South-Asian descent (typically have a 40% greater risk of developing CHD)

✓ Patients with familial hypercholesterolaemia (particularly high risk of dying from CHD); the risk tables cannot be used for this group

The NNT (Number Needed to Treat) with statins for secondary prevention of death over five years is 16: ie 16 patients have to take a statin for five years to prevent one death. NNT for primary prevention is 69.

For the primary and secondary prevention of CHD, statin treatment should be adjusted to lower the serum total cholesterol concentrations to below 5 mmol/l or by 20–30% (or LDL-cholesterol concentrations to below 3 mmol/l or by 30%), whichever results in the lower concentration. However, these targets may imminently be changed; in their 2003 annual congress, the European Society of Cardiology proposed new targets of total cholesterol (TC) < 4.5 mmol/l and LDL-cholesterol < 2.5 mmol/l for patients with established atherosclerotic disease or diabetes.

Primary Prevention Trials

There are some key trials supporting the use of statins.

The West of Scotland Coronary Prevention Study (WOSCOPS)
(J. Shepherd, et al. New Engl J Med 1995;333:1301–7)

Randomised controlled trial involving 6,595 men (many of whom were smokers) aged 45–64 years with high cholesterol levels (average 7.0 mmol/l) and no previous history of myocardial infarction (MI). They received either placebo or pravastatin and were followed up for five years.

Pravastatin was found to reduce the risk of:
- ✓ First heart attack or coronary death by 31%
- ✓ Non-fatal heart attack by 31%
- ✓ Cardiovascular death by 32%
- ✓ Death from any cause by 22%
- ✓ Revascularisation procedures by 37%

The Air Force/Texas Coronary Atherosclerosis Prevention Study
(J. R. Downs, et al. JAMA 1998;279:1615–22)

Randomised, double-blinded trial involving 5608 men and 997 women with average cholesterol levels of 5.71 mmol/l and no previous history of cardiovascular disease. They received either placebo or lovastatin and average follow-up was for 5.2 years.

Lovastatin was found to reduce the risk of:
- ✓ First acute major coronary event by 37%
- ✓ Incidence of CHD by 40%
- ✓ Revascularisation procedures by 33%

Both these studies illustrate that lipid levels alone (except for those with familial disease resulting in extremely high levels) are relatively weak individual predictors of cardiovascular risk.

Secondary Prevention Trials

 The Simvastatin Survival Study (4S)

(*Study Group, Lancet 1994;344:1383–9*)

This was the first landmark trial of LDL-cholesterol lowering with statins for the secondary prevention of CHD. It was a randomised, controlled, double-blinded trial involving 4444 men and women aged 35–69 years and from 94 centres in Denmark, Finland, Norway and Sweden. Patients were randomised to take placebo or simvastatin. All patients had a history of myocardial infarction and/or angina and mild to moderately high total cholesterol levels of 5.8–8.0 mmol/l. The patients were followed up for a mean of 5.4 years.

Simvastatin was found to reduce the risk of:
- ✓ Death by 30%
- ✓ Coronary death by 42%
- ✓ Major coronary events by 34%
- ✓ Revascularisation procedures by 37%

 Cholesterol and Recurrent Events (CARE)

(*F. M. Sacks, et al. New Engl J Med 1996;335:1001–9*)

Another randomised controlled trial of 4159 men and women aged 21–75 years, all of whom had suffered a heart attack in the previous two years and had an average total cholesterol of 5.4 mmol/l. Patients were randomised to receive either pravastatin or placebo and were followed up for five years.

This trial was especially important as it showed the value of cholesterol reduction in patients with what was previously considered to be a 'normal cholesterol'.

Pravastatin was found to reduce the risk of:
- ✓ CHD death/non-fatal MI by 24%
- ✓ CHD death by 19%
- ✓ Fatal MI by 37%
- ✓ Stroke by 28%
- ✓ Revascularisation procedures by 26%

 ## The Long-term Intervention with Pravastatin in Ischaemic Disease (LIPID)

(*Study Group, New Engl J Med 1998;339:1349–57*)

This trial was similar to CARE but with higher patient numbers. This double-blinded, randomised, controlled trial compared the effects of pravastatin with those of placebo over a mean follow-up period of 6.1 years in 9014 patients who were 31–75 years of age. The patients had a history of MI or unstable angina and cholesterol levels of between 4 and 7 mmol/l.

Pravastatin was found to reduce the risk of:
- ✓ CHD death/non-fatal MI by 24%
- ✓ CHD death by 21%
- ✓ Overall mortality by 22%
- ✓ Revascularisation procedures by 20%

Cerebrovascular accidents were significantly reduced in the treatment arms of both the CARE and LIPID studies.

 ## The Heart Protection study

(*Lancet 2002;360:7–22*)

This is the biggest ever lipid-lowering study and looked at 20,000 patients with a history of IHD, CVA, TIA, PVD or diabetes, and included participants with normal and low cholesterol levels.

Participants were randomised to 40 mg simvastatin per day or to placebo for five years. Benefits of lipid lowering included:

✓ 12% RRR for total mortality ($p < 0.001$)

✓ 18% RRR in coronary mortality ($p = 0.0005$). Benefits were seen in all groups, including: those with IHD and CVA, diabetics, women, the elderly and those with a low baseline cholesterol (eg TC < 5 mmol/l; LDL-cholesterol < 3 mmol/l)

Put another way, five years of treatment with a statin prevents a major event in:

✓ 1 in 10 people with previous MI

✓ 7 in 100 people with DM

✓ 7 in 100 people with previous CVA

✓ So convinced was he by these results, that one of the authors made the now famous quote: 'statins are the new aspirin'

✓ No benefit was found with antioxidant vitamins

 The Anglo-Scandinavian Outcomes Trial, lipid lowering arm (ASCOT study)

(*Lancet 2003; 361:1149*)

Randomised trial involving 10,305 patients with non-fasting cholesterol levels < 6.5 mmol/l and at least three risk factors for CHD. They were given atorvastatin or placebo. Treatment was stopped after a median period of 3.3 years because interim analysis showed clear benefits of statin therapy.

Atorvastatin was found to reduce the risk of:

✓ Fatal and non-fatal CVA by 27%

✓ Total cardiovascular events by 21%

The CARDS (Collaborative AtoRvastatin Diabetes Study) (*BMJ 2003; 326:1014–17*) trial looked at lowering cholesterol in 2838 type 2 diabetics with no history of CVA or coronary disease. It has been ended early because of convincing evidence of substantial benefit.

Should every patient with any cardio-vascular risk factor receive a statin?

This is potentially a very expensive question to answer! It is clear that priority for treatment must be given to those whose arterial disease is already evident, but the relative benefit from treatment is remarkably constant across all groups of patients.

It is clear that it is the cardiovascular risk that is important rather than the actual level of cholesterol. If a patient is at a high enough cardiovascular risk, then it is worth considering statin treatment regardless of their actual cholesterol level.

The authors of the Heart Protection Study have said that statins could benefit three times the number of patients currently receiving them – thus tripling the statins drug bill but potentially saving 10,000 lives from cardiovascular disease. The Department of Health is apparently considering reviewing the current guidance in light of this study, which may lead to a new publication by NICE.

It is obviously possible to argue that virtually anyone who needs to take aspirin really ought to be taking a statin as well!

Currently, the advice is to treat all patients with clinically overt atherosclerotic disease with a statin, aiming to reduce cholesterol to < 5 mmol/l or by 30%, whichever is greater; this is endorsed by the NSF, but currently not by NICE, who controversially suggest checking cholesterol at 12 weeks', post-MI and not treating people with a cholesterol < 4 mmol/l.

For primary prevention, statins are recommended for all patients whose 10-year risk is > 30%, or 15–30% if 'local resources allow'.

Important additional measures to drug treatment

Appropriate lifestyle modifications should be identified and continued indefinitely in all patients worthy of risk assessment (even if their risk is below 30% over 10 years). In primary prevention, stopping smoking alone may often reduce the CHD risk sufficiently to eliminate the need for statin treatment; although patients should be considered smokers for five years after they quit (*Br J Gen Pract 1999;49:217–18*). Other appropriate measures include weight reduction, reducing the intake of saturated fat and increasing that of polyunsaturated fat, regular physical exercise and, when appropriate, additional measures to reduce BP and control blood glucose.

Diet can decrease levels of both cholesterol and triglycerides. However, patients at high CHD risk should not be denied statin treatment – diet should be regarded as an adjunct therapy. Patients should reduce their saturated fat intake and replace the calories with complex carbohydrates. It has recently been suggested that an 'ape' type diet – high in oats, almonds, soy protein, soluble fibre and green leafy vegetables – might be as beneficial in terms of lipid lowering as statin therapy (although compliance would almost certainly be poorer!).

Omega-3 fatty acids are known to be important in secondary prevention of CHD, and omacor (a highly purified and concentrated omega-3 fatty acid capsule, with high concentrations of EPA and DHA) is now licensed for use post-MI (at a dose of one capsule per day), following the GISSI-P trial (*Lancet 1999;354:447–455*); this followed up 11,000 post-MI patients for 3.5 years and found that omacor reduced the absolute risk of death by 2%; largely due to a reduction in the number of sudden deaths. No reduction was noted in the rate of non fatal MI.

Omacor is also licensed for treatment of hypertriglyceridaemia, at a dose of 2–4 capsules per day, in combination with statins and diet.

Which statin should be used?

The DTB (March 2001) recommends simvastatin as routine first-line treatment; the HPS would seem to endorse this. The dose required to lower LDL-cholesterol concentrations varies substantially between the different statins. At current maximum doses, rosuvastatin (newly licensed) appears the most effective, followed by atorvastatin, simvastatin then pravastatin and fluvastatin (*Am J Cardiol 1998; 81:582–7*). There have, however, been allegations that the research into rosuvastatin was biased (*Lancet 2003;362:1341*). Atorvastatin and simvastatin appear to have the greatest effect in lowering plasma triglyceride concentrations.

Ezetimibe (ezetrol) is a new type of lipid-lowering agent, which works by inhibiting cholesterol absorption from the small intestine. It is very effective in combination with statins, but is less so on its own.

Patients should be prescribed the lowest licensed dose initially, which should be taken in the evening for maximum effect. Measurement of total or LDL-cholesterol concentrations should be performed six weeks after dosage adjustments are made, and then annually when the desired lipid concentrations are achieved.

USEFUL WEBSITES

www.bcs.com – British Cardiac Society
www.pccs.org.uk – Primary Care Cardiovascular Society
www.hyp.ac.uk/bhs – British Hypertension Society
(includes copies of CHD risk charts)
www.bhf.org.uk – British Heart Foundation

SUMMARY POINTS FOR HYPERCHOLESTEROLAEMIA

✓ Treat for primary prevention if CHD risk >30% or 15–30% if local resources allow
✓ Treat all for secondary prevention
✓ Cost of statin prescribing is increasing fast
✓ Less than one-third of patients with CHD currently receive statins
✓ Women and the elderly also benefit from statins

Diabetes Mellitus

The prevalence of diagnosed diabetes within the UK is about 3%. The incidence is rising, especially as a result of the expanding ageing population and an increasing incidence of obesity. Up to 25% of people of Asian origin > 60 years have diabetes.

Diabetes is a leading cause of blindness, kidney failure and limb amputation and greatly increases the risk of coronary heart disease and stroke. Diabetes accounts for > 8% of the acute sector costs – it has been estimated that the average cost of inpatient care for a diabetic patient is more than six times that for a non-diabetic.

How is the diagnosis of diabetes confirmed?

The WHO introduced new criteria for the definition, diagnosis and classification of diabetes in June 2000. The methods for diagnosing diabetes are as follows:

With symptoms (polyuria, thirst, unexplained weight loss):

✓ A random venous plasma glucose concentration ≥11.1 mmol/l

or

✓ A fasting venous plasma glucose concentration ≥7.0 mmol/l

or

✓ A two-hour venous plasma glucose concentration ≥11.1 mmol/l two hours after 75 g anhydrous glucose in an oral glucose tolerance test (OGTT)

With no symptoms

Diagnosis must not be based on a single glucose determination. At least one additional glucose result on another day with a value in the diabetic range is essential. This can be either fasting, from a random sample or from the two hour OGTT. If the fasting or random values are not diagnostic, the two hour value should be used.

Why is diabetes important in primary care?

The majority of diabetic patients are routinely managed in primary care. GPs have a crucial role in both the management and follow-up of their patients with diabetes.

Secondary care diabetes services are stretched and many patients still complain of long clinic waits and insufficient time with clinical staff. It is therefore very unlikely that secondary care will be able to cope with the expanding numbers of diabetic patients.

What are the implications of the NSF for diabetes?

The Standards for the NSF were published in December 2001 and the delivery strategy in January 2003. Key proposals of the diabetes delivery strategy are as follows:

- ✓ Regular (annual) check-ups for everyone with diabetes to detect complications early (by 2006)
- ✓ Systematic eye screening programme to national standards (100% coverage by 2007)
- ✓ Local diabetes networks – that include diabetic patients – should be set up to plan local services
- ✓ All diabetics should be on a practice-based register (by March 2006)
- ✓ 'Systematic treatment regimens' in place by 2006.

There is no mention of screening, which was widely expected, especially for high-risk people, such as South Asians. Also, perhaps in response to previous criticism, the NSF leaves it up to PCTs to decide on the best approach for local delivery of care.

Diabetes UK has welcomed the NSF, but has raised concerns about the lack of benchmarks (apart from eye screening and regular check-ups). The Government has announced that it would not ring-fence funding for diabetes care, which has obviously angered both GPs and patients. It is likely to suggest that primary care takes on the routine care of most patients with diabetes; payment for this would be part of the quality framework of the new contract.

What are the Standards of the NSF?

There are 12 Standards presented:
1.	Prevention of type 2 diabetes
2.	Identification of people with diabetes
3.	Empowering people with diabetes
4.	Clinical care of adults with diabetes
5/6.	Clinical care of children and young people
7.	Management of diabetic emergencies
8.	Care of diabetics during their admission
9.	Diabetics and pregnancy
10/11/12.	Detection and management of long-term complications

NICE has recently produced guidance on screening type 2 diabetics for renal complications and retinopathy, which recommend eye tests and renal function tests annually. GPs should be screening all type 2 diabetics for microalbuminuria annually, ideally with an early-morning urine test for albumin to creatinine ratio. If this ratio is above 2.5 mg/mmol in men or 3.5 mg/mmol in women on two different occasions, further assessment should take place.

What are the key elements of effective diabetes care?

These can be summarised as having:
- A planned programme of care for all patients with diabetes
- Clear management plans agreed with each patient, tailored to meet the needs of the individual and their carers
- Practice-based diabetes registers to facilitate regular call and recall of patients

Healthcare professionals have a responsibility to provide appropriate education to equip people with diabetes with the knowledge, skills, attitudes and motivation to effectively manage their diabetes care and modify their lifestyle in such a way as to maximise their wellbeing.

Is there evidence that improved glycaemic control leads to a reduction in complications?

The British Diabetic Association recommends that HbA_{1C} be controlled to < 6.5 for 'excellent control'. An HbA_{1C} of > 7.5 represents poor control. There is increasing evidence to confirm that meticulous glycaemic control can prevent or delay the onset of the complications of diabetes. The impact of these complications can also be greatly reduced if they are detected early and appropriately managed. Thus, regular surveillance for, and early diagnosis of, the complications of diabetes are also important. There are two very important studies regarding this:

1. DCCT (Diabetes Control and Complications Trial)
This demonstrated that type 1 diabetics receiving intensive insulin treatment had fewer microvascular complications (*Diabetes 1996; 45:1289–98*). The long-term follow-up of these patients was later published (*New Engl J Med 2000;342:381–5*), which showed that these benefits persisted with time. However, the improved glycaemic control was not completely advantageous to patients as it resulted in the need for more frequent blood glucose monitoring and increased frequency of insulin injections. Many patients also gained weight and had an increased frequency of hypoglycaemic episodes.

2. UKPDS (UK Prospective Diabetes Study)
This was a massive study involving over 5000 type 2 diabetic patients over a 20-year period, one arm of which studied whether intensive control of blood glucose after diagnosis of diabetes was beneficial (*Lancet 1998;353:837–53*). It demonstrated that better glycaemic control reduced microvascular complications and that intense management of cardiovascular risk factors reduced macrovascular complications. Essentially, the lower the levels of blood glucose, HbA_{1C} and BP, the lower the risk of complications, with metformin being particularly beneficial in overweight patients. It is worth noting however, that intensive BP control was found to be at least as important as intensive glycaemic control; indeed, some experts have claimed that the evidence of the benefit of tight glycaemic control is, at best, modest and confined only to metformin (*BMJ 2000;320:1720*). The main contribution of the UKPDS trial in terms of diabetes management is the highlighting of the importance of tight BP control.

Should there be a screening programme for type 2 diabetes?

The UKPDS study also showed that about 50% of patients had early signs of complications at the time of diagnosis of their diabetes. This therefore raises the question of whether screening for diabetes should be introduced; if diabetes is diagnosed earlier then, theoretically, there would be a reduced incidence of complications. This issue is clearly discussed in a BMJ Education and Debate article (*BMJ 2001;322:986–8*). This article concludes that, at present, there is no justification for universal diabetes screening in the UK. However, there is some support for screening in those population subgroups in which undiagnosed diabetes is especially prevalent and the cardiovascular risk is high, provided the systems for organisation and management are optimised; however, this is not mentioned in the NSF.

How important is treating hypertension in diabetic patients?

A study using the UKPDS data showed that any reduction in blood pressure for type 2 diabetic patients reduces the risk of complications (*BMJ 2000;321:412–20*). Intensive BP control is at least as (probably even more) important as intensive treatment of glucose levels in the reduction of complications in diabetic patients. The blood pressure target from the UKPDS study has been set at 140/80 mmHg, which is what the British Diabetic Association recommends.

The HOT study confirmed that tight BP control (130/80 mmHg) was more effective in diabetics than non-diabetics. The European Society of Cardiology has recently recommended that the BP of diabetics be controlled to < 130/80. However, whether or not these targets are realistic is debatable; it has been estimated that the number of diabetics taking antihypertensive medication would need to double even to meet the current targets of 140/80 mmHg!

Should we give all diabetics ACE inhibitors?

The HOPE (Heart Outcomes Prevention Evaluation) study looked at 3500 diabetics with other cardiovascular risk factors, and showed that giving ramipril to high-risk diabetic patients provides vasculoprotective and renoprotective effects independent of its effect on hypertension (*Lancet 2000;355:253–9*). Cardiovascular events were reduced by 25% and nephropathy by 24%. The NNT was 15 over 4.5 years to prevent one significant outcome.

How do we treat diabetic nephropathy?

ACE inhibitors slow the progress of diabetic nephropathy. Patients with an elevated albumin:creatinine ratio or microalbuminuria on dipstick should be offered either an ACE inhibitor or an angiotensin antagonist; and possibly a combination of these drugs. The CALM study (*BMJ 2000; 321:1440*) showed that dual blockade was more effective than either drug individually at reducing BP and albuminuria.

What is the evidence for statin use in diabetics?

Patients with diabetes, especially type 2, have a greatly increased risk of cardiovascular disease compared with non-diabetics. This is clearly illustrated in the Joint British Societies Coronary Risk Prediction charts. Four out of five deaths in patients with type 2 diabetes are caused by cardiovascular disease. The current recommendation is to prescribe statins to diabetic patients who have a 15% risk over 10 years. Other modifiable CHD risk factors such as smoking and obesity should also be addressed regularly. The UKPDS ranked increased LDL cholesterol as the most important modifiable risk factor for CHD.

The Heart Protection Study (*Lancet 2000;360:7–22*) is the world's biggest ever lipid-lowering study and is covered in the hyperlipidaemia chapter. A total of 3500 diabetics took part and were randomised to placebo or 40 mg simvastatin daily. It was shown that simvastatin significantly reduced the risk of vascular events for diabetic patients, even if they didn't have vascular disease, at any initial cholesterol concentration. If 100 diabetics are treated for five years, seven are prevented from having a major event. This suggests that all type 2 diabetics 'above average risk' should be given a statin.

The CARD study was stopped early because of the substantial benefits found in treating type 2 diabetics who had no history of CHD (see Hyperlipidaemia section).

What are the glitazones?

A new class of drugs for type 2 diabetics, the thiazolidinediones have recently been introduced; rosiglitazone (Avandia) and pioglitazone (Actos) were launched in 2000. They work by reducing the body's resistance to the action of insulin and enable it to be used more efficiently. They are licensed for combination use with a sulphonylurea or metformin and also for use as monotherapy.

The glitazones are expensive however, and NICE has recently issued guidance suggesting that the use of these drugs should be limited to patients who cannot tolerate metformin and a sulphonylurea in combination, because of intolerance or a contraindication to one of these drugs. Glitazones are not licensed for triple therapy (ie with metformin and a sulphonylurea) or in combination with insulin.

What about the meglitinides?

Repaglinide and nateglinide stimulate insulin secretion. Both have a rapid onset of action and have a short-lasting effect. They are licensed for combination therapy with metformin in type 2 diabetes and repaglinide is also licensed as monotherapy. These drugs are effective in reducing post-prandial glucose concentrations; however, it is not yet known whether this effect is clinically beneficial in terms of cardiovascular outcomes. A recent *Drug and Therapeutics Bulletin* concluded that these drugs are more expensive than sulphonylureas and that there is no evidence yet of improved efficacy. They therefore have only a limited role, usually in patients with erratic meal times (*Drug Ther Bull 41;7:July 2003*).

Other advances

Insulin glargine is a very long-acting insulin that can be given once a day to provide a steady, basal level of insulin without causing hypos.

The subcutaneous insulin pump is used to provide a basal dose of insulin at a rate dependent on the patient's needs. Research is being carried out on inhaled insulin and islet-cell transplantation.

What does all this mean for patients?

It is well known that in practice it is very difficult to maintain any reductions in glucose concentrations and blood pressure, even with multiple drug combinations. It is a daunting prospect for any diabetic patient to consider taking metformin, an ACE inhibitor, a statin, aspirin, other oral hypoglycaemics and other antihypertensives on a regular basis!

Many diabetes experts are calling for proposed clinical targets in the diabetes NSF (*BMJ 2002;324:1577–80*) to be practical and geared towards individual patients. One consultant has estimated that the targets of an HbA_{1C} of 7% and a BP of less than 140/90 mmHg (as recommended by the British Hypertension Society) could mean up to 10% of patients needing nine different medications.

The compliance of diabetic patients is poorer than expected. One study (*Diabet Med 2002;19:279–84*) collected anonymous information on prescriptions from diabetic patients in Dundee, which showed that only one-third of patients comply with single medications and about one-tenth comply with two medications!

The future of diabetes care in the UK will be challenging to primary care. Although clear therapeutic goals have been defined, doctors may need to negotiate realistic goals with individual patients regarding their optimal treatment.

USEFUL WEBSITES

www.diabetes.org.uk – Diabetes UK (formally the British Diabetic Association)
www.audit-commission.gov.uk – Audit Commission report
www.nsc.nhs.uk – National Screening Committee website – evaluation of type 2 diabetes mellitus screening against the National Screening Committee Handbook criteria

SUMMARY POINTS FOR DIABETES

✓ Incidence of diabetes is rising
✓ New criteria for diagnosis of diabetes (June 2000)
✓ 75% of diabetic patients are routinely managed in primary care
✓ Meticulous glycaemic and BP control can reduce complications
✓ Careful management of other cardiovascular risk factors is essential

Obesity

Obesity is rapidly becoming a major threat to health. The prevalence of obesity (defined as a body mass index (BMI) > 30 kg/m^2) in the UK is increasing; approximately one in five of the UK population is now obese. According to a recent report from the Royal College of Physicians, if current trends continue, conservative estimates are that at least one third of adults, one fifth of boys and one third of girls will be obese by 2020.

What are the problems with obesity?

Obesity results in a huge financial burden to healthcare. Each year 30,000 premature deaths can be linked to obesity. A recent National Audit Office report estimated that in 1998 treating obesity cost the NHS at least £500m and a staggering £2 billion in sickness absence.

Obesity is a significant aetiological factor in many common diseases. These include diabetes, hypertension, hyperlipidaemia, ischaemic heart disease, stroke and some cancers (eg breast, colon). Obesity is associated with increased mortality, particularly from cardiovascular disease (New Engl J Med 1999;341:1097–105). An obese woman is 3.2 times more likely to have an MI than a slim woman, and an obese man is 1.5 times more likely to have an MI than a slim man.

It is estimated that being obese increases the risk of developing type 2 diabetes by a factor of 12.7 in women and 5.2 in men, and triples the risk of developing colon cancer.

The National Audit Office published a report in January 2004 entitled 'Tackling Obesity in England', which stated that national guidelines should be produced for the management of overweight and obese patients in primary care.

It has been recognised for several years that a large waist circumference is also a predictor for type 2 diabetes. Carrying excess fat, particularly deposition of visceral fat, is known to promote insulin resistance and other features of the metabolic syndrome. A large waist circumference is also a predictor for future CHD and should be included in any risk assessment.

Deprivation is known to be associated with obesity; in 1996, 25% of women in social class 5 were classified as obese, compared to 14% in social class 1.

Is obesity increasing in children?

Reports suggest that the prevalence of obesity among children is also increasing – presently one in five 9-year-olds and one in three 11-year-old girls are overweight. This trend towards obesity in British children has produced the country's first recognised cases of type 2 diabetes in White adolescents. There are high levels of insulin resistance in even normal weight South-Asian children in the UK.

The American Heart Association Committee has recently recommended that doctors should increase children's physical activity, prevent or treat obesity, counsel children and their parents, as well as checking for high blood pressure and high cholesterol concentrations in the obese (*Circulation 2002;106:143–60*). This is likely to be appropriate for British children in the not-to-distant future; which is both alarming and has huge resource implications for GPs.

What are the benefits of a modest weight reduction?

For many obese people, achieving their ideal body weight is unrealistic and impossible. However, significant benefits can be gained from even a 10% loss of body-weight, which is more achievable and sustainable. These benefits include reductions in blood pressure and in total cholesterol (including a rise in HDL-cholesterol) and a reduced risk of developing diabetes.

What is the role of the primary healthcare team in obesity treatment?

Unfortunately, only one in five obese patients ever receives treatment for their obesity, and those who do have a 90% chance of failure.

Primary healthcare teams often feel very frustrated when dealing with patients with weight problems, mainly because treatment is long-term and relapse is very common. The National Obesity Forum has produced guidelines for the management of obesity in primary care. Many GPs responded to the Forum by stating they are not responsible for patients' weight and it is not really part of their job to help people tackle their weight problems. A paper in the *BMJ* discussed the importance of treating obesity as a chronic disease and the need for population interventions (*BMJ 2002;325:757–61*).

A report produced in February 2004 by the Royal College of Physicians, the faculty of Public Health and the Royal College of Paediatrics and Child Health has stated that action needs to be taken at every level to address obesity – national, local, community and individual. The report, which was developed at the request of the Chief Medical Officer, also states that health professionals need to be more involved in tackling obesity. It recommended that all NHS plans, policies, and Clinical Care strategies include the prevention and management of overweight and obesity.

It is easy to argue either way; however, it may be useful to compare losing weight with stopping smoking and there are proven benefits from this. In the longer term, it may well prove to be cost-effective to consider helping our obese patients to lose weight.

The Atkins diet

This is mentioned here because of its huge popularity. It advocates high protein and fat intake with low carbohydrates. The diet allows quick weight loss and certainly appears to be more effective than conventional low-fat diets after six months, according to two recent randomised controlled trials (*New Engl J Med 2003;348:2074–81* and *New Engl J Med 2003;348:2082–90*); however, most of the weight is usually regained within a year. The first of these trials included only 79 patients, and it is difficult to draw any firm conclusions from either in terms of the diet's long-term safety profile; in particular, effects on the kidneys and vitamin deficiencies (fruit is not allowed). In the trials so far, it appears that there is no significant increase in total cholesterol, BP or fasting glucose levels (insulin resistance may even be decreased). HDL levels seem to be improved by the Atkins diet (*Bandolier review July 2003*). Until there is more safety data, it should not be recommended in preference to conventional low-calorie, low-fat diets.

What drugs are available to treat obesity?

Orlistat
Orlistat is an intestinal lipase inhibitor that blocks the absorption of about 30% of dietary fat. In clinical trials of up to two years' duration it resulted in an average weight loss of about 10%, compared with 6% in the placebo group (*Lancet 1998;352:167–72*). There is good evidence to support its effect on weight reduction both in short term and 1–2 years' post-treatment. Other benefits of orlistat include a reduction in LDL and total cholesterol, a reduction in blood pressure and improvements in insulin resistance and blood glucose control in diabetic patients.

The licensing criteria for the drug require patients to lose at least 2.5 kg in four weeks prior to starting treatment. In addition, they should only continue with the drug if they achieve a weight loss of at least a further 5% of their body weight after the first 12 weeks of treatment and a cumulative weight loss of at least 10% after the first six months.

NICE have produced guidance on the use of orlistat. They have agreed it can be prescribed, as long as doctors abide by the strict conditions of its product licence and that it is only used for patients who are either clinically obese or overweight (BMI $\geq$28 kg/m^2) with other health-related problems (such as type 2 diabetes or hypertension).

Sibutramine

Another new antiobesity drug, sibutramine (Reductil), became available in June 2001. A UK, general practice-based study assessed its long-term weight reduction efficacy, tolerability and safety with encouraging results (*J Fam Pract 2001;50:505–12*). While 20% of placebo patients lost at least 5% of their body weight, this figure was 39% of patients taking 10 mg sibutramine and 57% taking 15 mg sibutramine.

The STORM (Sibutramine Trial of Obesity Reduction and Maintenance) trial differs from other weight-loss trials as its objective was to test whether treatment with sibutramine could prevent weight regain among patients who had already achieved a weight loss of more than 5% of their body-weight (*Lancet 2000;356:2119–25*). The study showed that 43% of the patients treated with sibutramine maintained at least 80% of their body-weight loss compared with only 16% in the placebo group. In addition, significant changes in cardiovascular disease risk factors were noted, including reduced triglyceride concentrations, increased HDL-cholesterol concentrations and reduced cholesterol:HDL-cholesterol ratio.

Sibutramine works by inhibiting the reuptake of the neurotransmitters noradrenaline and serotonin, thereby leading to increased feelings of satiety after eating. The UK licence for sibutramine specifies a maximum treatment period of 12 months and has similar constraints for its use as orlistat (although no initial weight loss is necessary). It is contraindicated in patients with coronary heart disease, peripheral vascular disease and inadequately controlled hypertension or hyperthyroidism.

NICE has also produced recommendations on the use of sibutramine. However, the *Drug and Therapeutics Bulletin* has questioned this guidance. It reviewed the clinical trial data and announced that the drug's 'limited' benefits, coupled with its many side-effects, contraindications and stringent requirements for monitoring, make it 'difficult and impractical' for GPs to prescribe (*Drug Ther Bull 2001;39:89–91*).

USEFUL WEBSITES

www.nice.org.uk – NICE guidelines
www.nao.gov.uk – 'Tackling Obesity in England' report
www.nationalobesityforum.org.uk – National Obesity Forum

SUMMARY POINTS FOR OBESITY

✓ Prevalence of obesity dramatically increasing
✓ Obesity is a huge financial burden to healthcare
✓ Primary care teams need to be more involved
✓ Numerous benefits gained from losing small amounts of weight
✓ Orlistat and sibutramine have been approved by NICE

Coronary Heart Disease
– other risk factors

Healthcare professionals tend to overemphasise the benefits of medication (eg statins) and neglect lifestyle factors (eg smoking, diet). The most effective intervention in reducing risk of CHD seems to be stopping smoking, which results in a 50% risk reduction over two years; as shown by the MONICA study, commissioned by the WHO. This was a large epidemiological study looking at 100,000 people aged 35–64 from 21 countries over 10 years. In this chapter, we will examine other risk factors for CHD.

Impaired glucose tolerance

Although diabetes is obviously a strong risk factor for CHD, the association between glycaemia 'in the normal range' and CHD risk has previously been controversial. However, one study has shown that glycosylated haemoglobin levels are positively correlated with the risk of future coronary heart disease independent of body mass index (BMI), cholesterol level, age, sex, blood pressure or smoking history (*BMJ 2001;322:15–18*). This study looked at 4662 men aged between 45 and 79 years and found that the HbA_{1C} concentration significantly predicted all-cause mortality, even below the threshold commonly accepted for a diagnosis of diabetes.

Impaired glucose tolerance (defined as a fasting plasma glucose of < 7 with a 2 h oral glucose tolerance test value of 7.8–11.1 mmol/l) is a common condition affecting up to 17% of people aged 40–65 in the UK. People with impaired glucose tolerance have increased cardiovascular mortality; the Whitehall study (*Lancet 1980;1:1373–6*) showed that impaired glucose tolerance doubled the risk of death from CHD among middle-aged male civil servants.

Insulin resistance can lead to impaired glucose tolerance and is a major risk factor for CHD and type 2 diabetes. Indeed, it is thought to be the aetiological factor behind the 'metabolic syndrome' which consists of type 2 diabetes, hyperinsulinaemia, central obesity, hypertension, dyslipidaemia and atherosclerotic cardiovascular disease. A recent study (*BMJ 2002;324:635–8*) showed, rather worryingly, that South-Asian children aged 8–11 years in the UK already had higher levels of insulin and insulin resistance than White children. Insulin resistance is certainly a huge problem in the South-Asian population, and may help to explain why the mortality rate from CHD in this group is 40–50% higher than in their Caucasian counterparts.

Interventions which have been shown to be of benefit, include exercise and weight loss; approximately seven people need to be treated for one year with a 150-min exercise programme per week and a suitable low-calorie diet, in order to prevent one case of diabetes (*New Engl J Med 2002;346:393–403*). This NNT is certainly more impressive than for most drugs.

Sedentary lifestyle

Physical inactivity roughly doubles the risk of coronary heart disease and is also a major risk factor for stroke. Regular exercise has numerous benefits, including reducing hypertension and CHD. Short bouts of exercise (for at least 20 minutes) can be just as effective at protecting the heart as longer workouts; however, getting the heart rate up is a key factor as light activity offers no cardiac benefit (*Circulation 2000;102:975–80, 981–7*).

Diet

Folic acid and B vitamins antagonise the effect of homocysteine. A meta-analysis in 2002 (*BMJ 2002;355:12606*) concluded that there was a significant, positive association between homocysteine levels and cardiovascular disease. One randomised controlled trial (RCT) (*New Engl J Med 2001;345:1593*) has confirmed that giving folic acid and B vitamins to patients after angioplasty, reduces the restenosis rates. Folic acid should be given at a dose of 800 microgrammes per day. It is difficult to achieve these levels through diet alone.

Deprivation

Deprivation is known to double the risk of coronary heart disease; this is equivalent to the increased risk produced by smoking. Nonetheless, GPs in deprived areas have significantly lower referral rates for angiography and revascularisation services.

Why are patients not more motivated in reducing their risk of CHD?

One of the biggest barriers for implementing evidence-based practice may be convincing patients that they need to take part in lifelong measures for the prevention of coronary heart disease. In one study, 30% of patients declined to participate in a nurse-led prevention programme (*BMJ 1998;316:1434–7*); although some such programmes are inaccessible to patients because of conflicting work commitments. Patients often perceive a 'heart attack' to be an acute, self-limiting condition rather than the onset of a high-risk chronic disease.

A very interesting qualitative study looked at identifying factors influencing the use of health services by people with angina (*BMJ 2001;323:214–17*). It found that fear, denial and low expectations in patients from lower socioeconomic classes are important barriers to accessing health services. This may also account for some of the regional and socioeconomic differences in the incidence and prevalence of CHD in the UK.

 USEFUL WEBSITES

www.bcs.com – British Cardiac Society
www.pccs.org.uk – Primary Care Cardiovascular Society
www.hyp.ac.uk/bhs – British Hypertension Society (includes copies of CVD risk charts)
www.cardiacrehabilitation.org.uk – Information regarding rehabilitation
www.riskscore.org.uk – New scoring system for assessing cardio-vascular disease risk

The Coronary Heart Disease National Service Framework

This was published by the Department of Health in March 2000 and has been designed to 'transform the prevention, diagnosis and treatment of coronary heart disease'.

Coronary heart disease is among the biggest killers in this country. More than 1.4 million people suffer from angina. Some 300,000 have heart attacks every year. Heart disease is much more common in deprived areas, yet treatment and care are often better in more prosperous areas. This 'postcode' lottery of care is unacceptable and the NSF attempts to end it.

What do National Service Frameworks (NSFs) do?

National Service Frameworks have been created to set national standards and define service models for a specific service or care group, put in place programmes to support their implementation and establish performance measures against which progress within an agreed time-scale will be measured. This was the second NSF to be produced.

What does the CHD National Service Framework state?

This Framework sets out a programme designed to achieve the Government target of cutting coronary heart disease and stroke by an ambitious 40% by 2010. It sets 12 standards for the prevention, diagnosis and treatment of coronary heart disease; describes service models; and explains how the standards can be delivered and how progress will be monitored, with milestones and goals.

What does this mean for GPs?

GP teams have had to identify patients who are at risk of CHD and offer them appropriate advice and treatment. Regular audits on this information have to be performed. This has meant a considerable amount of work in many practices.

A major survey has revealed a large gulf between milestones set out in the NSF and the standards actually being reached in general practice (*BMJ 2001;321:1463*). In this study, research nurses analysed the records of 548 GPs across the UK and found 24,431 patients with a diagnosis of CHD. The study showed that 35% of men and 52% of women had no record of cholesterol levels; and at least 40% of patients actually tested had total cholesterol levels greater than 5 mmol/l. About one-half of post-MI patients were taking aspirin, one-fifth were taking beta-blockers and less than one-fifth of the disease population were taking statins. These findings obviously suggest that many GPs still have alarming amounts of work to do if they are to meet the NSF milestones.

It has been estimated that the NHS statin prescribing bill will increase by at least £2b a year if GPs stick to the NSF targets. Prescribing for statins has already risen by 78% since the NSFs launch in 2000.

Should all age groups be targeted?

A study has shown that no hypertensive patients under 45 years have a 10-year cardiovascular risk > 30% (*Br J Gen Pract 2001;51:571–4*). Virtually no health benefits result from assessing and treating blood pressure in patients less than 45 years of age. If the assessment and treatment of blood pressure were confined to patients over 65 years, this would prevent 85% of cardiovascular disease.

What are the negative parts of this NSF?

This is a very lengthy document consisting of 124 pages with another 283 pages containing eight appendices! It is written with a lot of repetition and contains a large amount of 'management jargon', which is not always easy to follow. The main document is not referenced, although it does claim to provide evidence-based advice.

Many of the current deficiencies in providing adequate secondary prevention care to coronary heart disease patients is often due to poor funding; for example, low prescription rates for statins, long waiting times for exercise ECGs and angiograms. It is unclear how undertaking regular audits will actually improve this! The NSF has been described as a blueprint for audit rather than a guideline for patient management, and the main audit burden is going to fall on general practices.

An interesting editorial in the *BMJ* (*BMJ 2001;323:246–7*) comments on how unrealistic the NSF targets are. In addition, it states that if patient-centred medicine is accepted as a desirable core of general practice, patients should then have the right to make their own health choices.

USEFUL WEBSITE

<u>www.doh.gov.uk/nsf/coronary.htm</u> – National Service Framework for Coronary Heart Disease

AIMS OF THE NATIONAL SERVICE FRAMEWORK:

✓ Create disease registers
✓ Produce locally agreed protocols
✓ Provide structured care
✓ Perform regular audits

SUMMARY POINTS FOR THE NSF FOR CHD

✓ 12 standards covered in NSF
✓ Aims to reduce heart disease
✓ Involves primary and secondary care
✓ Provides clear and challenging targets

Heart Failure

Heart failure, like hypertension, is a very common but poorly managed condition. Some 50% of patients with heart failure are undetected, 50% of those detected are not treated and 50% of those treated are not adequately controlled.

Despite improvements in treatment the prognosis for patients with heart failure remains poor: the risk of death annually is 5–10% in patients with mild symptoms and 30–40% in those with advanced disease.

Diagnosis

There is a poor correlation between symptoms and signs of heart failure and echocardiogram findings. Only 10–25% of patients presenting with shortness of breath have heart failure. Unfortunately, there are no particular characteristics of breathlessness which help to identify the patient with heart failure. Although the echocardiogram is the gold standard investigation for heart failure, GPs are limited by its accessibility.

Guidance has recently been produced by NICE (July 2003). It suggests that if the patients's ECG and blood levels of B-type natriuretic peptide (BNP) are normal, then the patient does not have heart failure. Patients with a totally normal ECG are unlikely to have heart failure. However, BNP testing is still not widely available in the UK. A recent study confirmed that the BNP test is cost around £15 per assay.

The NICE guidance states that all patients suspected of having heart failure should undergo echocardiography to diagnose the condition and be offered ACE inhibitors if they have left ventricular dysfunction. It also recommends that all patients should be monitored on a regular basis – at least every six months. Monitoring should include assessment of functional capacity, fluid status, cardiac rhythm, review of medication and measurement of urea and electrolytes.

GPs have a vital role in the early detection and treatment of the main factors for heart failure – namely, hypertension and ischaemic heart disease – and other cardiovascular risk factors, such as smoking and hyperlipidaemia. The Framingham study has shown a decline in hypertension as a risk factor for heart failure over the years, which probably reflects improvements in treatment. Early detection of left ventricular dysfunction in fibrillation, and treatment with angiotensin converting enzyme inhibitors can minimise the progression to symptomatic heart failure.

What are the best treatments for heart failure?

There are now so many different drugs known to benefit patients with heart failure that treatment can often become confusing and complex for both the patient and the doctor.

Lifestyle
Patients should be advised to eat a low-salt, low-fat diet, to stop smoking and to reduce alcohol consumption. It is important to remember that many drugs, including NSAIDs and prednisolone can exacerbate heart failure. More PCTs are funding exercise programmes; a systematic review (*Br J Gen Pract 2002;52:47*) has found that short-term exercise training has positive effects on physical performance, quality of life, mortality and readmission rates.

Diuretics
For many years, diuretics have been an important part of the symptomatic treatment for patients with heart failure and evidence of fluid retention. However, their long-term effects on mortality rates and other endpoints are not known (it would be unethical to trial now).

Angiotensin-converting enzyme inhibitors
ACE inhibitors (ACEIs) have been evaluated extensively in randomised controlled trials (eg CONSENSUS, SAVE, RESOLVD studies) comprising a large number of patients with heart failure, and were found to reduce mortality and morbidity, with an NNT of about 16. Benefits extend to different patient groups: the elderly, women and patients with and without coronary artery disease. Patients with different degrees of functional impairment and with a history of diuretic and digoxin use are also benefited. In the absence of clear contraindications these drugs should therefore be used as first-line agents in all patients with left ventricular dysfunction who do or do not have symptoms.

The HOPE study also found that ramipril reduces the risk of new-onset heart failure by about 23% in high-risk groups. It therefore seems to have a preventive effect as well as a therapeutic effect.

Many GPs still do not regularly monitor renal function, even in the most vulnerable patients (*BMJ 1999;318:234–7*). It has been recommended that patients should be screened for risk factors predisposing them to uraemia (for example, old age, peripheral vascular disease, or concomitant treatment with non-steroidal drugs). Renal function should be checked before and 7–10 days after ACEIs are started in all patients and thereafter annually only in those with risk factors.

Despite the evidence for their effectiveness, angiotensin-converting enzyme inhibitors are underused in primary care. Doctors' perceptions of the risks of these drugs in patients with heart failure are often exaggerated; however, the introduction of these drugs has been shown to very rarely cause problems (*BMJ 2000;321:1113–16*). Remember that an ACEI is included in the 'poly pill'.

Angiotensin-II receptor antagonists (AII RAs)

The ValHeFT trial showed a 13% relative-risk reduction in the combined endpoint of all-cause mortality and morbidity in patients with chronic heart failure on valsartan compared with placebo. However, valsartan had no significant effect on the endpoint of mortality alone.

Recently, four papers have been published from the Candesartan in Heart Failure Assessment of Reduction in Mortality and Morbidity (CHARM)-Overall Programme – the largest trial programme ever undertaken in heart failure patients (*Lancet 2003;362:759–81*). The CHARM investigators compared the angiotensin-receptor blocker, candesartan, with a placebo in three different populations with class II–IV heart failure followed up for at least two years. CHARM-Added studied 2548 patients with ejection fractions of 40% or less who were already being treated with optimum doses of angiotensin-converting-enzyme inhibitors (ACEIs). CHARM-Alternative studied 2028 patients with ejection fractions of 40% or less who were intolerant of ACEIs. CHARM-Preserved studied 3025 patients with ejection fractions of more than 40%. These three trials were combined for analysis and showed that candesartan led to a 1·6% absolute reduction in the primary endpoint of mortality. The addition of candesartan to ACEIs leads to a reduction in cardiovascular events in patients with both reduced left ventricular ejection fraction and heart failure. Candesartan was generally well tolerated and the ejection fraction or treatment at baseline does not seem to alter its effects.

However, the VALIANT trial found that there was no additional reduction in mortality among patients taking both an AIIRAs and an ACE inhibitor, compared to patients taking only one or other of these drugs (*NEJM 2003;349:1893–906*).

The ELITE II study (*J Card Fail 1999;5:146–54*) showed that losartan is no more effective than captopril in reducing mortality in elderly patients with heart failure.

Beta-blockers

Beta-blockers have been evaluated in more than 15,000 patients with mild to moderate heart failure, in over 20 randomised clinical trials (eg MERIT-HF [*Lancet 1999;353:2001-7*] and CIBIS-II [*Lancet 1999; 353:9–13*] trials). They have been shown to decrease mortality, cumulatively by about 30–40%, and also to reduce morbidity. About three or four deaths are prevented during the first year of therapy for every 100 patients treated. These benefits were attained in patients already taking ACEIs and diuretics, with ischaemic and non-ischaemic disease and with different degrees of functional impairment, although clinical trials have generally carefully selected stable patients. The consensus, now, is that beta-blockers should be prescribed to all patients who have symptomatic heart failure, and are in a stable condition.

However, even in carefully selected patients there is often an initial deterioration in symptoms, followed by a subsequent improvement. Owing to the complexities of initiating, titrating and monitoring treatment with β-blockers in patients with heart failure, this treatment should generally be given only by experienced doctors or in specialised clinics; the β-blocker is usually started at a very low dose, then titrated up, sometimes over several months. The choice of β-blocker (selective versus non-selective, eg metoprolol versus carvedilol) remains controversial and is currently under investigation in randomised trials. There is evidence for carvedilol, bisoprolol and metoprolol. β-blockers may also be beneficial in severe heart failure; as shown by the BEST (*New Engl J Med 2001;344:1659–67*) and COPERNICUS trials (*New Engl J Med 2001;344:1651–8*).

The BEST trial (*New Engl J Med 2001;344:1659–67*) looked at 2708 patients with class 3 or 4 heart failure for two years and found that the β-blockers bucindolol reduced the risk of the secondary end point of death from cardiovascular causes (odds ratio 0–86, 95% confidence interval 0.74–0.99), although there was no overall significant survival benefit.

The COPERNICUS trial (*New Engl J Med 2001;344:1651–8*) demonstrated a 35% reduction in risk of death with carvediol in patients with severe heart failure, over an average follow-up period of 10.4 months (95% confidence interval 19–48%).

Digoxin
One study has shown that digoxin can provide some symptomatic benefit in patients in sinus rhythm with heart failure. However, it does not appear to improve mortality (*New Engl J Med 1997;336:525–33*). It is of much more benefit in patients with heart failure who are in AF.

Spironolactone
The RALES study (*Lancet 1999;341:709–17*) showed that patients who received spironolactone in addition to their usual treatment had a decreased mortality of 30%. The patients in this study had severe heart failure persisting despite standard therapy. More trials are still needed before spironolactone can be recommended as a routine treatment for heart failure. Care should be taken in terms of interactions, for example hyperkalaemia with ACEIs.

Summary

General practitioners have a vital role in the early detection and treatment of the main risk factors for heart failure – namely, hypertension and ischaemic heart disease – and other cardiovascular risk factors, such as smoking and hyperlipidaemia. The Framingham study has shown a decline in hypertension as a risk factor for heart failure over the years, which probably reflects improvements in treatment. Early detection of left ventricular dysfunction in 'high risk' asymptomatic patients (eg those who have hypertension or atrial fibrillation) and treatment with angiotensin-converting enzyme inhibitors can minimise the progression to symptomatic heart failure.

ACRONYMS OF IMPORTANT CARDIOVASCULAR TRIALS

CONSENSUS –   Co-operative North Scandinavian Enalapril Survival Study

RESOLVD –   Randomised Evaluation of Strategies for Left Ventricular Dysfunction

ValHeFT –   Valsartan Heart Failure Trial

VALIANT –   Valsartan in Acute Myocardial Infarction trial

ELITE –   Evaluation of Losartan in the Elderly [study]

MERIT-HF –   Metoprolol CR/XL Randomised Intervention Trial in Congestive Heart Failure

CIBIS –   The Cardiac Insufficiency Bisoprolol Study

RALES –   Randomized Aldactone Evaluation Study

USEFUL WEBSITE

www.bsh.org.uk/bshx – British Society for Heart Failure

SUMMARY POINTS FOR HEART FAILURE

✓ Heart failure is underdetected and undertreated
✓ Affects 10% of people over 75-years-old
✓ ACE inhibitors are the standard treatment
✓ A normal ECG and BNP value excludes heart failure
✓ patients with abnormal ECGs and raised BNP values should have an echo
✓ ACE inhibitors are still under-prescribed
✓ Target risk factors in all patients

Atrial Fibrillation

There is an increased incidence of atrial fibrillation (AF) with increasing age: One study suggests a prevalence of 2.4% in patients over the age of 50 years (*Br J Gen Pract 1997;47:285–9*). Atrial fibrillation is an independent risk factor for developing a stroke; its presence increases the risk of stroke fivefold. Patients with atrial fibrillation who do sustain a stroke have a higher mortality rate, greater disability, a longer duration of hospital stay and a lower rate of discharge to their own home.

The prevalence of atrial fibrillation increases with age, which obviously means the proportion of strokes attributable to atrial fibrillation also increases with age – about 24% in people aged 80–89 years. However, community-based studies show that atrial fibrillation is still underdiagnosed and undertreated.

Is rate as important as rhythm?

Traditionally, doctors have concentrated on cardioverting patients in AF, either medically (eg with amiodarone) or surgically, with DC cardioversion. However, drugs that regulate heart rate are just as effective as drugs that control rhythm, as well as being cheaper and safer, according to two new studies (*New Engl J Med 2002;347:1825–33* and *New Engl J Med 2002;347:1834–40*). This approach may also lead to fewer hospital admissions. One of these studies was carried out in North America and looked at 4060 patients with AF, followed up for 3.5 years on average. They were randomised to rate control (with β-blockers, verapamil or diltiazem or digoxin) or rhythm-control. At the end of the study, 356 patients in the rhythm-control group had died, compared to 310 in the rate-control group. The other study, which looked at 522 patients, was set in The Netherlands and again showed a reduced mortality in the rate-controlled group.

Should patients with atrial fibrillation be prescribed warfarin?

It is recommended that patients who are at a high risk of stroke should be identified and targeted for anticoagulation in the absence of contraindications (*Lancet 1999;353:4–6*), see Box at end of chapter. This risk should be reviewed at regular intervals, at least annually. High-risk patients (ie those with an annual risk of CVA of 8–12%) should receive warfarin (International Normalised Ratio, 2.0–3.0) if possible; patients at moderate risk (ie annual risk of CVA, 4%) should receive either warfarin or aspirin, depending on each individual case; and low-risk patients (risk of CVA, 1%) should receive aspirin at a dose of 75–300 mg daily.

Randomised trials have established that anticoagulation with warfarin is associated with a relative reduction in risk of stroke of 68% (*Lancet 1996;648:633–8*). Aspirin has been shown to be less effective in stroke reduction among high-risk patients, but is more convenient and theoretically safer then warfarin. One systematic review of long-term anticoagulation and aspirin in patients with AF showed for the first time that aspirin is probably as effective at preventing fatal and non-fatal cardiovascular events as warfarin (*BMJ 2001;322:321–4*). However, larger trials need to be undertaken before a change in the current practice can be recommended. There is no evidence that adding aspirin to warfarin confers any additional benefit.

Anticoagulation in those aged over 75 is associated with a greater risk the higher the INR. The SPAF III (Stroke Prevention in Atrial Fibrillation) trial showed that maintaining a lower INR of 1.5–3.0 is both safe and effective in reducing the risk of stroke in this age group.

New guidelines for the management of AF have recently been produced by the American Academy of Family Physicians and the American College of Physicians (*Am Intern Med 2003;139:1009–33*). They state that rate control is more important than rhythm control. In addition, dignoxin should be given second-line after atenolol, veraponil ditialem as it is not effective for rate control during exercise.

Why are some patients with atrial fibrillation not anticoagulated?

Despite evidence in the published literature, anticoagulation is underused in clinical practice, partly because it is not known whether trial efficacy translates into clinical practice. The patients in the trials were highly selected and had very close monitoring and follow-up. Although the trials were designed to provide an estimate of treatment efficacy, they have been widely interpreted as being studies of warfarin treatment. There is a counter-argument that the benefits of warfarin were actually underestimated, since patients randomised to the warfarin arms of the studies who actually did sustain a stroke often had subtherapeutic INRs. However, a community-based study showed that stroke and haemorrhage rates were comparable to those in randomised studies (*BMJ 2000;320:1236–9*).

Other reasons for the poor prescribing of warfarin to patients with atrial fibrillation may include concern over cerebral haemorrhage, the problems associated with initiating therapy in elderly housebound patients and the inconvenience of safely monitoring anticoagulation in the community. One small study demonstrated that patients on warfarin could manage their INR at home as safely as at a hospital anticoagulation clinic (*Lancet 2000;356:97–102*). This was made possible by reliable, easy-to-use machines using capillary blood samples. Longer term studies are needed to assess the feasibility of this method, but home management would obviously have many advantages.

One study has highlighted a considerable variability between physicians and patients in their weighing up of the potential outcomes associated with anticoagulation for atrial fibrillation (*BMJ 2001;323:1218–21*). It showed that for anticoagulation treatment to be acceptable, patients required less reduction in risk of stroke and were more tolerant of an increase in the risk of bleeding than physicians.

However, a study of elderly patients in general practice showed that nearly 40% of patients with atrial fibrillation preferred not to receive anticoagulation when they were given information about the stroke risk and consequences of treatment (*BMJ 2000; 320:1380–4*). The findings of this study suggest that guidelines for the management of atrial fibrillation should be modified to incorporate the patients' preferences in their treatment decisions, particularly with regard to the consequences of anticoagulation treatment.

Risk of Stroke in Non-Rheumatic Atrial Fibrillation

High Risk (8-12% annually)
- All patients with a previous history of a transient ischaemic attack (TIA) or cardiovascular accident (CVA)
- All patients aged over 75 years with diabetes, hypertension or ischaemic heart disease
- All patients with clinical evidence of valve disease or heart failure

Medium Risk (4% annually)
- All patients under 65 years with diabetes, hypertension or ischaemic heart disease
- All patients over 65 years who have not been identified in the high risk group

Low Risk (1% annually)
- All other patients under 65 years

SUMMARY POINTS FOR ATRIAL FIBRILLATION

✓ Risk of AF increases with age
✓ Associated with a fivefold risk of stroke
✓ Rate control is as important as rhythm control
✓ Patients at high risk of stroke need warfarin
✓ Patient education regarding risks and benefits of warfarin is important
✓ Many patients would choose not to take warfarin

Stroke

Stroke is the third highest cause of death in the United Kingdom and the biggest single cause of major disability. Treatment in the UK is far from satisfactory. Stroke can occur at any age, but half of all strokes occur in people over 70-years-old. About 80% of all acute strokes are caused by cerebral infarction; the remainder are caused by haemorrhage. More than 50% of patients are physically dependent on others six months after a stroke.

It has been estimated that there will be a 30% absolute increase in the number of patients experiencing their first stroke in 2010 compared with the figures for 1983. The International Stroke Trial highlighted that UK centres had the poorest survival rates from stroke in the world.

The cost to the NHS and Social Services of stroke is about £2.3b per year, nearly twice that for coronary heart disease. However, the government and charities spend around £5m per year on stroke research, compared to £43m on heart disease. Stroke prevention is actually one of the most cost-effective of all cardiovascular interventions in primary care.

The Department of Health produced the National Service Framework for elderly people in April 2001, which contains a substantial chapter on stroke. A better service for stroke is supposed to be delivered by April 2004.

Of what value are stroke units?

Stroke units are known to improve outcome by concentrating patients in a unit with the appropriate expertise. Patients treated in stroke units are less likely to die and more likely to recover fully or partially from a stroke (*BMJ 1997;314:1151–9*).

The Third National Sentinel Stroke Audit for 2001–2 has been published by the Royal College of Physicians, which provides an overview of progress in the management of stroke. It highlights the failure of the NHS to provide adequate numbers of beds in stroke units – the mean number of acute stroke beds was four and the median number zero!

Even in the community, the audit has shown that only 31% of Primary Care Trusts have specialised community stroke teams. Evidence from randomised controlled trials shows that a focused community rehabilitation team with adequate resources, linking with a state-of-the-art stroke unit, reduces the length of stay and, in moderately and severely disabled patients, reduces disability and institutional care, when compared with management by a stroke unit alone (*Stroke 2000;31:2989–94*).

National Service Framework for Elderly People and Stroke
Stroke is covered in Standard Five of the NSF. This aims to reduce the incidence of stroke in the population and ensure that those who have had a stroke have prompt access to integrated stroke-care services (ie on a stroke unit). It states there are four key areas for the development of integrated stroke services, namely: prevention; immediate care; early and continuing rehabilitation; and long-term support.

Primary prevention

Hypertension is the most prevalent and modifiable risk factor for stroke in primary prevention, with its treatment substantially reducing the risk of stroke. As the risk factors for stroke are similar to those for coronary heart disease, primary care teams have a very important role in primary stroke prevention.

The NSF emphasises the need for GPs to identify patients at high cardiovascular risk and it proposes the creation of GP registers, based on those created through implementing the NSF for coronary heart disease. In addition, GPs should put in place models of care to enable the systematic recording of risk factors in high-risk patients, provide and document the delivery of appropriate advice, support and treatment, and offer a regular review to those at risk of stroke.

Secondary prevention

The main interventions with proven benefit are aspirin, cholesterol reduction and carotid endarterectomy in people with severe carotid artery stenosis. In addition, people with atrial fibrillation have been shown to benefit from oral anticoagulation (or aspirin in the case of contraindications to anticoagulants).

Hypertension persisting after one month should be treated according to the British Hypertension Society guidelines (see below for evidence on treating hypertension). All patients should receive aspirin (if there are contraindications, then dipyridamole or clopidrogel could be considered). There is some evidence that clopidrogel may be better than aspirin (CAPRIE study. *Stroke 2000;31:1779*) for secondary prevention, but overall, the current recommendation is to use it only in aspirin-intolerant patients.

The benefits of cholesterol reduction in patients who have suffered from a CVA, even with no history of CHD, have been shown by the Heart Protection study (*Lancet 2002;360:7–22*).

Immediate care

The NSF states that all patients with acute stroke require urgent admission to hospital and should have a computed tomography (CT) brain scan within 48 hours. There is strong evidence that patients treated in stroke units are less likely to die and more likely to recover fully or partially from a stroke (*BMJ 1997;314:1151–9*). The NSF therefore states that all patients with an acute stroke should be managed on an acute stroke unit (currently, less than one-quarter of patients are being treated in specialist stroke units).

Interventions for acute ischaemic stroke

These are summarised in the Box on p. 59. Early use of aspirin reduces the chance of death and dependency and improves the chance of a complete recovery (*Lancet 1997;349:1569–81*). There has been no evidence to show that immediate anticoagulation is beneficial.

Thrombolysis trials have shown very conflicting results. Tissue plasminogen activator is used widely in the USA and seems to reduce the risk of disability from a CVA but increases the risk of death (from intracerebral haemorrhage and from any cause). It is recommended that tPA is only given in specialist centres, within three hours of the stroke and as part of randomised controlled trials.

An interesting qualitative study in the *BMJ* highlighted that knowledge of stroke is still very poor amongst both stroke patients and the general public (*BMJ 2002;324:1065–8*). None of the available written patient information about stroke actually conveys the importance of early presentation to hospital.

Early and continuing rehabilitation

The NSF emphasises the need for efficient liaison between hospitals and primary care. Secondary prevention measures are a key part of any care plan, and must continue following discharge. By April 2002 every general hospital that cares for stroke patients should have drawn up plans for a specialised stroke service.

Long-term support

The NSF states that patients and carers needing long-term, ongoing support after the stroke should have access to a stroke-care coordinator who can provide advice, discuss discharge needs and facilitate access to further rehabilitation services.

By 2004, Primary Care Trusts will have to use protocols to identify, treat and refer stroke patients, and every general practice will have established clinical audit systems for stroke. It is still unclear at present how this is going to be fully implemented. Success can obviously only be achieved if there is adequate provision of staff, education, training and finance to carry out the programme.

Antihypertensives for stroke prevention

The PROGRESS (Perindopril pROtection aGainst REcurrent Stroke Study) trial has shown that for secondary prevention of CVA, the lower the level of BP achieved, the more events are prevented (*Lancet 2001; 358:1033*). It enrolled 6100 patients who had suffered a haemorrhagic or ischaemic stroke or transient ischaemic attack within the past five years. They were randomised to receive placebo or drug therapy (perindopril plus indapamide). After four years of follow-up, the primary endpoint of stroke recurrence had been reduced by 28% in the drug-treated group. There were also significant reductions in stroke recurrence in both the hypertensive and non-hypertensive patients. This study demonstrated a benefit of ACE inhibition that was independent of any blood-pressure lowering effect, and also showed that cognitive and functional outcomes after repeat CVA were better in the perindopril group than the placebo group.

The HOPE study (*BMJ 2002;324:699*) looked at the role of ramipril in prevention of CVD in high-risk patients and diabetics; 10,000 patients were followed up for about 4.5 years. The results looking at CVA specifically were published in March 2002. The participants were all under 55 and had pre-existing vascular disease or diabetes and one other risk factor, but they were not hypertensive. Patients were given either ramipril 10 mg or placebo. Only a modest reduction in BP was seen (mean reduction 3.8 mmHg in systolic pressure and 2.8 in diastolic pressure), but the incidence of fatal and non-fatal CVA was significantly lower in the treatment group than the placebo group (0.4% compared to 1% after 4.5 years); note, however, that the NNT to prevent a stroke is about 167 for 4.5 years. ACE inhibitors therefore seem to have some preventive effect on both CHD and cerebrovascular disease over and above their blood-pressure lowering effect, possibly due to anti-inflammatory and anti-oxidant effects on the vessel wall.

The LIFE (Lorsartan Intervention For Endpoint reduction in hypertension) study was recently published. This showed that blocking angiotensin-II receptors reduced the risk of stroke by 25% compared to atenolol (*Lancet 2002;350:995–1003*).

USEFUL WEBSITES

www.rcplondon.ac.uk/pubs/strokeaudit01-02.pdf – Summary report on the National Sentinel Stroke Audit, Royal College of Physicians
www.dcn.ed.ac.uk/csrg/ – Cochrane Stroke Group website
www.basp.ac.uk – British Association of Stroke Physicians
www.doh.gov.uk/nsf/olderpeopleindex.htm – National Service Framework for Older People
www.stroke.org.uk – The UK Stroke Association

INTERVENTIONS FOR ACUTE ISCHAEMIC STROKE

Beneficial
✓ Stroke units
✓ Aspirin

Trade-off between benefits and harms
✓ Thrombolytic treatment

Likely to be ineffective or harmful
✓ Immediate systemic anticoagulation
✓ Acute reduction of blood pressure

Chapter 2:

Respiratory Diseases

Chapter 2: Respiratory Diseases

Asthma

Asthma is still underdiagnosed and poorly treated despite an increased awareness of the condition. In 2002, asthma was estimated to cost the NHS £850m a year, with half of these costs arising as a result of acute asthma attacks. Over 18 million working days are lost to asthma each year. Most patients with asthma are managed in primary care.

How safe are inhaled steroids?

The amount of inhaled steroid absorbed in the body is very low, but systemic side-effects can occur – eg osteoporosis and growth retardation. Side-effects are unlikely to occur with low-dose inhaled steroids (< 400 μg beclometasone/day in children and < 1000 μg/day in adults). All children receiving inhaled steroids should have their height measured regularly, and any children needing high maintenance doses are best supervised by a paediatrician. Children with a viral-associated wheeze should not be prescribed inhaled steroids. The most important safeguard for patients is to have their asthma controlled regularly, and the dose of inhaled steroid stepped down once control of symptoms is achieved (*Drug Ther Bull; Jan 2000*).

The Cochrane Airways Group has reviewed six randomised, controlled trials (RCTs) looking at patients with asthma or chronic obstructive airways disease (COAD) who were on steroids. No significant rise in bone turnover was found in any of the studies up to three years after steroids were first prescribed, provided they had been given at recommended British Thoracic Society (BTS) levels. Although there is usually some concern in prescribing inhaled steroids, especially to children, a recent study has shown that if inhaled corticosteroids are used at the recommended dosages, then there is no association with risk of future fracture (*Am j Respir Crit Care Med 2004;169:83*). There was an increased risk of fracture for patients who had used inhaled steroids above 2000 mcg a day.

There has also been concern about under-recognized symptoms of adrenal suppression resulting from steroid use, such as anorexia, tiredness, headaches, etc. An association has also been found between inhaled steroids and cataract formation in elderly patients (*Br J Ophthalmol 2003;87:1247–51*). These effects can occur at doses of beclometasone and fluticasone > 400 µg daily and budesonide > 800 µg daily.

A recent UK study has found that doubling the dose of inhaled cortico-steroids is an ineffective way of preventing asthmatic exacerbations (*Lancet 2004;363:271–5*). It is interesting to note that the recommendation of doubling the dose of inhaled corticosteroids when asthma control deteriorates is not in the latest version of the BTS guidelines.

Which new drugs are available to treat asthma?

Leukotriene-receptor antagonists (LRAs) – montelukast (Singulair) and zafirlukast (Accolate) – are a class of oral asthma therapies that have anti-inflammatory and bronchodilator properties. Currently they seem to be best used as add-ons to low- or high-dose inhaled steroids where control of persistent asthma symptoms has not been achieved, or instead of steroids for children under five years.

A systematic review recently examined the evidence for the efficacy and glucocorticoid sparing effect of oral antileukotrienes in asthmatic patients (*BMJ 2002;324:1545–8*). This found that there is a shortage of relevant trials testing antileukotrienes as add-on treatment, but showed that these drugs may modestly improve the control of asthma compared to glucocorticoids alone. A more recent trial has shown that adding montelukast to the treatment regimes of asthma patients whose symptoms were uncontrolled with fluticasone provided equivalent control to adding salmeterol (*BMJ 2003;327:891–5*).

There is still little evidence however, to support the use of LTRAs as a substitute to inhaled glucocorticoids. A systematic review (*BMJ 2003; 326:621*) compared LRAs to inhaled steroids and found that inhaled steroids were more effective (at a dosage equivalent to 400 µg beclometasone per day), with a 60% lower risk of exacerbation.

Another study showed that adding monteleukast to the treatment regimen of asthma patients whose symptoms were uncontrolled with fluticasone provided equivalent control to adding salmeterol (*BMJ 2003;327:891–5*). This is the first time these two treatments had been directly compared with each other.

Do self-management plans have a role in asthma management?

Asthma lends itself to the use of guided self-management plans based on the BTS guidelines. There is plenty of evidence which shows that the use of self-management plans for asthma can lead to a reduction in hospitalisation rates and time off work, and to an improvement in symptom control.

However, according to one study, the concept of patient self-management plans receives a lukewarm response from GPs, practice nurses and from patients themselves (*BMJ 2000; 321:1507–10*). Many patients are not actually interested in formal self-management plans; they believe that they are already managing their asthma adequately! Asthma patients generally do not regard their condition as a chronic disease that needs regular monitoring and therapeutic adjustments, they prefer to manage it as an intermittent acute disorder. Many patients do not even wish to attend for regular asthma reviews – 45% of patients questioned said they neither had nor wanted regular asthma reviews.

How well is asthma controlled in primary care?

The ultimate goal is to help patients lead a normal life, free from symptoms and with no limitations on activities. According to the 'National Asthma Campaign's Needs of People with Asthma' survey, there are as many as 1.4 million people in the UK whose asthma control is less than satisfactory (*Asthma 2000;5:133–7*). This study showed that 42% of asthmatics have their daily life affected by symptoms related to their asthma, 44.5% report activity limitation and 87.5% experience asthma symptoms during the night. Surprisingly however, 87% of patients were either very satisfied or fairly satisfied with their asthma care (*Asthma 2000;5:141–4*).

A recent systematic review and meta-analysis of trials of educational programmes for the self-management of asthma in children and adolescents was performed (*BMJ 2003;326:1308*). This found that educational programmes improve lung function and feelings of self-control, reduce absenteeism from school, number of days with restricted activity and number of visits to hospital.

Similar results were found in another recent survey – the ACE (Asthma Control and Expectations) survey – which highlighted that patients have much lower expectations of asthma control and treatment than are laid out in asthma management guidelines (*Int J Clin Pract 2002;53:89–93*). As a result, many accept a life with unnecessary symptoms and activity limitations (see Box on p. 68). Healthcare professionals therefore have a role in improving asthma management by helping to raise patient expectations of what is achievable in terms of asthma control.

What is the best way of identifying suboptimal control of asthma?

Although objective measurements of the peak expiratory flow rate are important in assessing the severity and control of asthma, a symptom-based assessment is also very useful in clinical practice (*Br J Gen Pract 2000;50:7–12*). The three best questions to ask are:

✓ Have you had difficulty sleeping because of your asthma?

✓ Have you had your asthma symptoms during the day?

✓ Has your asthma interfered with your usual activities?

New BTS guidelines for asthma (2003)

The British Thoracic Society guidelines for the management of asthma have been updated (*Thorax 2003;58:(suppl 1):1*). They are clearly written, the summary charts are improved, the references are extensive, and useful additional chapters are included on topics such as pregnancy, occupational asthma, concordance or compliance, and audit datasets.

The major change is in the approach to step 3, where the guidelines are now consistent with current practice of using a long-acting broncho-dilator as the first approach when low dose inhaled steroids are inadequate. The previous alternative of an increase in the inhaled steroid dose to the 800–2000 µg range has been moved up to step 4.

The leukotriene receptor antagonists (LTRAs), which may offer a small improvement in lung function and symptoms and a small decrease in exacerbations, should now be considered as add-on drugs as step 4.

Step 1: Inhaled short-acting β_2-agonist as required. If needed more than once per day on average, go to step 2.

Step 2: Add inhaled steroid 200–800 µg/day. Start at dose of inhaled steroid appropriate to the severity of disease. In children under five years, an LRA (leukotriene-receptor antagonist) could be considered instead of the steroid. In 5–12-year-olds, add inhaled steroid to a maximum of 400 µg/day.

Step 3: Add a long-acting β_2-agonist (LABA) or consider an LRA in children under five years. If inadequate response, continue LABA, but increase the inhaled steroid dose to 800 µg per day (400 µg in children aged 5–12) If no response to LABA, stop LABA and increase the inhaled steroids to 800 µg/day (400 µg in children). If control is still inadequate, consider LRAs/theophylline in adults and children. Refer children under two years of age at this stage or at stage 4 if between two to five years.

Step 4: Consider trials of:

✓ Increasing inhaled steroids up to 2000 µg/day (800 µg in children aged 5–12 years)

✓ Addition of a fourth drug, eg LRA, SR theophylline, β_2-agonist tablet

Step 5: Prescribed daily steroid tablet the lowest dose providing adequate control, whilst maintaining a high-dose inhaled steroid at 2000 µg/day (or 800 µg in children aged 5–12). Consider referral in most adults and all children under 12 years of age.

USEFUL WEBSITES

www.gpiag.com – General Practice Airways Group
www.brit-thoracic.org.uk – British Thoracic Society
www.asthma.org.uk – National Asthma Campaign

SUMMARY POINTS FOR ASTHMA

✓ Essential to learn BTS guidelines
✓ CFC-free inhalers are replacing CFC inhalers
✓ Patient expectations of asthma control are very low
✓ Leukotriene receptor antagonists may not always be beneficial
✓ Patients are not always keen on self-management plans

KEY FINDINGS OF THE ACE SURVEY

Of patients who said they usually felt well:
• around 1/3 experienced daily symptoms
• 51% accepted limitations to their lifestyle
• 32% of patients modify their behaviour when they feel their asthma is getting worse to avoid symptoms
• 89% of patients do not discuss their lifestyle limitations with their healthcare professional

Chronic Obstructive Pulmonary Disease (COPD)

Over 26,000 people died of COPD in England and Wales in 1999. It is estimated that COPD accounts for as many as one in every eight hospital admissions.

COPD VS ASTHMA

	COPD	Asthma
FEV_1	Always reduced (FEV_1/FVC < 70%)	Variable
Diurnal variation	Minimal	Morning dip
Increase in FEV_1 post bronchodilator	< 200 ml	> 500 ml
Response to steroid trial	Partial response in 10–20%	Good

If a patient is suspected of having COPD, then it is worth measuring their PEFR; a PEFR of < 80% of the predicted value will detect > 90% of patients with COPD, and probably everyone with moderate or severe disease. The specificity of PEFR is approximately 82% (*BMJ 2003; 327:653*).

BTS Guidelines

The BTS guidelines from 1997 state that inhaled steroids should only be used after a 'steroid trial' in patients with moderate to severe disease. This can be done either by giving prednisolone 30 mg daily for two weeks or high-dose inhaled steroids (eg 1000 μg beclometasone per day) for six weeks. An increase in FEV_1 of > 200 ml and > 15% above baseline indicates a positive response; this is expected in 10–20% of patients.

Smoking cessation is the most effective intervention in terms of stopping the decline of respiratory function, although it does not restore lost function.

The Royal College of Physicians have recommended that long-term oxygen therapy should be considered in severe cases of COPD where $pa(o_2)$ < 7.3 kPa, or moderate cases ($pa(o_2)$ 7.3–8 kPa) in the presence of secondary polycythaemia, nocturnal hypoxaemia, peripheral oedema or pulmonary hypertension. Oxygen therapy only increases survival if used for > 15 hours per day, when it is most economical to prescribe a concentrator as well.

What evidence is there for inhaled steroids?

This is quite controversial. Some RCTs have shown that there is no significant difference between inhaled steroids and placebo in lung function (ie FEV_1) over 10 days to 10 weeks. However, a meta analysis looking at 3715 patients with COPD, monitored for two years, found that long-term steroid reduced the annual rate of fall of FEV_1, by 13–17% in smokers and 26–33% in non-smokers (*Thorax 2003;58:937–41*). The ISOLDE study (*BMJ 2000;320:1297–1303*), a large RCT, found that inhaled fluticasone (500 µg bd) reduced the median exacerbation rate in patients with severe COPD by 25% (although there was no significant difference in the annual rate of decline of FEV_1). The TRISTAN study group published a trial (*Lancet 2003;361:449–56*) which showed that treatment of COPD with combined fluticasone and salmeterol significantly increased FEV_1 after 12 months of treatment; more than either drug used individually.

The DTB suggests that a trial of inhaled steroids should be reserved for patients who have an FEV_1 of < 50% and who have frequent exacerbations or those who have had a spirometric response.

Which is better – inhaled anticholinergics or β_2-agonists?

RCTs have shown that FEV_1 is improved more with inhaled anticholinergics compared to β_2-agonists over a three-month period. There are inconsistent results when comparing LABAs with anticholinergics. The long-acting anticholinergic drug tiotropium is licensed as once-daily therapy for maintenance treatment of COPD. Trials show that it improves FEV_1 compared to placebo and reduces the number of exacerbations. It appears more effective than ipratropium in reducing the number of exacerbations, and initial data suggest it might be more effective than salmeterol (*Drug Ther Bull Vol 41, Feb 2003*).

Exercise programmes and rehabilitation

A review of the effects of exercise (*Br J Gen Pract 2002;52:574*) in patients with mild to moderate COPD showed improved exercise tolerance and health status. A meta-analysis in *The Lancet* (*1996; 348:1115–19*) concluded that pulmonary rehabilitation (lasting at least four weeks) comprising graded exercise training, education and psychological/behavioural therapy (including smoking cessation advice) reduces breathlessness and increases quality of life. This may be feasible in primary care (*Br J Gen Pract 2002;52:567*).

Mucolytics

N-acetylcysteine is prescribed in mainland Europe and seems to be effective in reducing the number and frequency of exacerbations in patients with chronic bronchitis. Mucodyne can now be prescribed on the NHS.

COPD causes a great deal of social and psychological morbidity: 80% of patients with advanced COPD are housebound. Approximately 90% of patients with severe COPD are depressed, but this is rarely addressed.

SUMMARY POINTS

✓ COPD is a common, disabling condition, often associated with co-existing depression

✓ The argument about whether to prescribe inhaled steroids remains contentious

✓ Smoking advice is vital

✓ Pulmonary rehabilitation is very effective

✓ Anticholinergics are more effective than short-acting β_2-agonists

✓ Long-acting anticholinergics are probably more effective than LABAs

✓ Long-term oxygen therapy for at least 15 hours daily improves survival in severely hypoxaemic patients ($Pao_2 < 7.3$) and in patients with moderate hypoxaemia with other features as described above

Smoking Cessation

Smoking is the single most important cause of preventable illness and premature death in the UK, and leads to direct medical costs of £1.7b each year. Cigarette smoking will cause about 450 million deaths worldwide in the next 50 years. It is therefore a top healthcare priority, especially as there has been a recent increase in the number of smokers. The NHS Plan states that a comprehensive smoking cessation service has been in place since 2001.

Around one in four adults smoke, with much higher levels in deprived sections of society. However, giving up permanently is difficult; although two-thirds of smokers want to quit, and about one-third try each year, only 2% actually succeed. A recent study has found that 16% of English smokers are 'hardcore' – defined as having had less than a day without cigarettes in the past five years, no desire to quit and no intention to quit (*BMJ 2003;326:1061*). They are more likely to be older and from more socio-economically deprived backgrounds. In addition, they are more likely to dismiss any effects of smoking on their health.

On average, 70% of smokers consult their GP each year, so primary care teams need to be involved with smoking cessation programmes. The authors of the Sheffield table have even estimated that the statin bill could be reduced by 85% if everyone stopped smoking!

In December 2000, *Thorax* published updated guidelines for tackling cigarette dependence (*Thorax 2000;55:987–99*). They recognise that GPs have a pivotal role if the NHS is to deliver a noticeable drop in smoking rates. These guidelines are based on strong evidence from randomised trials supplemented by studies examining what can be achieved in routine clinical practice. A systematic review has since been published, which is discussed below (*Tob Control 2003;12:21–7*).

What are the advantages of stopping smoking?

There are obviously huge benefits from stopping smoking. Widespread cessation of smoking in the UK has already approximately halved the lung cancer mortality that would have been expected if former smokers had continued to smoke.

Underscoring the health benefits of smoking cessation is the report by Doll et al based on a comparison of two case-control studies conducted

40 years apart in the United Kingdom (*BMJ 2000;321:323-9*). Even smokers who stop at age 50 or 60 years avoid much of their excess risk of developing lung cancer. The benefits of cessation become progressively greater with a younger age of quitting; stopping smoking before middle age avoids more than 90% of the risk attributable to tobacco.

How effective are smoking cessation treatments?

Helping smokers to stop is actually one of the most cost-effective interventions in the NHS today (*BMJ 2001;323:1140-1*). The cost-effectiveness of smoking cessation treatments has been calculated at just over £600 per life-year gained for treated smokers aged 35-44 and £750 for those aged 45-54 years. By comparison, statin therapy to lower blood cholesterol concentrations ranges from about £4,000 to £13,000 per life-year gained.

The NHS Centre for Reviews and Dissemination (University of York) has produced a systematic review of smoking cessation treatments. The results also show that both NRT and bupropion are cost-effective treatments in terms of cost per life-year saved.

Smoking cessation treatments have been established throughout the NHS and are an integral part of the Government's plans to reduce deaths from coronary heart disease and cancer. Statistics show that between April 2001 and March 2002, there was an increase in successful quitters from 64,000 to 119,800; an overall increase of 84%. There was a doubling of prescriptions for smoking cessation drugs in 2002.

Nicotine replacement therapy (NRT)

This treatment aims to replace the nicotine obtained from cigarettes, thus reducing withdrawal symptoms when stopping smoking. Nicotine replacement is available as a chewing gum, transdermal patch, nasal spray, inhaler, sublingual tablet and lozenge. A Cochrane review of over 90 trials found that nicotine replacement helps people to stop smoking. Overall, it increases the chances of quitting by about 1.5-2 times, whatever the level of additional support and encouragement.

There is little direct evidence that one nicotine product is more effective than another. Thus, the decision about which product to use should be guided by individual preferences. Combining a patch with other forms of NRT may be more effective than a patch alone and appears to have a good safety profile. A systematic review found that over-the-counter nicotine replacement therapy works as well as prescribed NRT, even if prescription is combined with a behavioural programme (*Tob Control 2003;12:21–7*).

What is bupropion (Zyban)?

This was initially developed as an antidepressant. One hypothesis of its mode of action is that it works by increasing levels of dopamine and noradrenaline in the brain, thereby counteracting the reductions in these chemicals that result from nicotine withdrawal. The efficacy of bupropion as an aid to smoking cessation has been investigated in two randomised, double-blinded, placebo-controlled trials (*New Engl J Med 1997; 337:1195–202* and *New Engl J Med 1999;340:685–91*). These patients received regular counselling sessions in addition to bupropion. Results have indicated that up to 30% of smokers succeed with bupropion and that these results are sustained over a year.

Bupropion is relatively well tolerated; contraindications to its use include epilepsy, pregnancy and concomitant antidepressants. The risk of fits has been estimated at about 1 in 1000 people, which is actually the same risk as for amitriptyline and imipramine. It may also increase the risk of fits through interactions with other drugs that lower the seizure threshold, including antipsychotics, antidepressants, systemic steroids, antimalarial drugs and theophylline.

There is little evidence to support the superiority of bupropion over NRT for smoking cessation; one double-blind study indicated that the NRT patch is less effective than bupropion, while another study found no difference between NRT gum and bupropion; further RCTs are clearly needed. There is currently not enough evidence to recommend the use of NRT and bupropion together.

What are the NICE recommendations for smoking cessation treatments?

In April 2002, NICE recommended the use of bupropion and NRT for smokers who wish to quit. The guidance states that NRT or bupropion should normally only be prescribed when smokers have made a commitment to stop smoking on or before a certain date ('target stop date'), in conjunction with advice and encouragement to help them quit.

First prescriptions of NRT or bupropion should only be enough to last until two weeks after the target stop date. Normally, this will be two weeks for NRT. For bupropion it will be 3–4 weeks, because bupropion should be taken for about one week before the target stop date. Smokers should only be given a second prescription for NRT or bupropion if they can show they are still trying to stop smoking.

Other treatments

The effectiveness of other treatments – namely: aversion therapy, acupuncture, hypnotherapy and exercise – is as yet uncertain.

What is the cycle of change and how can it be used for smoking cessation?

There are undoubtedly certain times when a patient will be more receptive to advice on stopping smoking. Smoking cessation should not be regarded as a dichotomous process (cessation or not), but rather as a continuum that entails several stages. DiClemente and Prochaska's cycle of readiness to change (see Figure on p. 71) has been used to describe the psychological processes involved in many patterns of human behaviour and lends itself very well to smoking cessation (*J Consult Clin Psychol 1991;59:295–304*). It is important to know the 'cycle of change' as it can be applied to various aspects of clinical practice, and can be very useful to discuss in the viva examination!

Precontemplation
This is the stage at which the patient is happy at being a smoker and does not contemplate stopping. Although brief intervention at this stage may not persuade them to give up, it may help them question their habit and move them nearer to the next stage.

Contemplation
This is the stage at which the patient is dissatisfied with being a smoker and is thinking about giving up (70% of adult smokers are at this stage!). During this stage, it can be effective to make the idea of quitting relevant to the patient, for example a patient recently diagnosed with heart disease.

Preparation
This is the stage at which the smoker is making serious plans to stop. It is therefore important to be supportive; discussion about smoking cessation treatments is most beneficial at this stage.

Action

This is the stage when maximum support should be given, as it is at this stage when the attempt to stop smoking is made.

Maintenance

This is the stage at which the patient tries to prevent relapse. This is often the most difficult time as enthusiasm often wears off quicker than withdrawal symptoms.

Relapse

This is obviously when the patient's attempt to stop smoking has been unsuccessful. This can either mean permanently giving up the idea of quitting smoking or thinking about it again in the future, when the patient would then re-enter the cycle at the precontemplation stage.

If the doctor or healthcare professional is unaware of where their patient is in this cycle of change, then any time and effort given regarding smoking cessation may be wasted.

USEFUL WEBSITES

www.update-software.com/abstracts/mainindex.htm – Cochrane reviews
www.nhs.uk/nhsplan – The NHS Plan
www.mca.gov.uk – Medicines and Healthcare products Regulatory Agency (MHRA) (for further information on the CSM)
www.nice.org.uk – NICE guidance

DICLEMENTE AND PROCHASKA'S CYCLE OF CHANGE

SUMMARY POINTS FOR SMOKING CESSATION

✓ Over 75% of smokers consult their GPs annually
✓ Only 2% smokers manage to give up by themselves
✓ Smoking cessation clinics have promising results
✓ Bupropion can help up to a third of smokers stop smoking
✓ Assessing smokers' motivation to quit is important
✓ Consider the 'cycle of change'

Influenza

During the winter months there is usually an outbreak of influenza, caused by A or B virus, which results in a huge increased workload for both primary care teams and hospitals. Even when the incidence is low, it has been estimated that 3–4000 deaths in the UK each year are from influenza-related causes. These deaths occur mainly in older people, but young children and immunosuppressed people are also at increased risk.

What are the benefits of the influenza vaccine?

There is plenty of evidence to support the effectiveness of the vaccine; it reduces mortality and morbidity in high-risk groups. Overall, the vaccination gives up to 70–80% protection against strains related to the vaccine, and helps prevent pneumonia, hospital admission and death (*New Engl J Med 2000;343:1778–87*). Another study also showed a marked reduction in hospital admission of people who had received the vaccination (*Lancet 2001;357:1008–11*). In particular, there was a 46% reduction in admissions for influenza and a lower mortality from all causes (53–56% reduction).

In May 2000 the policy on influenza vaccination was altered and the vaccine is now recommended for:
✓ All people over 65 years
✓ All people in long-stay residential accommodation
✓ All people with:
  • Chronic respiratory disease, including asthma
  • Chronic heart disease
  • Chronic renal disease
  • Diabetes mellitus
  • Immunosuppression due to disease or treatment.

Health authorities were set a target of achieving a minimum of 65% uptake of immunisation in their over-65-year-old patients for the winter of 2001/2, and 70% for the winters of 2002/3 and 2003/4.

What are the treatments for influenza?

Although vaccination remains the most important measure for reducing the burden of influenza, the influenza virus inhibitors, zanamivir (Relenza) and oseltamivir, are additional agents for the treatment and prevention of influenza.

Neuraminidase inhibitors have been shown to be clinically effective for the treatment of influenza in otherwise healthy adults and children, as well as for the prevention of the disease (*BMJ 2003;326:1235–40*). When taken as prophylaxis they can decrease the likelihood of developing influenza by 70–90%. This systematic review showed that treating otherwise healthy adults and children with zanamivir and osteltamivir reduces the duration of symptoms by between 0.4 and 1.0 days. The treatment also lowers the risk of complications by 29–34% when given within 48 hours of the onset of symptoms. However, evidence is still limited for the treatment of high-risk populations and these medications are expensive. There is also still a lack of data on their efficacy in preventing serious influenza-related complications and mortality in groups at highest risk – elderly and people with co-morbidity.

Community studies have shown that seasonal prophylactic use of neuraminidase inhibitors administered after exposure in households and residential care would be clinically effective (*Vaccine 2002;20: 2562–78*). No studies have been conducted to compare the response to treatment in vaccinated versus non-vaccinated people.

Oseltamivir, like zanamivir, is a neuraminidase inhibitor, but unlike zanamivir it is readily absorbed from the gut so is an oral medication. A study of 548 elderly people in residential homes were randomised to receive either oseltamivir or placebo for 6 weeks, starting when influenza was confirmed in the home or nearby (*J Am Geriatr Soc 2001; 49:1025–31*). Oseltamivir was found to reduce the incidence of influenza from 4.4% with placebo to 0.4%. It seems to offer protection from influenza over and above that of the vaccination. It may be worthwhile, therefore, offering prophylaxis with osteltamivir to residents and staff in the event of an outbreak in residential homes (*Drug Ther Bull 2002;40:89–91*).

When should zanamivir be prescribed?

In November 2000, NICE recommended that zanamivir should be used to treat 'at risk' adults when influenza is circulating in the community and if they present within 36 hours of developing symptoms.

Flu is considered to be circulating in the community when consultations for influenza rise above 50 a week per 100,000 population, as monitored by the Royal College of General Practitioners' weekly returns' monitoring service. The Public Health Laboratory Service must also have identified the circulation of a flu virus.

'At risk' adults are defined as those with:
- ✓ Chronic respiratory disease
- ✓ Significant cardiovascular disease
- ✓ Diabetes mellitus
- ✓ Age over 65 years

This recommendation reverses the NICE's previous ruling that there was insufficient evidence of the drug's efficacy in high-risk individuals to make it worth prescribing on the NHS (*BMJ 1999;319:1024*).

It has been estimated that only 30% of self-diagnosed flu is actually due to influenza. As there is no cheap, effective diagnostic test available, many people may therefore be unnecessarily prescribed or unnecessarily request zanamivir.

Why is there opposition to prescribing zanamivir?

The evidence to support its use is still from small studies and many of the trials did not specifically recruit high-risk patients. Its own product characteristics' statement said it had been unable to determine that the drug was effective in elderly patients and those with chronic conditions such as asthma and diabetes. In addition, there has been no published trial comparing its effect on influenza symptoms with symptomatic therapy (eg ibuprofen and paracetamol).

There have been reports of fatal adverse reactions in patients with COPD and asthma in the USA. It has therefore been recommended that if zanamivir is to be prescribed for patients with airways disease, it should only be done under careful supervision and with short-acting bronchodilators available.

NICE originally refused to allow the drug to be prescribed on the NHS in 2000 and the *BMJ* has criticised NICE on its U-turn for responding to 'political clout'.

The Drug and Therapeutics Bulletin will continue not to recommend zanamivir as part of the treatment of influenza as it is 'unconvinced of the benefits'. Certainly, the complications zanamivir reduces are minor –

eg sinusitis. There is no evidence of benefit for major complications like hospitalisation and death.

Finally, one study has found that most elderly people cannot use the zanamivir inhaler device correctly (*BMJ 2001;322:577–9*). One of the authors of the study has advised that GPs need to spend at least 15 minutes teaching their elderly patients how to use the device, which is not really realistic. A nasal spray is also available.

USEFUL WEBSITES

www.rcgp-bru.demon.co.uk   –   Influenza   surveillance   website
www.nice.org.uk – NICE guidelines available online

SUMMARY POINTS FOR INFLUENZA

✓ Influenza leads to about 3000 deaths annually
✓ Influenza vaccine is safe and effective
✓ NICE recommends the use of zanamivir
✓ Weak evidence to support the use of zanamivir

Chapter 3:

Psychiatry

Chapter 3: Psychiatry

Mental health national service framework

✓ Sets national standards for mental health services
✓ Based on clinical evidence and sets out best practice for promoting mental health and treating mental illness
✓ Accompanied by £700m for mental health services (1999–2002)
✓ Aims to iron out unacceptable variations around the country
✓ Proposes further integration of health and social services

Standards of care

1. Combat discrimination against individuals and groups with mental health problems, and promote their social inclusion.

2. Any service user who contacts their primary healthcare team with a common mental health problem should:
   - Have their mental health needs identified and assessed
   - Be offered effective treatments, including referral to specialist services if they require it.

3. Any individual with a common mental health problem should:
   - Be able to make contact 24 h a day with local services
   - Be able to use NHS Direct, as it develops, for first-level advice and referral on to specialist helplines or to local services.

4. All mental health service users should have a Care Programme Approach (CPA) and have a copy of a written care plan that:
   - Includes the action to be taken in a crisis by the service user, their carer and their care coordinator
   - Advises their GP how they should respond if the service user needs additional help
   - Is regularly reviewed by their care coordinator.

5. Each service user who is assessed as requiring a period of care away from their home should have timely access to an appropriate hospital bed or alternative bed or place, which is:
    *   In the least-restrictive environment consistent with the need to protect them and the public
    *   As close to home as possible.

6. All individuals who provide regular and substantial care for a person on CPA should:
    *   Have an assessment of their caring, physical and mental health needs, repeated on at least an annual basis
    *   Have their own written care plan, which is given to them and implemented in discussion with them.

7. Prevent suicide. Ensure that health and social services play their full part in the achievement of the target in saving lives. Reduce the suicide rate by at least one-fifth by 2010.

Criticisms

For many, the NSF arrived far too late. After years of chronic under-funding the expectation of achieving far-fetched idealistic targets within a short period seems unattainable.

Much of the document could easily be a party political broadcast on mental health. Should politics play such a large role?

Can 24 h access be sufficiently foolproof with the use of NHS Direct? Discrimination is not an easily audited subject, how can you show you have improved it, in a reliable and reproducible way?

 Reforming The Mental Health Act, December 2000

This White Paper sets out the Government's plans for new mental health legislation. It comprises two parts. This is to distinguish arrangements for high-risk patients.

Reforms are a response to:
✓ Media publicity regarding dangerous and severely personality-disordered (DSPD) patients and the tragic toll of homicides and suicides (rare though this is)

✓ The current 1983 Mental Health Act is largely based on a review of mental health legislation which took place in the 1950s; outmoded laws have failed to protect the public, patients or staff

✓ Under existing mental health laws, the powers for compulsory treatment are for patients in hospital only, whereas the majority of patients today are treated in the community

✓ Severely ill patients have been allowed to drift out of contact with mental health services and have been able to refuse treatment

✓ Existing legislation has also failed to provide adequate public protection from those whose risk to others arises from a severe personality disorder

Half of the White Paper is devoted to 'high risk' patients, with more emphasis on protection of the public. It is proving to be generally controversial and has not yet become law in England and Wales.

New procedures for use of compulsory powers (previously called 'sections').

There will be a new three-stage process that applies in all cases, except for offenders (for whom assessment will be ordered by the Court, and for prisoners by the Home Secretary). The aim is to simplify the template for 'formal assessment', making it easier for staff and patients to understand.

Stage 1 – Preliminary examination

✓ When a patient might be at risk of serious harm or pose a risk of serious harm to other people

✓ Decisions to begin assessment and initial treatment of a patient under compulsory powers will be based, as it is now, on a preliminary examination by two doctors and a social worker or another suitably trained mental health professional.

Stage 2 – Formal assessment and initial treatment under compulsory powers

✓ Patients will be given a full assessment of their health and social care needs, and receive treatment set out in a formal care plan

✓ Initial period of assessment and treatment under compulsory powers will be limited to a maximum of 28 days

✓ After that, continuing use of compulsory powers must be authorised by a new independent decision-making body, the Mental Health Tribunal, which will obtain advice from independent experts as well as taking evidence from the clinical team, the patient and his or her representatives and other agencies, where appropriate. This is to safeguard the patients' rights

Stage 3 – Care and treatment order
The Tribunal (or Court in the case of mentally disordered offenders) will be able to make a 'Care and treatment order', which will authorise the treatment specified in a care plan recommended by the clinical team. The first two orders will be for up to six months each; subsequent orders may be for periods of up to 12 months. The criteria for a Care and treatment order are an unwilling patient and the presence of a 'mental disorder that warrants specialist care and attention and which without treatment might lead to a risk for others'. Of particular significance, personality disorder is included within the definition of mental disorder. It is also worth making note of the fact that the Tribunal, although ostensibly there to safeguard the patient's rights, may 'exceptionally' reserve the right not to accept the clinical team's decision to discharge the patient.

Care and treatment in the community
✓ Introduction of new provisions so that care and treatment orders may apply to patients outside hospital
✓ Will mean that patients need not be in hospital unnecessarily and need not suffer the possible distress of repeated unplanned admissions to acute wards
✓ There will, however, be no powers for patients to be given medication forcibly except in a clinical setting
✓ Steps will be specified in community orders to prevent patients becoming a risk to themselves, their carers or the public if they do not comply with their order
✓ New legislation will also introduce a new duty covering the disclosure of information about patients suffering from mental disorder between health and social services agencies and other agencies, eg housing agencies or criminal justice agencies

It remains unclear whether community orders are intended to be short- or long-term measures.

Better information and advice
✓ Every patient will be informed about the particular powers that apply in his or her case
✓ Patients who want to challenge the use of compulsory powers will continue to have the right to free legal representation

✓ Will also give them a new right of access to advice and support from independent specialist advocacy services – 'The New Patient Advocacy Liaison Service'

New safeguards
✓ New independent body – the Mental Health Tribunal – to determine all longer term use of compulsory powers
✓ New right to independent advocacy
✓ New safeguards for people with long-term mental incapacity
✓ New Commission for Mental Health
✓ Statutory requirement to develop care plans

A new Commission for Mental Health
✓ Will be set up to look after the interests of all people who are subject to care and treatment under powers laid down in the Act
✓ Will carry specific responsibilities for monitoring the use of formal powers, providing guidance on the operation of those powers and assuring the quality of statutory training provided for practitioners with key responsibilities under the new legislation and for specialist advocacy services

New safeguards for children and young people
✓ The Mental Health Tribunal will be required to obtain specialist expert advice on both health and social care aspects of the proposed care plan, and to consider whether the location of care is appropriate
✓ Decisions taken in respect of children will be subject to a clear principle that the interests of the child must be paramount
✓ Changes will be made in the provisions regarding the right of a young person between the ages of 16 and 18 years to refuse consent to care and treatment for mental disorder

High-risk patients
✓ Those who need treatment primarily in their own best interests will be dealt with separately from those who need treatment because of the risk they pose to others
✓ If the care plan cannot directly address the mental illness of those who need treatment because of the risk they pose to others, it may instead address the 'behaviours arising from that disorder'. This means that 'treatability' is no longer necessary as it was in the 1983

Mental Health Act. Patients with a personality disorder may be considered high risk

The most contentious issue is whether the Mental Health Act is being cynically used to detain difficult, often violent individuals under a veneer of so-called 'health care'.

When will it become law?

 Draft Mental Health Bill, July 2002

Following the initial White Paper on reforming the Mental Health Act, the Draft Mental Health Bill was published in July 2002. Proposed legislation is the first major overhaul of the system since the 1950s and has been published in draft form. In Scotland, the new Mental Health Act has received Royal Assent, and the Scottish executive is currently asking for views on it, in order to implement the act by 2005. Implementation in England and Wales is much more uncertain, with much opposition from human rights groups.

 Department of Health. Draft Mental Health Bill. London, Stationery Office, 2002

The Bill can be accessed at the Website below and was discussed in an editorial (*BMJ 2002;325:2–3*) entitled 'Detaining dangerous people with mental disorders'.

 USEFUL WEBSITE

www.doh.gov.uk/mentalhealth

SUMMARY

✓ The White Paper on reforming the Mental Health Act that preceded the Draft Bill attracted a great deal of attention because of its overriding emphasis on public safety

✓ The fact that it was not well received is hardly surprising, and proposals for managing dangerous people with severe personality disorder were described as glaringly wrong and unethical

✓ The ministerial foreword accompanying the Draft Bill seeks to reassure us that the new law will promote patients' rights and protect them

✓ The term 'dangerous people with severe personality disorder' often used in the White Paper does not receive a single mention in the Draft Bill

✓ The procedure for compulsion in the Draft Bill is similar to that described in the White Paper. This involves a single pathway with three distinct stages: a preliminary examination; a period of formal assessment lasting up to 28 days; and then treatment under a Mental Health Act order

✓ Certain conditions must be satisfied before any compulsory powers can be used:
1. There must be a mental disorder
2. This must be of a nature or degree warranting medical treatment
3. Treatment must be necessary for the health or safety of the patient or the protection of others

✓ 'Mental disorder' is defined as 'any disability or disorder of mind or brain which results in impairment or disturbance of mental functioning'

✓ The broad definition of mental disorder means that dangerous people with severe personality disorder are included; it also raises the possibility of compulsory treatment for sexual deviancy and alcohol/drug dependence

Summary (cont.)

Summary (cont.)

✓ The 'treatability test', which many will recall is used to exclude some patients with psychopathic disorder and mental impairment from treatment under the current Act, is also absent

✓ The Draft Bill may not go as far as the White Paper in advocating compulsory powers to manage behaviours arising from the disorder, but the broad 'medical treatment' definition probably allows for this

✓ Principles require that patients are involved in decisions made about them, decisions are made fairly and openly and that any treatment given imposes the minimum level of intrusion. In certain circumstances, however, including matters of public protection, these principles may be 'disapplied'

✓ Another important difference is that a patient who is at substantial risk of causing serious harm to others can be given medical treatment if this is necessary for the protection of those other persons

✓ In all other instances the condition that treatment cannot be provided without using the Act must also be satisfied

✓ The development of services for dangerous people with severe personality disorder at Whitemoor and Frankland prisons shows that this must be on the Government's agenda

✓ The Draft Bill has safeguards including rights of appeal, as one would expect

✓ Access to advocacy services and safeguards for certain patients treated informally who are not capable of consenting are welcome additions, but it is doubtful whether the proposed safeguards are robust enough

Criticisms

✓ The Mental Health Alliance, a group of over 50 voluntary organisations that has worked with the Government to try to update the Mental Health Act 1983, says that it is disappointed with the Government for ignoring its concerns and that it fears the new proposals will make the current services even worse

✓ Mental health experts have rejected the Government's proposals to lock up hundreds of people with untreatable personality disorders who may not have committed a crime

✓ The Royal College of Psychiatrists together with the Law Society has called the proposals 'fundamentally flawed' as well as 'costly and complex' and almost impossible to implement

✓ It has been said that 600 extra full-time psychiatrists would be required to run the new 'Mental Health Review Tribunals' alone, clearly an almost impossible task

Depression

As GPs we see distressed, tearful people everyday and can sometimes wrongly label them as being depressed. Conversely, many of the patients whom we regularly treat for chronic, physical disease have an underlying depression, which we do not diagnose. It is known that patients with depression tend to ration themselves to a limited amount of time with their GP, even though they would value the chance to talk more, because they are anxious about time restrictions (*BMJ 2002;325:687*).

It is possible that we as GPs could be doing more to help our depressed patients. A study in America (*BMJ 2002;325:934*) has shown that ongoing intervention in patients with depression (in the form of regular telephone calls from the practice nurse to monitor the patient's mood) improved symptoms and function after two years of treatment. Whether this is realistic in practice however, is debatable.

UK studies in the 1980s showed that 5% of people have major depression and a further 10% have milder depressive symptoms. In a more recent study in the USA in 1994, the prevalence of major depression in patients seeing their family doctor was estimated to be 13.5%.

✓ Much of the published research in primary care revolves around the poor pick-up of depression and lack of treatment instigation. However, it remains unclear whether it is worthwhile picking up milder cases of depression (see below); many cases of depression that we miss as GPs might resolve spontaneously. A recent BMJ study (*BMJ 2002;325:1016–17*) suggested that although many patients with depression do not receive an initial diagnosis, most are diagnosed at subsequent consultations, or recover spontaneously. This small study estimated that about 14% of patients with clinically significant features of depression remain undiagnosed after three years.

Many studies look at various short questionnaires that can be used in clinical practice. These allow for the screening and therefore detection of people with depression. Using validated tools allows GPs to be more accurate in their diagnosis. A recent study in Germany (*BMJ 2003; 326:200–1*) suggested that using the WHO-5 Well-being Index Questionnaire as a routine screening test for depression could be feasible, since it offers high sensitivity with a high negative predictive value. However, using routine screening tests might lead to over-treatment (see the section on mild depression).

📖 Detection criteria (simplified): (Oxford Textbook of Medicine: third edition)

Over the last two weeks, one of the following features should be present for a diagnosis of major depression:
* Depressed mood
* Anhedonia – loss of interest or pleasure

And at least four of the following:
✓ Weight or appetite change
✓ Early waking and diurnal mood variation
✓ Psychomotor agitation or retardation
✓ Fatigue
✓ Feelings of worthlessness/guilt
✓ Reduced ability to concentrate
✓ Recurrent thoughts of death/suicidal ideas

Mild depression

As GPs, we see more cases of 'mild' than 'major' depression. This may be nothing more than a self-limiting reaction to adverse life events, but still results in significant morbidity and loss of working days. Little is known about the natural history of mild depression and about how we should treat it.

It seems that in most patients, symptoms of depression improve within six months to a year. Long-term, follow-up studies (over 10–11 years) have found that 50–60% of patients have, at most, a single recurrence of depression, but up to 30% experience relapsing and remitting symptoms and 18% have chronic symptoms (*BMJ 1996;313:26–8*).

There is no convincing evidence of benefit from antidepressant therapy in patients who do not meet the criteria for major depression, although limited evidence exists for the treatment of 'dysthymia' (presence of at least three of the symptoms from the above list, including depressed mood, for most days for at least two years). Most patients prefer counselling to medication.

The *Drug and Therapeutics Bulletin* (*Drug Ther Bull Vol 41, No 8, August 2003*) concludes that a supportive 'watchful waiting' approach is reasonable and an immediate prescription for an antidepressant rarely justified. However, GPs do need to monitor patients with mild depression, in order to pick up the 20% who develop a chronic problem.

Papers

1. *Effects of a clinical-practice guideline and practice-based education on detection and outcome of depression in primary care: Hampshire Depression Project (HDP) randomised controlled trial*

(*C. Thompson, et al, Lancet 2000;355:185–91*)

✓ This large, well-constructed RCT tested the hypothesis that 'the most effective strategy to reduce depression is education of GPs'

✓ They tested this assumption by assessing the effectiveness of an educational programme based on a clinical-practice guideline in improving the recognition and outcome of primary-care depression

✓ Education was delivered to practice teams and quality tested by feedback from participants and expert raters. This involved four hours of education for GPs in the intervention group

✓ The primary endpoints were recognition of depression, defined by the Hospital Anxiety and Depression (HAD) scale, and clinical improvement. Analysis was by intention to treat

✓ 21,409 patients were screened, of whom 4192 were classified as depressed by the HAD scale

✓ The education was well received by participants, 80% of whom thought it would change their management of patients with depression

✓ The sensitivity of physicians to depressive symptoms was 39% in the intervention group and 36% in the control group after education

✓ The outcome of depressed patients as a whole at six weeks or six months after the assessment did not significantly improve

✓ Results were disappointingly negative, failing to show any increase in recognition or patient recovery rates

✓ In an editorial (*Lancet*) GPs were accused of not following the guidelines

Shortly afterwards, an editorial entitled 'Why can't GPs follow guidelines on depression?' appeared in the *BMJ* discussing the issues raised by the study (*BMJ 2000;320:200*).

Issues discussed and points raised:

✓ Findings of the HDP herald the need for a major change in thinking about improving the management of depression in primary care

✓ Results conflict with the positive findings of other studies (note the HDP had more participants)

✓ Such intensive training as used in the HDP cannot be delivered through our existing education systems

2. Antidepressant drugs and generic counselling for treatment of major depression in primary care
(*C. Chilvers, et al, BMJ 2001;322:772–5*)

✓ Objective was to compare the efficacy of antidepressant drugs and generic counselling for treating mild to moderate depression in general practice

✓ RCT with patient-preference arms (ie allowed to choose rather than be randomised), followed up at eight weeks and 12 months

✓ 31 general practices in the Trent region with 103 patients randomised and 220 patients in preference arms

✓ Study looked at the Beck Depression Inventory Score (validated), time to remission and global outcome assessed by a psychiatrist

Conclusions

✓ Statistical tests showed no significant differences in effectiveness, so authors state that generic counselling seems to be as effective as antidepressants for mild to moderate depressive illness

✓ Patients receiving antidepressants may recover more quickly

✓ GPs should allow patients to have their preferred treatment

✓ 12 months after starting treatment, generic counselling is as effective as antidepressants

✓ Patients who choose counselling may benefit more than those with no strong preference

Criticisms

✓ Data interpretation should be regarded with caution due to small sample sizes and difficulties in follow-up

✓ Study placed few constraints on either the drug treatment or the type of counselling, other than that the counselling should be provided by an experienced mental health professional in six sessions

✓ Therefore compared non-standardised antidepressant use with non-standardised counselling by experienced professionals

3. Effectiveness of teaching general practitioners skills in brief cognitive behaviour therapy (CBT) to treat patients with depression: randomised controlled trial

(*M. King, et al, BMJ 2002;324:947–50*)

✓ In brief, this study looked at whether a short period of education on CBT would have an impact on patients suffering from depression

✓ CBT is as effective as pharmacotherapy for treating depression, with the benefit of reduced rates of long-term relapse

✓ It is also effective in depressed patients presenting to GPs

✓ CBT is effective when delivered by GPs who have received extensive instruction

✓ It was an RCT involving 84 GPs and 272 patients in North London

✓ The patients enrolled had scored above the threshold for psychological distress on the Hospital Anxiety and Depression scale

✓ A training package of 4.5 days on brief cognitive behaviour therapy was given to GPs

✓ The GPs and patients then completed the Depression Attitude Questionnaire (GPs) and the Beck Depression Inventory (patients)

✓ The results, not surprisingly, showed doctors' knowledge of depression and attitudes towards its treatment led to no major difference between intervention and control groups after six months. The training had no discernible impact on patients' outcomes

✓ They concluded that GPs may require more training and support than a basic educational package on brief CBT to acquire the skills to help patients with depression

✓ We, however, already know from other studies that most doctors do not have the time or inclination to carry out such comprehensive training

✓ Problems with the study related to a small sample size due to loss of follow-up, although power calculations suggested the data was still reliable

✓ Also, they found that trained doctors probably referred more patients to secondary care, suggesting training may have had a paradoxical effect in making GPs feel unable to deal with more complex cases

4. General practice based intervention to prevent repeat episodes of deliberate self-harm: cluster randomised controlled trial

(O. Bennewith, et al, BMJ 2002;324:1254–7)

✓ This large English study looked at whether a GP-based intervention on self-harm can reduce its incidence. We know that:

- About two-thirds of patients consult their GPs in the three months after an episode of deliberate self-harm

- Deliberate self-harm is a serious clinical problem in England and Wales, accounting for an estimated 140,000 hospital presentations each year

- 15–23% of patients will be seen for treatment of a subsequent episode of deliberate self-harm within one year

- 3–5% of those who harm themselves die by suicide within 5-10 years

✓ RCT involving 98 practices, which were assigned in equal numbers to an intervention or a control group

✓ The intervention comprised a letter from the GP inviting the patient to consult, and guidelines on the assessment and management of deliberate self-harm for the GP to use in consultations. Control patients received the usual GP care

✓ 1932 patients participated. The patients were registered with the study practices and had attended accident and emergency departments at one of the four hospitals after an episode of deliberate self-harm (patients lived within the catchment area of four general hospitals in Bristol and Bath)

✓ Primary outcome was an occurrence of a repeat episode of deliberate self-harm in the 12 months after the index episode. The study also looked at the number of repeat episodes and time to first repeat

✓ The results showed the incidence of repeat episodes of deliberate self-harm was not significantly different for patients in the intervention group compared with the control group

✓ Similar findings were obtained for the number of repeat episodes and time to first repeat

✓ The treatment seemed to be beneficial for people with a history of deliberate self-harm, but it was associated with an adverse effect in people for whom the index episode was their first episode

✓ The authors concluded that the hypothesis that patients who had previously harmed themselves benefited from the intervention was inconsistent with previous evidence and should be treated with caution

✓ As usual, more research is needed on how to manage patients who deliberately harm themselves, to reduce the incidence of repeat episodes

✓ As to what is the most effective management in general practice of patients who self-harm, nobody knows

✓ The role of the GP is very important in the aftercare of patients who deliberately harm themselves, as more than half of them will receive no psychiatric follow-up

5. Suicide rate in young men in Scotland is twice that in England and Wales

(Framework for the Prevention of Suicide and Self Harm can be found at www.show.scot.nhs.uk)

✓ Action is to be taken in Scotland in an attempt to halt an alarming rise in suicides among men, which have increased by more than 70% in the past 30 years

✓ Deaths from suicide of men under the age of 34 in Scotland now accounts for more deaths of young men than road traffic accidents

✓ More than 50% of 600 suicides/year in Scotland occur in men under 44 years of age, rates are twice as high as those in England and Wales

✓ Poverty and unemployment in Scotland are considered to be important factors

✓ Suicide rates among women in Scotland have fallen slightly since the 1970s and are now three times lower than rates among men

✓ But the rate of women succeeding is twice that in England and Wales

✓ The Scottish Health Department has published a consultative report that sets out a series of proposals on how the problem can be tackled

✓ Practical suggestions include making popular sites for suicide less accessible

✓ Plans to establish a telephone helpline and referral service

6. Spiritual beliefs may affect outcome of bereavement: prospective study

(*K. Walsh, et al, BMJ 2002;324:1551*)

✓ This study looked at the whether spirituality can help with bereavement

✓ Religious belief affects the outcome of bereavement in families coping with the death of a child and in older people who are bereaved of a spouse

✓ Research is often retrospective, and causal connections are difficult to establish

✓ It was a prospective cohort study of people about to be bereaved with follow-up continuing for 14 months after the death

✓ 135 relatives and close friends of patients admitted to the centre with a terminal illness from a Marie Curie centre for specialist palliative care in London participated

✓ Outcome was based upon Core Bereavement Items, a standardised measure for the intensity of grief, measured 1, 9 and 14 months after the patients' death

✓ They found that people reporting no spiritual belief had not resolved their grief by 14 months after the death

✓ Participants with strong spiritual beliefs resolved their grief progressively over the same period

✓ People with low levels of belief showed little change in the first nine months, but thereafter resolved their grief

✓ Strength of spiritual belief remained an important predictor after the confounding variables were controlled for (age, sex, etc)

✓ Although the degree of closeness to the person who died and the level of emotional distress before the death increased feelings of grief, neither affected the rate at which the grief was resolved

✓ They concluded that people who profess stronger spiritual beliefs seem to resolve their grief more rapidly and completely after the death of a close person than do people with no spiritual beliefs

Limitations

✓ Fell short of statistical significance, but strength of spiritual belief remained an important predictor

✓ Sample size was small and so restricts the number of potential confounders that can be explored

✓ The difficulty of recruiting a large sample of people for what is obviously a difficult and emotive time

7. Burden of chronic illness and suicide in elderly people
(*BMJ 2002;324:1455*)

✓ Most elderly people who commit suicide suffer from depression, although physical illness is common (56% of suicide cases, vs 16% of matched controls). Visual impairment, malignancy and neurological illness were most strongly associated with suicide.

✓ Many who committed suicide had consulted their GP shortly before their death, but had not communicated their despair to their doctor.

Medical treatments for depression

A review of 45 guidelines for depression showed they all have three common recommendations:

✓ Practitioners should seek cases of 'major depressive disorder'

✓ Treatment is advised if patients have enough symptoms for long enough (even if social causes are identified)

✓ Most recommend tricyclics antidepressants (TCAs) as first-line treatment (in dose equivalents of 125 mg/day of amitriptyline and continuing for four months after recovery)

Problems exist with these recommendations:

✓ Diagnosis is not easy to make in primary care, symptoms change quickly and the cut-off levels for duration are somewhat arbitrary

✓ Practitioners vary significantly in the threshold at which they treat. Many practitioners doubt the effectiveness of antidepressants in the face of social problems. Guidelines are based on an RCT of amitriptyline versus placebo: patients with 'major' depression responded, whilst those with minor depression did not, irrespective of whether the depression was endogenous or non-endogenous (ie attributed to social problems). Other research shows social factors in the short-term are associated with persistence of depression

✓ Patients are often reluctant to accept drugs. Much of the public believe that depression is due to adverse life events and that counselling should be offered. Most think that antidepressants are addictive. This explains why patients take subtherapeutic doses of tricyclics and discontinue early. Advent of selective serotonin-reuptake inhibitors (SSRIs) has increased the proportion taking therapeutic doses, but they still do not continue treatment for the recommended duration

Selective serotonin-reuptake inhibitors (SSRIs)

Recently, there has been much controversy surrounding the use paroxetine after a spate of adverse publicity, including a *Panoroma* documentary. There are certainly concerns about the difficulty that certain patients have in coming off it. SSRIs are no longer recommended by the CSM for children under 18 years. Their efficacy is comparable (*BMJ 2003;326:1014*).

Whichever drug is chosen, treatment should be continued for 4-6 months after recovery; this is rarely done in general practice at present, probably in part due to patient reluctance to continue treatment. A Canadian paper (*BMJ 2001;323:666*) has shown that SSRIs might increase the risk of gastric bleeding but do not seem to increase the risk of CHD.

Tricyclic antidepressants (TCAs)

Low-dose TCAs (usually at 75–100 mg/day) may be just as effective as TCAs at standard dose (*BMJ 2002;325:991*), but have fewer side-effects and hence lead to increased compliance.

There has been some concern about the association of TCAs and CHD. Findings from a UK study of 1000 patients with CHD showed that patients who had taken dosulepin (dothiepin) were 67% more likely to develop CHD than those who had not (*BMJ 2001;323:655–8*). However, there has been some research on whether having depression in itself increases the risk of CHD; this is what a six-year cohort study in the USA found (*Circulation 2000;102:1773*).

There has also been a suggestion that certain, genotoxic TCAs such as dosulepin (dothiepin) and imipramine (as opposed to non-genotoxic TCAs such as amitryptiline) are associated with an increased risk of breast cancer. Newer TCAs such as lofepramine and trazodone may have fewer side-effects.

Postnatal Depression

 (Drug Ther Bull, May 2000)

✓ Common, affects 70,000 women/year in the UK, approximately 13% of deliveries

✓ Little evidence for aetiology; antenatal, personal and social factors are more relevant

✓ Many recover spontaneously

✓ 50% are still depressed at six months

✓ One-third go on to develop a chronic, recurrent mood disorder

✓ Associated with disturbances in the mother-infant relationship, which in turn has an adverse impact on child cognitive and emotional development

✓ Must distinguish between common maternity 'blues' (= emotional lability, peak between third to fifth day postpartum and over by day 10)

✓ Depression is more likely if she has previous psychiatric/family history, social problems, bereavement; this should be assessed antenatally

✓ Remember to routinely use 'The Edinburgh Post-natal Depression Score' (validated detection tool)

✓ Conclusion of *Drug Ther Bull* article states that the following are effective:
  - Non-directive counselling by the health visitor
  - CBT
  - Antidepressants all effective
  - TCAs appear to be safe with breast-feeding
  - SSRIs are only secreted in small quantities in breast milk; the article states they are probably OK at the usual doses, but baby should be closely monitored and mother advised to stop breast-feeding if she is on a high dose
  - Refer if psychotic/suicidal to mother-and-baby unit

Schizophrenia

How to manage the first episode of schizophrenia
(*Editorial, BMJ 2000;321:522–3*)

- ✓ The article quoted a '1% lifetime prevalence'
- ✓ Is among the leading causes of disability worldwide
- ✓ Affects 2–4 per 1000 patients (*Clin Evid 2001*)
- ✓ £2.6b estimated to be the cost in the UK per year
- ✓ First onset typically in twenties
- ✓ Insidious onset hinders diagnosis, particularly when there is a 'background of premorbid disorders'
- ✓ There is growing evidence that early stages of schizophrenia are critical in forming and predicting the course and outcome of the disorder. Rapid diagnosis and early referral is therefore very important, as is initiating early treatment
- ✓ However, it typically remains undetected for 2–3 years; often insidious onset. Also, there may be reluctance to make this stigmatising diagnosis. Diagnosis is often made later in socially deprived groups (*BMJ 2001;323:1398*)
- ✓ Aim of primary treatment is rapid remission, and strategies that cause a minimum of side-effects should be used
- ✓ 80% will recover, but 70% will have a second psychotic episode within 5–7 years
- ✓ Early withdrawal of drug is not recommended and should be slowly tailed off
- ✓ Clozapine is used if typical antipsychotics do not help
- ✓ Most patients have difficulty reintegrating into the community
- ✓ CBT is useful in reducing persistent delusions and hallucinations
- ✓ Focusing on early detection and intervention in schizophrenia offers the opportunity to make a real difference to the lives of our patients and their families
- ✓ We cannot afford to miss it

The New Antipsychotic Drugs

Reviewed in Br J Gen Pract September 1999
(*T. Kendrick, Br J Gen Pract 1999;49:745–9*)

Benefits of the atypical antipsychotics

✓ They cause fewer extrapyramidal side-effects; this represents a major advance in the treatment of schizophrenia

✓ Clozapine is effective in 30–70% of patients resistant to traditional treatments; it remains to be seen whether the other atypical drugs also confer this benefit

✓ Clozapine also seems to be beneficial for the negative symptoms of schizophrenia, including apathy and social withdrawal. Time will tell whether this is a true effect and whether it extends to other atypicals

✓ Risperidone may be more effective among younger patients who have a depressive component to their psychotic illness

✓ The atypicals are expensive, but may be more cost-effective if they reduce specialist treatments and hospital admissions

Prescribing issues for the atypical antipsychotics

✓ Clozapine is restricted to treatment-resistant patients; however, the other atypicals, especially risperidone and olanzapine, are increasingly being used as first-line agents, especially among treatment-naive patients

✓ All other psychotropic drugs must be withdrawn before clozapine can be commenced

✓ Co-prescribing of traditional antipsychotics negates the benefits of the atypical drugs

✓ Clozapine-treated patients must have regular blood counts, initially weekly

✓ ECGs before and during treatment are mandatory when prescribing sertindole (available on a named-patient basis for those patients already stabilised on the drug in whom other antipsychotics are inappropriate)

✓ Extreme caution is advised when prescribing atypicals for patients with heart disease

✓ Avoid concurrent prescribing of antihistamines, diuretics, tricyclics and antiarrhythmics, especially in the elderly
✓ Hypokalaemia must be corrected before prescribing an atypical
✓ Patients should be warned to avoid concurrent use of over-the-counter antihistamines

NOTE

Also see *Clin Evid* 2001 for further evidence from systematic reviews.

Atypical antipsychotics, patients value the lower incidence of extrapyramidal side-effects
(*S. Kapur and G. Remington, BMJ 2000;321:1360*)

This editorial appeared in the BMJ alongside a systematic review of atypicals, points raised were:
✓ No clinically significant evidence found of superiority in efficacy, or for that matter tolerability, for atypical antipsychotics as a group
✓ Atypical antipsychotics account for nearly three out of four new prescriptions for antipsychotics in North America
✓ Atypicals have a lower incidence of extrapyramidal side-effects
✓ Extrapyramidal side-effects are not just incidental 'side' effects but the central factor in many patients' agendas
✓ Extrapyramidal effects by themselves have been related to a poor outcome, a compromised compliance, secondary negative symptoms, cognitive parkinsonism and depression, as well as the long-term risk of tardive dyskinesia
✓ May turn out that the real superiority of atypicals is not in their antipsychotic abilities but in their ability to control ancillary symptoms related to mood, cognition, hostility and a higher level of compliance
✓ Atypical agents have their own new side-effects such as weight gain and diabetes

NICE guidance 2002

✓ NICE has recommended the more widespread use of atypical antipsychotic drugs for patients with schizophrenia, on the grounds of fewer side-effects and equal efficiency

✓ The recommendations were made after a review of over 200 trials

✓ NICE has said that older antipsychotic drugs were associated with a higher incidence of extrapyramidal side-effects compared with newer antipsychotics (such as amisulpride, olanzapine and risperidone)

✓ If, however, patients are achieving good control without unacceptable side-effects with typical antipsychotics, they should not change their medication

✓ The National Schizophrenia Fellowship said more than 80% of the 210,000 people with schizophrenia are currently denied access to antipsychotics, on grounds of cost

✓ Direct treatment costs of schizophrenia in England and Wales are estimated to be in excess of £1b (about 3% of the total NHS expenditure)

✓ The yearly cost of maintenance on older style antipsychotics is £70, whereas for atypical drugs it is £1220

✓ NICE estimates that the cost for the NHS of making these drugs freely available will be £70m a year. The cost will be offset by an expected shift away from inpatient care to cheaper community-based care

✓ All patients should have a care plan and GPs should function in multidisciplinary teams. Patients should be involved with decisions about their care, as should family/carers. There is no evidence that carrying hand-held records improves outcomes, although they are useful as communication tools (*Br J Gen Pract 2003;53:197*)

✓ Patients should have access to psychological treatments such as CBT and family therapy, which improve long-term social functioning

✓ Patients should have their physical health as well as mental health regularly monitored; the guidelines suggest six-monthly physical health checks. Physical health in schizophrenics is often bad, perhaps due to high rates of substance abuse, poor diet, poor housing, etc

Eating Disorders

✓ Rates: 1/2000 anorexia, 20/2000 bulimia, 40/2000 'partial' syndromes (*Br J Gen Pract 2000;50:38083*)
✓ Psychological interventions such as cognitive behavioural therapy (CBT) and antidepressants such as SSRIs have been shown to be effective treatment options
✓ Early intervention produces better outcome
✓ Binge eating – eating an amount of food that is larger than most people would eat in a similar period/situation. May have a sense of lack of control
✓ Standards 2 and 3 of the NSF for mental health outline the need to improve health care for patients with eating disorders

Diagnostic criteria for anorexia nervosa

✓ Overconcern with shape and weight, with intense fear of becoming fat
✓ Active maintenance of low weight (body mass index < 17.5) by strict dieting, excessive exercising and possibly self-induced vomiting
✓ Amenorrhoea for a minimum of three months (if not taking the combined oral contraceptive pill, COCP)

Diagnostic criteria for bulimia nervosa

✓ Characteristic overconcern with shape and weight
✓ Frequent binges (bulimic episodes)
✓ Extreme behaviour to prevent weight gain (self-induced vomiting, purgative and diuretic abuse, fasting)

Atypical eating disorders

✓ Disorders that do not fulfil the above criteria (ie binge eating without extreme weight-controlling behaviour)

The SCOFF questionnaire: assessment of a new screening tool for eating disorders

(*J. F. Morgan, et al, BMJ 1999;319:1467*)

The SCOFF QUESTIONS (one point for every yes; a score of greater than or equal to 2 indicates a likely case of anorexia nervosa or bullimia).

1. Do you ever make yourself Sick because you feel uncomfortably full?
2. Do you ever worry you have lost Control over how much you eat?
3. Have you ever lost more than one stone over a one-month period?
4. Do you believe yourself to be Fat when others say you are thin?
5. Would you say Food dominates your life?

The researchers found that 'setting the threshold' at two or more positive answers to all five questions provided 100% sensitivity for anorexia and bulimia, separately and combined (all cases, 95% confidence interval 96.9% to 100%; bulimic cases, 92.6% to 100%; anorexic cases, 94.7% to 100%), with specificity of 87.5% (79.2% to 93.4%) for controls.

A further study (*BMJ 2002;325:755–6*) assessing the SCOFF questionnaire in primary care, again showed excellent sensitivity when a threshold of two or more positive answers was set. All cases of anorexia nervosa and bulimia were identified, although two out of nine cases of 'non-specified eating disorder' were missed. The positive predictive value of the SCOFF questionnaire is low, because of the relatively low prevalence of eating disorders.

Alcohol

✓ We know from population studies that non-drinkers and heavy drinkers have higher all-cause mortality rates than light drinkers; this is known as the 'U-shaped curve'

✓ The RCP/RCGP/RCPsych advise men and women to drink less than 21 and 14 units a week, respectively

✓ The UK government, however, recommends no more than 28 and 21 units a week, respectively

✓ 1 unit is 8–10 g of alcohol (8 units in a bottle of wine)

✓ It is estimated that 20/1000 people are physically dependent. 10% of men in social classes 4 and 5 were dependent on alcohol in 1994, compared to 5% in classes 1 and 2

✓ Alcohol dependence is associated with an 80-fold increase in male depression and suicide

✓ 14% of RTAs are caused by drinking

✓ In systematic reviews of all-cause mortality, the risk was lowest for men drinking 7–14 units a week and for women drinking under 7 units a week (*J Clin Epidemiol 1999;52:967–75*)

✓ In a recent review by a group of statisticians (*BMJ 2002;325:191*) the level of alcohol consumption that carries the lowest mortality ranges from zero in men and women aged under 35 to 3 units a week in women aged over 65 and 8 units a week in men aged over 65

✓ Alcohol problems are estimated to cost Scotland £1b a year through reduced productivity and the costs of crime, accidents, damage to property and health service costs from injury and illness

✓ Latest figures show that 1 in 3 men in Scotland and 1 in 7 women in Scotland are exceeding recommended drinking levels

✓ Most worrying is the increase in alcohol use amongst young people

✓ More 12–15-year-olds drink alcohol and at greater amounts than 10 years ago

✓ The heaviest drinking occurs among people aged 16–24 years

✓ The Health Education Board for Scotland stated, 'A 15 year old in France is likely to drink as frequently as a 15 year old in Scotland but is half as likely to get drunk as often'

KEY SOURCES

Royal Colleges of Physicians, Psychiatrists, and General Practitioners. *Alcohol and the heart in perspective: sensible limits reaffirmed.* London, Royal Colleges, 1995.

Inter-Departmental Working Group. *Sensible drinking.* London, Department of Health, 1995.

Currently, it is estimated that only one-third of problem drinkers are known to their GPs. Most GPs rely on the use of unstructured questions and blood tests, both of which are unreliable in detecting heavy drinkers. One study confirmed the poor reliability of blood tests and also compared five different alcohol screening questionnaires (*Br J Gen Pract 2001;51:206–17*), showing that they all performed much better than blood tests, except for the CAGE questionnaire. The Audit-C questionnaire is easy to use:

✓ How often do you have a drink containing alcohol?

✓ How many drinks do you have on a typical day when you are drinking?

✓ How often do you have six or more drinks on one occasion?

This questionnaire is estimated to have a sensitivity of approximately 75%, but is not particularly specific.

It is unclear whether routine screening for excessive alcohol intake could be effectively done in the primary care setting. A recent systematic review (*BMJ 2003;327:536–42*) concluded that of 1000 patients screened using a health questionnaire, only 25 were eligible for brief intervention in the form of advice, information or feedback. Of these 25, less than three reported that they had cut down their alcohol consumption to within recommended limits after a year.

Does AA work?

Attending Alcoholics Anonymous may improve the chances of staying abstinent: a small study (*Alcohol and Alcoholism 2003;38:421–6*) has recently demonstrated that after six months of attending AA meetings, participants drank significantly less alcohol, drank less often and reported fewer problems related to drink. They also had fewer psychological problems and enjoyed a better quality of life.

Important studies

1. Alcohol consumption and mortality from all causes, coronary heart disease, and stroke: results from a prospective cohort study of Scottish men with 21 years of follow up

(C. L. Hart, et al, BMJ 1999;318;1725–9)

✓ Comprised 5766 men aged 35–64 screened in 1970–3 who answered questions on their usual weekly alcohol consumption

✓ Aim was to define mortality from all causes, coronary heart disease, stroke and alcohol-related causes over 21 years of follow-up related to units of alcohol consumed per week

✓ Risk for all-cause mortality was similar for non-drinkers and men drinking up to 14 units/week

✓ Mortality risk then showed a graded association with alcohol consumption

✓ No strong relationship found between alcohol consumption and mortality from coronary heart disease

✓ Strong positive relationship found between alcohol and risk of mortality from stroke

✓ Men drinking 35 or more units have double the risk of stroke compared to non-drinkers

✓ No clear evidence found of any protective effect for men drinking less than 22 units/week

✓ Different relationships found between alcohol consumption and mortality than previous studies

✓ Some, but not all, of this could be accounted for by alcohol- related increases in blood pressure

✓ Overall, the risk of all-cause mortality was higher in men drinking 22 or more units/week

2. Editorial: Dying for a drink

(BMJ 2001;323:817–18)

Focused on developing strategies to reduce suicide amongst those with alcohol-use disorders.

KEY POINTS RAISED

- There is a consistently reported high prevalence of alcohol-use disorders among people who committed suicide (eg 56% in New York, 43% in Northern Ireland)
- Lifetime risk of suicide is 7% for alcohol dependence
- In the Northern Ireland suicide study (case-control psychological autopsy), the estimated risk of suicide in the presence of current alcohol misuse or dependence was eight times greater than in the absence of current alcohol misuse or dependence
- 89% of suicides with alcohol dependence in the Irish study had at least one other comorbid mental disorder
- The five-year report of the National Confidential Inquiry into Suicide and Homicide by People with Mental Illness recently revealed that 40% of people who committed suicide in England and Wales who had been in contact with mental health services within one year of death had a history of alcohol misuse (53% in Scotland) and 19% had misused both alcohol and drugs (26% in Scotland)
- 'The combination of mental illness and substance misuse is probably the greatest clinical problem facing general adult mental health services' suggests that 'a coordinated approach to training, service planning, and research is needed to improve the ability of the general service to address this problem'
- Therefore, after attempted suicide (deliberate self-harm) and presentation to mental health services, the detection and effective treatment of alcohol-use disorders are important aspects of suicide prevention
- The Irish study also revealed that a lower risk of suicide was associated with a higher religious commitment
- However, after adjustment for psychiatric disorders, the 'protective' effect did not remain, suggesting that the protective effect of religious commitment may be partially mediated by the reduced likelihood of a committed individual developing a psychiatric disorder (including alcohol-use disorder)
- The author states that healthcare professionals should be aware of the potential influence of religious commitment on behaviour affecting health

Drug Misuse

Drug Misuse and Dependence – Guidelines on Clinical Management. Department of Health, 1999

These guidelines, first published in 1991, were updated in 1999 in the light of recent advances. Great discrepancy exists throughout the UK in terms of provision of services. Many of the points in the plan caused a lot of controversy and still remain topical in the GP press. In summary from the guidelines:

- ✓ Total number of drug misusers presenting to treatment in the six months ending March 1998 was around 30,000
- ✓ 54% of those users presenting were in their twenties
- ✓ 1 in 7 (15%) were aged under 20 years
- ✓ Ratio of males to females was 3:1
- ✓ 55% reported heroin as their main drug of misuse
- ✓ Methadone was the next most frequently reported main drug of abuse (13%), cannabis (9%) etc
- ✓ Self-reported drug use amongst those aged 16–59 years in England and Wales in 1996, showed that approximately 1 in 10 had used illegal drugs in the last year, and that 1 in 20 (6%) had done so in the last month
- ✓ 60% of people arrested test positive for illegal drugs
- ✓ People who are involved in drugs may have multiple social and medical problems
- ✓ Doctors everywhere must expect to see drug misusers presenting for care, and will need to be vigilant in looking for signs of drug misuse in their patients
- ✓ It is the responsibility of all doctors to provide care for both general health needs and drug-related problems, whether or not the patient is ready to withdraw from drugs
- ✓ This should include the provision of evidence-based interventions such as hepatitis B vaccination
- ✓ Medical practitioners should not prescribe in isolation, but should seek to liaise with other professionals who will be able to help with factors contributing to an individual's drug misuse
- ✓ A multidisciplinary approach to treatment is therefore essential

✓ Where there are no local specialist services with which a shared care agreement can be developed, it is the responsibility of the health authority to ensure that appropriate services are in place

✓ There is good evidence for methadone maintenance treatment. Good initial assessment is important and there should be clear evidence of dependence, withdrawal and tolerance before treatment starts. Supervised consumption is recommended for the first three months and should be continued further if there are doubts about compliance

✓ Prescribing is the doctor's responsibility and cannot be delegated. Clear records should be kept, and the doctor should regularly liase with the dispensing pharmacist

✓ No more than one weeks' supply should be given at any one time, except in exceptional circumstances

✓ Regular clinical reviews are recommended, at least once every three months

Drugs used in opioid-dependence substitution treatment

Methadone
Methadone maintenance treatment (MMT) has been shown to reduce illicit opioid use, reduce crime, decrease injecting activity and enhance social productivity (*BMJ 1994;309:997*). There is a very real potential for toxicity however, and it is important to get the starting dose right, to avoid cumulative toxicity. After full assessment, oral liquid methadone should be started at 10–40 mg daily; particular care is needed above 30 mg as a starting dose, so the starting dose should be 10–20 mg if uncertainty exists. The patient should then be stabilised over the next six weeks, probably so they end up receiving between 60 and 120 mg daily. After stabilisation, dose reduction may be attempted, but only if the patient is willing to try; otherwise MMT can be continued indefinitely. The success rates of such outpatient detoxification programmes are quite low, but a supportive home environment helps.

Buprenorphine
This is an opioid partial agonist/antagonist and comes in a sublingual preparation. It is now licensed for treatment of opioid dependence. It has less potential for overdose and has low euphoric effects at high doses. A Cochrane review (Issue 1, 2002) has examined the short-term management of opioid withdrawal with buprenorphine and concluded that although it seems to be effective, there is limited evidence at present.

Lofexidine

This is a non-opioid α-agonist, which is licensed to relieve symptoms in patients undergoing detoxification. It has a similar action to clonidine, but causes less hypotension. It is only likely to be useful in patients whose average drug use is < 1 g heroin per day (50 mg methadone equivalent) and with short drug-taking histories.

Naltrexone

This is an opioid antagonist that should only be initiated in a drug addiction centre. It can only be used in highly motivated addicts who have remained drug free for 7–10 days. It is licensed as an 'adjunctive prophylactic therapy for maintenance of detoxified, formerly opioid dependent patients'.

And finally... Should we be prescribing heroin?

Recent Dutch research has looked at the safety and efficacy of supervised medical prescription of heroin to addicts not benefiting from methadone maintenance (*BMJ 2003;327:310–312*). A total of 549 heroin addicts were prescribed inhalable or injectable heroin over 12 months in two separate RCTs; heroin plus methadone was compared to methadone alone, in terms of physical and mental health and social functioning. Both trials found that 12 months of treatment with heroin plus methadone was significantly more effective than treatment with methadone alone whether given by injection or inhalation. The incidence of serious adverse events was similar across treatment conditions. The authors concluded that supervised co-prescription of heroin is feasible, more effective and probably as safe as methadone alone in reducing the many physical, mental and social problems of treatment-resistant heroin addicts.

USEFUL CONTACT NUMBERS FOR GPS AND PATIENTS

ADFAM – National charity for the families of drug misusers	020 7928 8900
Alcohol Concern	020 7928 7377
Cocaine Anonymous	020 7284 1123
Council for Involuntary Tranquilliser Addiction (CITA)	0151 286 9884
Drug Prevention Advisory Service, head office	020 7217 8631
Narcotics Anonymous (NA) UK Service Office	020 730 0009
National Drugs Helpline – provides 24 h free and confidential advice, including information on local services	0800 776600
Release – provides legal advice and infomation on safer use and substitution therapies and offer liaison with GPs and other treatment providers	0207 729 9904
TACADE – Teacher's Advisory Council on Alcohol and Drug education	0161 836 6850

USEFUL WEBSITE

www.talktofrank.com – linked to the National Drugs helpline this website provides confidential drugs information and advice 24 hours a day.

Cannabis trial launched in patients with multiple sclerosis (MS)

✓ The world's biggest clinical trial of the cannabis plant started in January 2001 at Derriford Hospital, Plymouth

✓ It is looking at the control of pain and tremors in multiple sclerosis

✓ The Cannabis in Multiple Sclerosis (CAMS) study is sponsored by the Medical Research Council

✓ Approved by the Government, which has arranged for the drug to be imported from Switzerland

- ✓ A parallel study will examine the effect of the drug on lower urinary tract symptoms
- ✓ Cannabis has been a Class C drug since January 2004, when the WHO pronounced it medically useless
- ✓ Two years ago a House of Lords select committee argued that more research was necessary in view of reports of the drug's efficacy in controlling pain and tremor in multiple sclerosis

Is cannabis safe?

There have been moves to decriminalise cannabis. People will no longer automatically be arrested for carrying 'small quantities for personal use only'. However, there are concerns about the safety of cannabis use, including a link between cannabis use in adolescence and an increased risk of psychosis in adulthood (*BMJ 2002;325:1212–13*). Early cannabis use (by the age of 15) confers a greater risk than does later use (by the age of 18), and this risk has been found to be specific to cannabis, as opposed to use of other recreational drugs, even after psychotic symptoms preceding the onset of cannabis use are controlled for. Cannabis use does not predict later depression.

 BMA calls for Government action on drugs and driving
(*BMJ 2002;324:632*)

- ✓ The BMA has called on the UK Government to develop a campaign to highlight that taking drugs, whether prescribed, over the counter or illegal, can impair driving capacity in a similar way to alcohol
- ✓ The BMA has recommended that the Government should coordinate scientific research to establish effective drug-testing devices and should educate the public on the association between taking some drugs and impaired driving ability
- ✓ To help publicise the problem, the BMA has developed a website that reviews trends in road traffic fatalities and injuries, as well as research on drugs and driving performance
- ✓ The website highlights research from the Transport Research Laboratory warning that the number of people involved in fatal collisions who tested positive for illegal drugs increased sixfold between 1985–7 and 1996–9

- ✓ The number of people testing positive for cannabis increased from 3% to 12%. Over the same period, the incidence of use of medicinal drugs and alcohol remained similar
- ✓ Driving while unfit under the influence of drugs is an offence in the United Kingdom, and a driver faces the same penalties as for driving under the influence of alcohol
- ✓ However, the law does not currently state any legal limits for drugs, as it does for alcohol, making it difficult to enforce legislation
- ✓ The BMA is calling for this dilemma to be resolved by the development of appropriate testing devices
- ✓ The BMA's initiative arose from a resolution passed at its annual meeting of representatives in 2001 to consider ways of supporting the police in their fight against drugs and driving

Illegal drugs are found in one in five of those killed on the road. Doctors have a responsibility to report to the authorities any patients they know to be driving whilst taking drugs that might impair their consciousness.

USEFUL WEBSITE

www.bma.org.uk – This allows access to the BMA's drugs and driving website

Counselling

What is counselling?

A. It is helping patients to identify, understand, come to terms and cope with their problems.

Skills needed:

Listening
Empathising
Reflecting
Clarifying

Summarising
Interpreting
Confronting
Motivating

Various counselling styles

Directive	Counsellor acts prescriptively
Informative	Counsellor provides information to help decision-making
Confrontational	Counsellor challenges unhelpful thinking/ behaviour
Cathartic	Counsellor encourages expression of hidden thoughts/fears/guilt
Catalytic	Counsellor encourages patient to establish own goal/take control
Supportive	Counsellor provides acceptance, empathy, concern for patient's anxieties and needs
Rogerian	Counsellor provides non-directive listening rather than advice, encouraging patient to make decisions based on own judgement

It has been known in the MRCGP exam to be asked for working examples of the above techniques, eg 'Give an example of the use of catalytic intervention'.

Who does it?

✓ GP – uses counselling skills generally in the course of normal surgery
✓ Attached counsellor – longer interviews with protected time
  • need to ensure competence
  • need to ensure integration in the primary healthcare team (PHCT)

Does it work?

Evidence suggests counselling in general practice is an effective therapy for psychosocial problems and minor affective disorders.

Some trials (not all) show that doctors:
✓ Identify more problems
✓ Prescribe fewer drugs
✓ Investigate less
✓ Refer less

Patients:
✓ Get relief from symptoms
✓ Cope better with feelings
✓ Cope better with life
✓ Consult less often

More information is needed on the value of types of counselling and the skills of counsellors.

What is the case against?

✓ It has been said that doctors may avoid contact with difficult patients by referring them on
✓ Patients may therefore feel rejected in some cases and fail to attend
✓ Some patients may feel worse after counselling
✓ Financial costs are sometimes prohibitive, nationally the service offered on the NHS is patchy

CHAPTER 4:

THE ELDERLY

Chapter 4:
The Elderly

National Service Framework (NSF) for Older People

The original document is over 100 pages long, therefore the salient points have been summarised here with respect to general practice. This NSF is a 10-year strategy to ensure fair, high quality, integrated health and social care services for older people. It is designed to support independence and promote good health. It aims to promote and engender that older people and their carers are always treated with respect, dignity and fairness.

The four themes in this NSF are:
1. Respecting the individual
2. Intermediate care
3. Providing evidence-based specialist care
4. Promoting an active, healthy life

Apart from this NSF, other initiatives to help the elderly include:

Extending access to services

✓ Provide free NHS sight tests for those aged 60 and over
✓ Improved access to cataract services
✓ Extension of breast screening to women aged up to 70
✓ Carers' access to services in their own right has been ensured through the Carers and Disabled Children Act 2000
✓ Care Direct (Government pilot), a one-stop shop gateway to information about social care, health, housing and social security benefits, which will complement NHS Direct
✓ DoH issued Fair Access to Care Services guidance to councils in Spring 2001 setting out how they should develop fair and consistent eligibility criteria for adult social care services

Developing services which support independence

✓ Promoting Independence Grant to support councils to help more people retain their independence for longer.

✓ 'Supporting People' is a new initiative to help vulnerable people live independently in the community by providing a wide range of housing support services

Helping older people to stay healthy

✓ Free influenza immunisation for everyone who is aged 65 and over

✓ Improve oral health in older people and increase access to dentistry through Modernising NHS Dentistry

✓ Routine breast cancer screening is being extended to women up to the age of 70

✓ 'Keep Warm, Keep Well' campaigns to prevent deaths in winter and increased Winter Fuel Payments of £200, or £300 for the over 80s. This is paid to every household with someone over 60 years of age, regardless of whether they are retired or not

Ensuring fairer funding

✓ End the anomaly that people in nursing homes may have to pay for their nursing care; it will be provided on the same basis as other NHS services, free at the point of use

✓ Three months property disregard and by raising the capital limits when councils may step in with financial support

✓ Deferred payment scheme, to be introduced from October 2001, will give people more choice in how they pay for residential accommodation

✓ Aim to give people a valuable breathing space between entering a care home and selling their home, if that is their wish

Developing more effective links between health and social services

✓ The Health Act 1999 allowed partnership between Health Authorities and councils to improve services at the interface of health and social care

✓ Establishment of local Strategic Partnerships (LSPs) across the country since April 2001

✓ Committed to improving the quality of life

✓ Refocusing of mainstream services and resources

✓ LSPs will bring together the public, private, voluntary and community sectors and service users to provide a single over-arching local framework that will allow NSFs to be implemented

The NSF itself has eight standards as detailed below

(As you go through, note the standards that have any additional funding to aid implementation.)

Standard 1: Rooting Out Age Discrimination

NHS services will be provided, regardless of age, on the basis of clinical need alone. Social care services will not use age in their eligibility criteria or policies, to restrict access to available services.

✓ Negative staff attitudes also impact on the quality of care

✓ Palliative care services have not been available to older people in some areas

✓ This may be related to the fact that palliative care services have been concentrated on those with cancer rather than with terminal stages of a chronic disorder

✓ Elderly people from Black and minority ethnic groups can be disadvantaged and are likely to suffer more discrimination in accessing services

✓ Concerns have been raised about resuscitation policies, with older people more likely to be denied cardiopulmonary resuscitation (CPR) on the grounds of age alone. Guidelines from the BMA, RCN and Resuscitation Council suggest regular audits of local CPR policies to prevent age-related discrimination

✓ Denying access to services on the basis of age alone is not acceptable

✓ Age discrimination may not always be explicit

A recent study (*BMJ 2003;326:580*) carried out in Bristol, found that the quality of medical care for elderly people (> 65) is generally inadequate, in terms of underuse of beneficial drugs (eg β-blockers post-MI), monitoring of chronic disease and overuse of inappropriate drugs. The researchers found that quality of care was worse for patients in nursing homes than for those living at home; eg more nursing-home residents were inappropriately being prescribed neuroleptics and fewer had regular BP checks.

Standard 2: Person-Centred Care

NHS and social care services treat older people as individuals and enable them to make choices about their own care. This can be achieved through the single assessment process, integrated commissioning arrangements and integrated provision of services, including community equipment and continence services.

The plan focused on key areas of improvement, where need was identified; they are summarized below.

Personal and professional behaviour

✓ Staff should be polite and courteous at all times, eg using the older person's preferred form of address and relating to them as a competent adult

✓ Procedures are in place to identify and, if possible, meet any particular needs and preferences relating to gender, personal appearance, communication, diet, race or culture and religious/ spiritual beliefs

✓ Personal hygiene needs are met with sensitivity, intimate interventions carried out in privacy

✓ Patients allowed to wear their own clothes in hospital and able to have personal effects at their bedside (space/safety permitting)

Dignity in end-of-life care
✓ Control of painful and distressing symptoms
✓ Rehabilitation and support as health declines
✓ Social care to maintain access to safe and accessible living environments, practical help, income maintenance, social networks and information
✓ Spiritual care – availability of pastoral or spiritual carers reflecting the faiths of the local population
✓ Provide evidence-based complementary therapies
✓ Psychological care to anticipate, recognise and treat any psychological distress of the patient or carer
✓ Bereavement support and counselling

The single assessment process
✓ Proposed by The NHS Plan
✓ Introduced in April 2002, for health and social care for older people
✓ Standardised assessment process is in place across all areas and agencies
✓ Designed to identify all of the needs of the patient
✓ Less duplication and worry for the patient
✓ Can be carried out by one front-line professional
✓ If other professionals need to be involved this should be arranged to provide a seamless service
✓ Assessment scales and tools are validated

Integrated community equipment services
✓ Audit Commission estimated that nearly one million people need equipment to help them live independently
✓ Demand for disability equipment is increasing due to ageing population and user expectation
✓ The NHS Plan set out an intention to achieve single, integrated community equipment services by 2004 and to increase by 50% the number of people able to benefit; comes with increased funding

Integrated continence services
✓ Primary and community staff involved in the identification and initial assessment and care

✓ Specialist services to provide expert advice when condition does not respond to initial treatment

✓ Availability and provision of continence aids/equipment and access to bathing/laundry services

Standard 3: Intermediate Care

Older people will have access to a new range of intermediate care services at home or in designated care settings, to promote their independence by providing enhanced services from the NHS and councils to prevent unnecessary hospital admission and effective rehabilitation services to enable early discharge from hospital and to prevent premature or unnecessary admission to long-term residential care.

✓ A new layer of care added, between primary care and specialist services

✓ To prevent unnecessary hospital admission, support early discharge and reduce or delay long-term residential care

✓ To improve physical functioning, build confidence, re-equip with the skills they need to live safely and independently at home

✓ Rehabilitation reduces re-admittance to hospitals and long terms in residential care

✓ Rehabilitation improves survival rates and physical and cognitive functioning

✓ 63% of older people permanently enter nursing-home care, 43% of those entering residential care homes come direct from hospital

✓ Older people will be the main, but not exclusive, beneficiaries of these services

✓ Should involve rapid assessment, diagnosis and immediate treatment followed by appropriate referral

✓ Will include counselling, intensive support at home for a short period, community nursing and therapy services ('hospital at home')

✓ Well-managed intermediate care can improve recovery rates, increase patient satisfaction and reduce impact on the primary care team

✓ Strongest evidence is for stroke rehabilitation and for geriatric/ orthopaedic rehabilitation (more patients being discharged home compared with conventional care)

Standard 4: General Hospital Care

Older people's care in hospital is delivered through appropriate specialist care and by hospital staff who have the right set of skills to meet their needs.

Emergency response
✓ Older people should be transferred from the emergency department as soon as possible
✓ The NHS Plan commitment is that no patient should stay longer than four hours in the emergency department (by 2004)

Early assessment
✓ Should identify the further care the older person requires
✓ Will include investigation, observation and multidisciplinary assessment
✓ Input from geriatricians, specialists in stroke, falls and mental health or other disciplines including specialist nurses, therapists, pharmacists and social workers, may be required
✓ 'Clinical Leaders (Modern Matrons) for Older People' to oversee care

Appropriate surroundings
✓ Separate room always available for private discussions and to make personal telephone calls
✓ More four-bedded bays available
✓ Single rooms provided for the most vulnerable
✓ Space provided for therapy equipment, or a small gym, comfortable day rooms and specially adapted kitchens
✓ More than 95% of NHS hospital accommodation is single sex

Standard 5: Stroke

The NHS will take action to prevent strokes, working in partnership with other agencies where appropriate. People who are thought to have had a stroke have access to diagnostic services, are treated appropriately by a specialist stroke service, and subsequently, with their carers, participate in a multidisciplinary programme of secondary prevention and rehabilitation.

✓ Each year 110,000 people in England and Wales have their first stroke (30,000 have further strokes); biggest cause of severe disability and the third most common cause of death in the UK

✓ 30% of patients die in the first month after a stroke

✓ After a year, 65% of surviving stroke patients can live independently, 35% are significantly disabled

✓ Around 5% are admitted to long-term residential care

✓ Risk increases with age but young people affected too

✓ 10,000 people under 55 years and 1000 people under 30 years have a stroke each year

✓ Afro-Caribbean and South-Asian men are about 40% and 70%, respectively, are more likely to have a stroke

✓ Socioeconomic group V have a 60% higher chance of having a stroke than group I

✓ Mortality rates from stroke are 50% higher in socioeconomic group V than in group I

✓ There is strong evidence that people who have a stroke are more likely both to survive and to recover more function if admitted promptly to a hospital-based stroke unit

✓ Apparently the NSF states this can be achieved at no overall additional cost to health and social care!

✓ Every DGH which cares for people with stroke has plans to introduce a specialised stroke service. This has been in place since April 2002

✓ Royal College of Physicians guidelines for stroke care have been in place since 2003, and they are to be audited regularly.

✓ By April 2004 PCG/Ts will have ensured that:
- That every GP is using protocols agreed with local specialist services
- That patients identified as being at risk are identified and treated
- That rapid referral and management of those with a transient ischaemic attack (TIA) guidelines are in place

Population approaches to preventing stroke

✓ Similar to those for coronary heart disease – increasing levels of physical activity, encouraging healthy eating, supporting smoking cessation and identifying and managing high blood pressure

Preventing strokes in individuals at greater risk

MAIN RISK FACTORS:	
Cardiovascular disease	hypertension, atrial fibrillation, CHD, previous stroke or TIA, peripheral vascular disease, carotoid stenosis
Metabolic	diabetes, hyperlipidaemia and obesity
Lifestyle	alcohol misuse, poor diet, low level of physical activity and smoking

✓ Risk of stroke for people with hypertension can be reduced by 37% through treatment

✓ Atrial fibrillation increases the risk of having a stroke by 3–7 times

✓ 13% of people who have had a stroke are in atrial fibrillation

✓ In the younger population, risk factors include sickle cell-disease, congenital heart disease, abnormalities of blood clotting and arteriovenous malformations of the brain

Long-term support

Can continue over a long time and until maximum recovery has been achieved.

Some will need ongoing support and have access to a stroke care co-ordinator who can provide advice, arrange reassessment, co-ordinate long-term support or arrange for specialist care.

Any patient reporting a significant disability at six months should be re-assessed and offered further targeted rehabilitation, if this can help recover further function.

Standard 6: Falls

The NHS, working in partnership with councils, takes action to prevent falls and reduce resultant fractures or other injuries in their populations of older people. Older people who have fallen receive effective treatment and rehabilitation and, with their carers, receive advice on prevention through a specialised falls service.

✓ Falls are the leading cause of mortality due to injury in older people aged over 75 in the UK

✓ 14,000 people a year die in the UK as a result of an osteoporotic hip fracture

✓ Osteoporotic fractures occur most commonly in the hip, spine and wrist

✓ One-third of women and one-twelfth of men over 50 are affected by osteoporosis

✓ 50% of women have an osteoporotic fracture by the time they reach the age of 70

✓ Consequences for an individual of falling or of not being able to get up after a fall can include:
  • Psychological problems, for example a fear of falling and loss of confidence
  • Loss of mobility leading to social isolation and depression
  • Increase in dependency and disability
  • Hypothermia
  • Pressure-related injury
  • Infection

✓ After an osteoporotic fracture, 50% can no longer live independently

✓ Falls are a common symptom of previously unidentified health problems

Prevention

✓ Older people who have fallen are at risk of falling again. These patients should be observed as they stand up from a chair without using their arms, walk several paces and return ('get up and go' test). Those showing no difficulties or unsteadiness need no further assessment

✓ A specialist falls services should be established for older people

Population approach to falls' prevention

✓ Reduce incidence and impact of falls through encouraging appropriate weight-bearing and strength-enhancing physical activity, promoting healthy eating and reducing smoking

✓ Community strategy to prevent falls should also include:
  • Ensuring that pavements are kept clear and in good repair
  • Adequate street lighting
  • Providing information, such as 'Avoiding Slips, Trips and Broken Hips' by the Department of Trade and Industry (DTI)
  • Making property safer

Preventing falls in individuals
✓ Depends on identifying those most at risk
✓ Many who fall do not seek medical help but may be identified through risk factors
✓ Interventions should target both multiple risk factors for individuals (intrinsic risk factors) and environmental hazards to be successful

Intrinsic risk factors include
✓ Balance, gait or mobility problems, including those due to degenerative joint disease and motor disorders such as stroke and Parkinson's disease
✓ Taking four or more medications, in particular centrally sedating or blood-pressure lowering drugs
✓ Visual impairment
✓ Impaired cognition or depression
✓ Postural hypotension

Elderly women with chronic disease, eg circulatory disease, COPD, depression and arthritis may have a higher risk of falling (*BMJ 2003;327:712–15*). This may be more significant than polypharmacy.

Risk factors in the home environment include
✓ Poor lighting, particularly on stairs
✓ Steep stairs
✓ Loose carpets or rugs
✓ Slippery floors
✓ Badly fitting footwear or clothing
✓ Lack of safety equipment such as grab rails
✓ Inaccessible lights or windows

USEFUL WEBSITE
www.dti.gov.uk/homesafetynetwork/index.htm

Assessment of risk of osteoporosis

✓ Previous fragility fracture (eg wrists)

✓ Prolonged corticosteroid therapy

✓ Hysterectomy, premature menopause or history of amenorrhoea (not treated to reduce risk of osteoporosis)

✓ Risk factors such as liver or thyroid disease, malabsorption, alcoholism, rheumatoid arthritis and male hypogonadism

✓ Family history of osteoporosis (including maternal hip fracture)

✓ Low body mass < 19 kg/m^2

✓ Smoking

Treating osteoporosis

✓ When patients are identified as being at high risk, bone mineral density measurement should be carried out in line with the RCP Clinical Guidelines

✓ All patients get lifestyle advice on nutrition (eg calcium and vitamin D), regular weight-bearing exercise, stopping smoking and avoiding alcohol

✓ Drug interventions: HRT, selective [o]estrogen-receptor modulators (SERMS) and bisphosphonates will be most cost-effective when prescribed to high-risk older people

✓ Frail or housebound people with previous fragility fractures may benefit from supplements of calcium and vitamin D to help prevent hip fracture

Standard 7: Mental Health In Older People

Older people who have mental health problems have access to integrated mental health services, provided by the NHS and councils to ensure effective diagnosis, treatment and support, for them and for their carers.

✓ Alzheimer's Disease is the third most costly disease to treat in the developed world, after heart disease and cancer, writing the UK over £1600 million per year

✓ Considerable variation across the country exists in mental health services for older people

- ✓ Under-detection of mental illness in older people is widespread
- ✓ Depression in people aged 65 and over is especially under-diagnosed
- ✓ Mental and physical problems interact in older people making diagnosis and management difficult
- ✓ Older people from Black and minority ethnic communities need accessible and appropriate mental health services
- ✓ Assessments may be culturally biased
- ✓ Information about services may not be effective if this relies on translated leaflets or posters rather than more appropriate mechanisms of dissemination
- ✓ There may be distrust of agencies by some Black and minority ethnic communities
- ✓ Older people with learning disabilities may have difficulty obtaining appropriate mental health care
- ✓ Family or paid carers of disabled elderly may not be alert to their mental health needs

Promoting mental health

- ✓ Standard 8 sets out the interventions at population level to promote good mental health
- ✓ Additional interventions that will promote mental health include tackling social isolation, providing bereavement support and preventing suicide
- ✓ Key elements of suicide prevention will include health maintenance and promotion, treatment of depression in primary care and screening for suicidal ideation coupled with prevention
- ✓ Older people in residential care and nursing homes should be able to participate in a range of stimulating group or one-to-one activities

Depression

- ✓ 10–15% of the population aged 65 and over will have depression
- ✓ More severe states of depression are less common, affecting about 3–5% of older people
- ✓ Depression severely affects the quality of life, and may adversely affect physical health
- ✓ Depression may be triggered by a variety of factors such as bereavement and loss, life changes such as unemployment,

retirement and social isolation
- ✓ Older people can become depressed because of increasing illness or frailty, or following a stroke or a fall
- ✓ Early recognition can reduce distressing symptoms and prevent physical illness, adverse effects upon social relationships, self-neglect and self-harm or suicide

Dementia

Dementia is a clinical syndrome characterised by a widespread loss of mental function, with the following features:
- ✓ Memory loss
- ✓ Language impairment (having difficulty in finding words especially names and other nouns)
- ✓ Disorientation (not knowing the time or place)
- ✓ Change in personality (becoming more irritable, anxious or withdrawn; loss of skills and impaired judgement)
- ✓ Self-neglect
- ✓ Behaviour that is out of character (for example, sexual disinhibition or aggression)

Dementia has a number of causes, the most common of which are:
- ✓ AD – responsible for 60% of dementia cases, characterised by memory loss and difficulties with language becoming more severe over several years
- ✓ Vascular dementia – this is the consequence of strokes and/or insufficient blood flow to the brain and causes up to 20% of cases of dementia; signs depend on the area of brain involved
- ✓ AD and vascular dementia can coexist
- ✓ Dementia with Lewy bodies – this causes up to 15% of dementia cases and is characterised by symptoms similar to Parkinson's disease as well as hallucinations
- ✓ Approximately 600,000 people in the UK have dementia (5% of the total population aged 65 and over, rising to 20% over the age of 80)
- ✓ 17,000 people with dementia are in younger age groups
- ✓ 154,000 live alone with dementia
- ✓ By 2026 there will be 840,000 people with dementia in the UK, rising to 1.2 million by 2050
- ✓ People diagnosed with dementia should be assessed under the single assessment process

Standard 8: The Promotion Of Health And Active Life In Older Age

The health and wellbeing of older people is promoted through a co-ordinated programme of action led by the NHS with support from councils.

✓ NHS and local partners should re-focus on helping older people to continue to live healthy and fulfilling lives

✓ There is a growing body of evidence to suggest modification of risk factors late in life can have health benefits: longer life, increased/ maintained levels of functional ability, disease prevention and an improved sense of wellbeing

✓ Integrated strategies for older people aimed at promoting good health and quality of life and to prevent or delay frailty and disability can have significant benefits for the individual and society

Action can be taken by the NHS and councils to:

✓ Prevent or delay the onset of ill health and disability

✓ Reduce the impact of illness and disability on health and wellbeing

✓ Identify barriers to healthy living (for example cultural appropriateness of services)

✓ Working with council services such as leisure and lifelong learning

✓ Health promotion activity should take account of differences in lifestyle and the impact of cultural/religious beliefs, for example it would not be appropriate to advise a strict Muslim woman to take up a certain form of exercise that would mean she would have to wear scant clothes for exercise or be in the same room as men

Papers:

The first four articles appeared in the *BMJ* in March and April 2001. They focused on the care of elderly, their basis being extensive literature reviews that were undertaken to inform the development of the National Service Framework (NSF) for NHS care of older people in England and Wales. Some of the issues mentioned are covered in the NSF, therefore just the salient points are listed below, along with any general issues that may arise.

1. Care of older people – Maintaining the dignity and autonomy of older people in the healthcare setting

(*K. Lothian and I. Phile, BMJ 2001;322:668–70*)

✓ It appeared that there is not just a lack of autonomy of elderly people within the healthcare service, but a somewhat unsettling lack of respect for their dignity

✓ Autonomy and dignity, although related, are differing concepts

✓ 'Dignity' refers to an individual maintaining his or her self-respect and being valued by others

✓ 'Autonomy' refers to individual control of decision-making and other activities

✓ Both the dignity and the autonomy of older people are often undermined in healthcare settings

✓ Negative interactions between staff and patients, a lack of regard for patients' privacy and a general insensitivity to the needs and desires of an older population all affect their 'dignity'

✓ 'Autonomy is threatened when patients (and their carers) are not given adequate information or the opportunity to understand fully their diagnosis and to make informed choices about their care'

✓ Qualitative data cited in the article suggests that attitudes of staff greatly affect both the quality of treatment of older people and the regard given to maintaining their dignity and autonomy

✓ Older people are becoming disempowered in healthcare settings

✓ It is not just a problem of the UK but international

✓ Pessimistic viewpoints of healthcare professionals translates into a loss of dignity, identity and decision-making power for seniors

✓ Ageism, it appears, is as much of a problem within the NHS as it is within the population as a whole

✓ 'Tackling negative attitudes through exposure and education can help to preserve older patients' dignity and autonomy'

✓ 'Giving older people and their carers adequate information for them to make informed choices about care further increases autonomy'

The ironic realisation is that the issues facing our profession in caring for the elderly are the same as those the Western world so readily counts as one of its merits, namely 'autonomy', 'dignity' and 'equality'.

From articles such as those listed above and guidelines such as the NSF, it is envisaged we can go some way in closing the apparent gap that exists between the young and old.

2. Promoting health and function in an ageing population
(*G. R. Andrews, BMJ 2001;322:728–9*)

The second article was written by an Australian academic in 'Ageing Studies'. Through a review of literature he looked at the evidence of the effectiveness of strategies for promoting health and function, particularly the benefits of exercise in old age.

- ✓ The prevalence of disability in older people is declining
- ✓ In order to maintain health and function in the elderly, the social, mental, economic and environmental determinants of health in old age must be taken into account
- ✓ The health benefits of exercise may often relate to psychosocial as well as direct health gains
- ✓ Most health benefits can be gained from regular physical activity of moderate intensity
- ✓ Health and wellbeing at older ages is modifiable
- ✓ Promoting health and fitness throughout life could provide substantial gains
- ✓ The WHO has argued for a proactive and positive approach to dealing with the risk of chronic disease in old age
- ✓ The WHO proposed a 'life course' approach for dealing with the health issues associated with ageing, and recommended implementing programmes oriented towards positive interventions in earlier life

3. Care of older people – mental health problems
(*A. Burns, et al, BMJ 2001;322:789–91*)

The third article looks at the quality of mental health services for the elderly. The paper outlines the current evidence of benefit in four areas: services currently available; interventions that have been shown to be effective; rating scales that should be recommended to clinicians for detecting common mental health problems; and the needs of carers.

✓ Guidelines and standardised screening instruments improve recognition

✓ Carer interventions in people with dementia have been shown to be effective in RCTs

✓ Depression is the commonest mental health disorder and psychological therapies are underused

✓ Memory clinics significantly improve the quality of life in carers of people with dementia because of the treatment and advice they offer

✓ An RCT of a psychiatric liaison intervention for medical inpatients aged over 75, showed that those in the intervention group had improved physical function, fewer re-admissions to hospital or nursing home and a shorter length of stay

✓ A similar intervention was shown to be effective in frail, older people living at home

4. Falls in late life and their consequences
(*C. G. Swift, BMJ 2001;322:855–7*)

The last in this series of articles looked at falls in the elderly. The salient points were covered in the NSF, but it would be a relatively easy read if you wanted more detail.

The next few short topics were duplicated in the NSF.

5. Randomised factorial trial of falls prevention among older people living in their own homes
(*L. Day, et al, BMJ 2002;325:128*)

✓ This urban Australian, RCT study looked at the effect of three interventions to prevent falls among older people

✓ Multiple interventions are known to prevent falls among older people, but the relative importance of the different strategies is unknown

✓ The prevention of falls among older people living in their own homes is an established priority in many countries; in the UK it has a strong presence in the NSF for the elderly

✓ 1090 people aged 70+ years and living at home were recruited

- ✓ Most were Australian-born and rated their health as good to excellent; just over half lived alone
- ✓ Three interventions (group-based exercise, home-hazard management and vision improvement) were delivered to eight groups
- ✓ Seven out of the eight groups received at least one intervention (1 hour/week for 15 weeks); the eighth received no intervention until after the study had ended
- ✓ The main outcome measure was time to first fall, ascertained by an 18-month falls' calendar
- ✓ Changes to targeted risk factors were assessed using measures of quadriceps strength, balance, vision and the number of hazards in the home
- ✓ A significant effect ($p < 0.05$) was observed for those combinations of interventions that involved exercise
- ✓ Balance measures improved significantly among the exercise group
- ✓ Neither home-hazard management nor treatment of poor vision showed a significant effect
- ✓ The strongest effect was observed for all three interventions combined, producing an estimated 14.0% reduction in the annual fall rate
- ✓ Number-needed-to treat (NNT) to prevent one fall a year ranged from 32 for home-hazard management to seven for all three interventions combined
- ✓ Group-based exercise was the most potent single intervention tested, and the reduction in falls among this group seems to have been associated with improved balance
- ✓ The addition of home-hazard management or reduced-vision management, or both, further reduced falls

Problems

- ✓ Cost-effectiveness was not examined
- ✓ These findings are most applicable to Australian-born adults aged 70–84 years living at home who rate their health as good
- ✓ Whether or not this data can apply to the UK population is unknown (mainly middle class in Melbourne)
- ✓ The authors state that their programmes were of least intensity and, despite poor compliance, people still showed improvement (the

exercises were supposed to be undertaken daily but most did them twice-weekly)

✓ The reduction in falls may also have been mediated through social interaction, behavioural change, or both, as a result of heightened awareness during the classes

✓ The population studied may already have had many visual problems addressed by the free public healthcare system, since 48% of the intervention group did not require referral

✓ Participants in the intervention groups may also have under-reported falls, and those receiving a more intense intervention, such as the group-based exercise programme, may have been even more inclined to under-report

6. Should elderly patients be told they have cancer? Questionnaire survey of older people

(A. Ajaj, et al, BMJ 2001;323:1160)

✓ This English questionnaire-based study examined the views of the elderly as to the level of information they would like imparted if they had a diagnosis of cancer

✓ It was based on the premise that doctors fail to tell patients of their diagnosis, particularly if elderly

✓ The questionnaire elicited views on how much they would want to know if they were diagnosed with cancer, about the type of cancer, extent of spread, treatment and prognosis, and also their wishes about informing their families. They also enquired about mobility and living circumstances to determine any association

✓ Patients with dementia or a history of cancer were excluded

✓ Out of a total of 315 individuals approached, 270 (86%) completed the questionnaire

✓ Respondents ranged in age from 65 to 94 years

✓ Altogether, 238 (88%) respondents wanted to be informed of the diagnosis, whereas 11% did not and 1% were indifferent

✓ 6.4% under 75 and 13.7% over 75 did not want to be informed, which represents a significant difference

✓ Of those who expressed a desire to be informed, 62% ($n = 147$) wanted to know as much as possible about their cancer, whereas the remainder were more selective

✓ Over 70% (n = 194) of respondents wanted their relatives to be informed when the diagnosis of cancer was made

✓ No significant differences in attitude towards being told about cancer were found between those with different living circumstances and those who lived with a partner or not

✓ Individuals with limited mobility were significantly less interested in knowing they had cancer than those who walked independently either unaided or with a stick

✓ The authors state this may represent that mobility could be taken to reflect independence

✓ There was no relationship, however, to walking distance, as a substantial proportion (44%) could walk only 23 metres or less

Treatment Of Alzheimer's Disease (AD)

About 6% of people aged over 65 and 30% of people aged over 90 have some form of dementia. Alzheimer's disease is the commonest form of dementia, accounting for 35–50% of all cases. AD has an insidious onset. Life expectancy after diagnosis is approximately 7–10 years on average. It is difficult to accurately detect dementia in the pre-clinical phase. A recent study (*BMJ 2003;326:245*) looked at screening people aged 75–95 without dementia (using a single question about memory complaints, the Mini-Mental State Examination (MMSE) to test for global cognitive deficits and domain-specific neuropsychological cognitive testing), to see whether onset of dementia at three years follow-up could be accurately predicted. None of the three tests was found to be accurate when used alone, but when used in combination, a high positive predictive value was achieved. However, sensitivity was still very low, at approximately 18%. This suggests that although a positive result on the three tests implies a high probability of developing dementia at three years, a negative result is difficult to interpret.

 NICE Guidelines – on the use of donepezil, rivastigmine and galantamine for the treatment of AD (Jan 2001)

✓ Available on the NHS as part of the management for mild and moderate AD

✓ For patients with MMSE score of > 12/30

✓ Only specialists should initiate treatment

✓ Agreed shared-care protocol with GPs

✓ Reviewed at 2–4 months

✓ Continue only if MMSE > 12

Evidence
NICE performed a systematic review of five RCTs for donepezil, five for rivastigmine and three for galantamine. They also used unpublished studies from drug companies. All three drugs show statistically a significant improvement in cognitive function compared with placebo.

Typical average improvements of 1 to 2 points in MMSE (out of 30 points) over six months are usual compared with placebo, compared with an average decline of some 4 or 5 points per year in placebo-treated patients within trials.

RCT evidence of improvement in quality-of-life measures is less positive. No measure of quality of life for use in patients with dementia has proved universally satisfactory. Evidence that quality of life has been improved by any of these drugs has therefore been mixed.

Carers report functional benefits and improvement in behavioural symptoms, such as agitation and aggression, as well as in motivation, concentration, control and independence.

Placebo effects are quite large, with as many as 30% improving on baseline outcome scores at the next assessment.

Clinical Evidence 2002

Beneficial	Donepezil, galantamine
Likely to be beneficial	Selegiline (one systematic review), ginkgo (limited evidence from RCTs), oestrogen (in women; one systematic review found that in women with mild to moderate AD, oestrogen improved cognition over 7–12 months)
Trade-off between	Rivastigmine, physostigmine (side-effects benefits and harms include nausea, vomiting, anorexia)

Editorial: Drugs for Alzheimer's disease.
Cholinesterase inhibitors have passed NICE's hurdle
(*BMJ 2001;323:123–4*)

✓ Alzheimer's disease, the commonest cause of dementia in older people, affects 4% of the over-65s and 20% of the over-80s, with around 400,000 sufferers in the United Kingdom

✓ The prevalence of the condition will double over the next 50 years

✓ NICE has reviewed the available drugs for Alzheimer's disease and declared them clinically effective in reducing the burden of disease in some patients

✓ Within the past three years, three cholinesterase inhibitors (donepezil, rivastigmine and galantamine) have been licensed in the UK for use in patients with mild to moderate Alzheimer's disease

✓ These drugs are a rational therapy based on the core deficit in the disorder, that of cholinergic deficit

✓ These compounds represent symptomatic treatments and have been shown in several large, multicentre, randomised, double-blind, placebo-controlled trials to improve cognitive function, global outcome and activities of daily living (ADL)

✓ There is also accumulating evidence that they may improve non-cognitive symptoms such as psychosis and apathy

✓ The mean effect of drug over placebo represents an improvement in cognition roughly equivalent to stemming 6-12 months of natural decline in untreated patients

✓ When the drug is withdrawn the clinical gain is reversed, and there are no convincing clinical data that these drugs modify the disease

✓ 40–50% of patients show a definite clinical improvement ($\geq$4 points on the Alzheimer's disease assessment scale-cognitive subscale – ADAS-cog)

✓ 20% show a strong response ($\geq$ 7 points on the ADAS-cog, equivalent to stemming a year or more of natural cognitive decline)

✓ Responders are maintained above baseline for 12–18 months on both cognitive and non-cognitive measures

✓ NNT for significant clinical improvement are 3–7

✓ No reliable predictors of response have emerged, and in each patient careful assessment of benefit needs to be undertaken after 2–4 months of treatment

✓ Both efficacy and side-effects (mainly gastrointestinal problems) are similar between compounds

✓ Initial scepticism over these compounds was fuelled by the late publication of key trial data, initial lack of clear effects on ADL scores and difficulties in determining cost-effectiveness

✓ Most economic analyses clearly show either cost-neutrality or cost-effectiveness in favour of these agents

✓ Evidence to date suggests that the modest cost of these agents (£800–£1200 a year) would be more than offset by savings elsewhere, although not necessarily within the healthcare system

New treatments: NMDA-receptor antagonists

Glutamate neurones are the most prevalent in the brain. In AD they become inefficient due to leakage at the NMDA receptor, which interferes with the transmission of the glutamate signal and can affect cognitive function. Memantine (Ebixa), an uncompetitive NMDA-receptor antagonist, repairs this leakiness, hence protecting neurones from the toxic effects of elevated glutamate. Memantine is thought to be effective in moderate to severe AD, whereas the cholinesterase inhibitors can only be used in mild to moderate disease. Memantine can be used in combination with a cholinesterase inhibitor, either at the start of treatment or as the disease progresses.

Other treatments

Statins and NSAIDs
There has been much observational data about these drugs, but not much in the way of hard evidence. One RCT found that indometacin improved cognitive function after six months of treatment, but another found no improvement with the use of Arthrotec (dicofenal plus misoprostol).

Vitamin E (at high dose)
This may reduce the number of people who develop severe dementia and lose the ability to perform daily living tasks.

Sensory stimulation
Aromatherapy and bright-light therapy may be effective in reducing restlessness and sleep disturbance in patients with AD, and with far fewer side-effects than sedative medication!

 USEFUL WEBSITE

www.nice.org.uk – Guidance No 19, January 2001

Osteoporosis

Osteoporosis is defined as a skeletal disease characterised by low bone mass and deterioration of the microarchitecture of bone tissue, which makes bone more fragile and hence increases the risk of fracture.

Osteoporosis affects approximately 40% of women and 10% of men over 70 years of age in the UK; which is especially concerning given that it is estimated that by 2025 almost a quarter of the population in Europe will be over 65. It is emerging as one of the biggest health problems in postmenopausal women – resulting in more deaths in older women than cancer of the cervix, uterus and ovaries combined. The annual cost to the NHS of osteoporotic fractures has been estimated at £1.7 billion; a hip fracture costs about £20,000 per fracture. Approximately 20% of patients die within a year of sustaining a fractured neck of femur as a result of osteoporosis.

A low level of awareness for the benefits of early identification of risk factors, together with the pressure to reduce prescribing costs, often results in ineffective disease management. 'The Women's Health Report' was produced in February 2003 by the National Osteoporosis Society. This looked at women's knowledge of osteoporosis-related issues. Despite the fact that one in three women over the age of 50 years will be affected by osteoporosis, only 27% thought this was cause for concern. One in three women did not know that osteoporosis could be treated.

The National Service Framework (NSF) for older people addresses the need for action on the prevention and treatment of osteoporosis. It also acknowledges that preventing osteoporosis in high-risk patients has a significant effect on both the number and severity of fractures.

How are patients at high risk of osteoporosis identified?

Osteoporosis can be reliably identified by bone densitometry, which is still the 'gold standard' for both the measurement of disease and the response to therapy. Unfortunately, the availability of dual-energy, X-ray absorptiometry (DEXA) scanning machines is still very variable across the UK, despite only costing the NHS £20–45 per scan. DEXA scans have been shown to predict future fracture rate with a high specificity but low sensitivity. It is recommended that DEXA scanning should be used for patients at a high risk of developing osteoporosis rather than for screening the general population (see Box on p. 168).

A study has shown that quantitative ultrasound scanning is better than asking about risk factors for osteoporosis to select women for subsequent bone densitometry (*BMJ 2003;326:1250–1*). A combination of the ultrasound scan and assessment of risk factors identified 90% of the women with osteoporosis.

How important is corticosteroid-induced osteoporosis?

In most patients on long-term oral corticosteroid treatment, there is a fall in bone mass and bone mineral density. Longitudinal studies have shown that the most rapid rate of bone loss occurs in the first year of treatment, and thereafter it continues at a rate of two to three times normal in older subjects on long-term therapy. As many as 40% of patients on long-term steroids may develop a fracture secondary to osteoporosis.

The exact dose of corticosteroid that induces clinically significant bone loss is not yet well established. Studies in patients have consistently demonstrated a clinically important fall in bone density in patients taking 7.5 mg prednisolone a day; therefore, all such patients should ideally be given preventive treatment. However, one study indicated that only 14% of patients treated with oral corticosteroids are also prescribed therapy to prevent bone loss (*BMJ 1996;313:344–6*).

The National Osteoporosis Society has produced guidelines on the management of glucocorticoid-induced osteoporosis, which, where possible, are based on current clinical evidence (see their website). The most commonly used treatment for glucocorticoid-induced osteoporosis are hormone-replacement therapy and bisphosphonates.

What drug and other interventions can be used to prevent and treat osteoporosis?

The Royal College of Physicians issued guidelines in 1999 for the prevention and treatment of osteoporosis. In the 18 months following the release of these guidelines, new clinical trial data became available for existing and new drug interventions. Hence, an 'Update on pharmacological interventions for the prevention and treatment of osteoporosis' has been prepared by the original Guidelines Writing Group, in collaboration with the Bone and Tooth Society, and endorsed by the Royal College of Physicians. This report also includes a useful algorithm for the management of individual patients, derived from an evidence-based synthesis of different pharmacological interventions.

Prophylaxis against osteoporosis obviously needs to be continued long term. There is no evidence that bone protection lasts much beyond the current use of any treatment option, so long-term costs (both to the patient and financially) have to be considered. The side-effects and method of administration must therefore be acceptable to the patient if compliance is to be optimal. Thus the increasing range of treatments and the greater acceptability of these options are very important.

A study has shown that fracture prevention treatment is under-prescribed for those at greatest risk (*Ann Rheum Dis 2003;62:350–2*). GP records from 41 UK practices were investigated and it was found that elderly patients had the most prescriptions for corticosteroid treatment but the fewest for effective fracture-prevention therapy.

Bisphosphonates

Bisphosphonates block osteoclast action. Cyclical etidronate (Didronel), alendronate (Fosamax) and risedronate (Actonel) are all licensed for the prevention and treatment of osteoporosis (and corticosteroid-induced osteoporosis).

Alendronate reduces the incidence of both vertebral and non-vertebral fractures, as demonstrated by large, well-constructed randomised controlled trials (*Fracture intervention trial. Lancet 1996;348:1535–41*).

Symptomatic vertebral fractures were decreased by 28–36% over four years of treatment, whereas the risk of hip fracture was reduced by just over a half.

Risedronate similarly reduces the incidence of vertebral fractures (Vertebral efficacy with risedronate therapy – VERT trial) (*JAMA 1999;282:1344–52*). There seems to be less convincing evidence in terms of protection against hip fracture.

NICE have recommended the use of bisphosphonates to treat post-menopausal women with severe osteoporosis and with those women who have had a fragility fracture, even without a DEXA scan. Post-menopausal women under 65 would be eligible for treatment provided a DEXA scan showed they had a T-score below -3.2 SD or below -2.5 CD and a history of maternal hip fracture or long-term use of systemic steroids. The extra cost to the NHS is estimated to be £75 million a year. This guidance has not been well received, as bisphosphonates are used to prevent fractures, rather than starting in patients once they have sustained a fracture.

Selective oestrogen-receptor modulator (SERM) therapy

Raloxifene mimics the beneficial effects of oestrogen on the bone but blocks the oestrogen effect on the uterus and breast tissue. It reduces vertebral fractures by 30% over three years, but does not reduce the incidence of non-vertebral fractures. It does not cause uterine bleeding or gastrointestinal side-effects, and reduces the risk of breast cancer; however, it worsens certain menopausal symptoms such as hot flushes and increases the risk of DVT. Therefore, the precise place for raloxifene in the prevention and management of osteoporosis in general practice is still a matter for debate.

Hormone-replacement therapy (HRT)

Earlier assumptions that taking HRT would reduce the risk of fracture in the future have unfortunately not been confirmed; oestrogen-induced skeletal benefits probably disappear within 6–10 years of stopping treatment. Some 10 years after HRT has been stopped, bone density and fracture risk are similar in women who have not taken HRT. Therefore, women would need to take oestrogens from their menopause until at least their early 70s to reduce their risk of osteoporotic fractures.

There is grade A evidence that HRT does reduce the risk of both hip and spine fractures (by 30% and 50%, respectively) while women are taking it. The WHI (Women's Health Initiative study, *JAMA 2002;288:321*) study was a large randomised controlled trial involving 16,608 postmenopausal women over the age of 50, 21% of whom were over the age of 70. After 5.2 years of treatment, there were only 5 per 10,000 fewer cases per year of hip or spine fracture in the women given HRT (a relative risk ratio of 0.66, but a disappointing absolute risk reduction). This may be because most of the women studied were relatively old; it is known that HRT has less effect on bone mass in the elderly. A recent systematic review (*Bandolier 2002, Vol 19, Issue 2*) shows that the NNT with HRT is approximately 40 women for 1–10 years to prevent one fracture.

However, following the Million Women Study (*Lancet 2003;362:419*), the Committee of Safety on Medicines have advised that HRT should no longer be considered as the therapy of choice for preventing osteoporosis in women over the age of 50 years. It may still be used to prevent osteoporosis in women who cannot take other treatments or for whom these have become ineffective. It is also the treatment of choice for preventing osteoporosis in women under 50 who had a premature menopause.

Calcium and vitamin D

Calcium and vitamin D supplements may slow down the rate of bone loss in elderly women who already have a low BMD, and have been shown to reduce fractures, including hip fractures. However, in patients with established osteoporosis this effect is not enough. Calcium can, however, complement other treatments (SERMs, bisphosphonates, oestrogen). It is recommended that those people at risk of osteoporosis should maintain an adequate intake of calcium and vitamin D, and any deficiency should be corrected by increasing dietary intake or taking supplements. Elderly patients, especially those in residential or nursing homes, may routinely benefit from taking supplements (*BMJ Editorial, November 1998*), eg calcium and ergocalciferol 800 IU daily.

There seems to be a higher incidence of hypovitaminosis D in the elderly (*New Engl J Med 1998;338:777–83*), although this study looked at inpatients. However, vitamin D deficiency may certainly contribute to osteoporosis; a recent study has concluded that if everyone over the age of 65 were routinely offered an oral vitamin D supplement (100,000 IU) every four months, then the rate of fractures could be reduced (*BMJ 2003;326:469*). The NNT is approximately 250 for five years to prevent one fracture. The benefit is more pronounced in women.

Calcitonin
This is an endogenous inhibitor of bone resorption, which suppresses osteoclasts. Salmon calcitonin (10 times more potent than human calcitonin) is available as a nasal spray and as a subcutaneous injection. It seems to have only a modest effect on bone density, but reduces the vertebral fracture rate by 33%.

Parathyroid hormone (PTH)
Recombinant human PTH given as daily subcutaneous injections is promising. An American RCT (*New Engl J Med 2001;344:1434*) found that spinal fractures were reduced by 90% and other fractures by 50% in osteoporosis sufferers; this makes it more effective than any other treatment currently available. It has not yet got its UK licence. PTH does not seem to be more effective when used in combination with bisphosphonates.

Hip protectors
These seem to be effective in reducing the impact of falls when used properly, eg in institutionalised patients. However, in the community, compliance remains a huge problem.

Lifestyle factors
Encouraging people to cut down on smoking and alcohol intake, to eat a healthy diet and to do regular, weight-bearing or impact exercises can all help to reduce fracture rates.

Statins
Finally, one observational study found that the inhibition of hydroxy-methylglutaryl coenzyme A reductase with statin therapy may reduce the risk of fracture (*JAMA 2000;283:3205–10*). However, this was

recently disproved by a study from the USA (*Ann Intern Med 2003; 139:97–104*) which examined data from the Women's Health Initiative study and found that the fracture risk in the women taking statins was similar to that of women who were not taking statins.

USEFUL WEBSITES

www.doh.gov.uk/osteorep.htm – DoH guidelines on prevention and treatment (produced by the RCP)
www.nos.org.uk – National Osteoporosis Society
www.doh.gov.uk/nsf/olderpeople.htm – National Service Framework for Older People

RISK FACTORS FOR OSTEOPOROSIS

✓ Early menopause
✓ Hysterectomy < 45 years
✓ Long-term prednisolone 7.5 mg/day
✓ Malabsorption disorder (eg coeliac disease)
✓ Premenopausal episodes of amenorrhoea
✓ Lean body habitus
✓ Strong family history
✓ Cigarette smoking

SUMMARY POINTS FOR OSTEOPOROSIS

✓ Annual cost of NHS of treating osteoporatic fractures is 1.7 billion pounds
✓ Often underdiagnosed and suboptimally managed
✓ Several effective medical interventions available
✓ Poor compliance with treatment is a problem

Parkinson's disease

Parkinson's disease occurs worldwide with an equal incidence in men and women. Overall, the age-adjusted prevalence is 1% worldwide, rising from 0.6% at the age of 60-64, to 3.5% at age 85–89. Mean age of onset is 65. Tremor from PD always starts asymmetrically. Parkinson's disease is currently incurable and disability tends to be progressive. Treatment may slow down the rate of progression and reduce symptoms.

 Treatment options

Dopamine agonists (eg ropinirole, pramipexole)
It is beneficial to start treatment with dopamine agonists instead of L-dopa in the early disease, especially in younger patients. Although it is no more effective, this reduces the incidence of dyskinesias and fluctuations in motor response. Combination treatment can also reduce the risk of dyskinesia. Longer-acting dopamine agonists such as ropinirole and pramipexole are less likely to induce dyskinesias than shorter-acting formulations.

Selegiline
This likely to be beneficial in patients with early disease. However, one RCT showed increased mortality in the treatment group.

L-Dopa (with dopa-decarboxylase inhibitor)
Although L-dopa improves motor functioning, dyskinesias and fluctuations in motor response are irreversible. There is no benefit in taking modified-release preparations.

Co-enzyme Q10
Treatment with high-dose (1200 mg) co-enzyme Q10 seems to slow deterioration in the early stages of PD; at 18 months, one study (*Arch Neurol 2002;59:541*) showed a significant difference in functional status and disability. However, it is a very expensive treatment.

Deep brain stimulation
This may be helpful for severe dyskinesias.

Depression and PD

Depression is extremely common in PD, affecting up to 50% of patients. It is under-diagnosed, especially because sufferers often have a flat affect anyway, as a result of the disease. Drug treatment is often difficult, since patients are at risk of developing the serotonin syndrome, especially if they are already on selegiline. SSRIs are probably the safest option (*BMJ editorial 2000;320:1287*).

 SUMMARY POINTS

✓ Parkinson's disease is incurable and causes significant morbidity and mortality
✓ Various medications can help with symptoms
✓ A dopamine agonist is a better option in initial treatment than L-dopa
✓ Do not forget to screen for depression

Osteoarthritis

Osteoarthritis (OA) most commonly affects the hands, knees, hips and spine. It is a common and important cause of pain and disability, with about 10–20% of people over 60 being clinically affected, although radiographic changes in at least some joints are almost universal. The annual GP consultation rate is approximately 24.8/1000 for OA alone, and it accounts for 11% of all working days lost. The annual cost in the UK is estimated to be about £1.2 billion.

What is the evidence for glucosamine?

Glucosamine is claimed to have chondroprotective properties and is naturally occurring. There is evidence for its use, but this remains controversial; *Clinical Evidence* (2003) criticises the quality of many of the studies carried out so far and concludes that glucosamine is of 'unknown effectiveness'. *DTB* (November 2002) disagrees, and claims that glucosamine is a reasonable treatment option.

A systematic review (*Cochrane 2002, Issue 4*) looked at 16 RCTs of glucosamine 1500 mg daily compared to placebo or NSAIDs in patients with OA. It concluded that glucosamine is at least as good as NSAIDs (ibuprofen and piroxicam), and that it had a significant effect clinically. However, the trials were all short (mean duration 6 weeks).

One study in the *Lancet* (*2001;357:251–6*) showed that radiographic joint narrowing (of the tibiofemoral joint) was decreased with glucosamine (at 1500 mg/day) compared to placebo, over a three-year period. Symptom scores also improved by about 20% with glucosamine.

What about topical NSAIDs?

A systematic review in the *BMJ* in 1998 (*316:333–7*) concluded that topical NSAIDs are effective in chronic pain conditions such as OA, with an NNT of 3.1 after two weeks. Systemic side-effects are no greater than with placebo. Topical NSAIDs are therefore a reasonable starting point, especially if the pain is localised.

Who should be taking COX-2 inhibitors?
Some 15% of patients on long-term NSAIDs develop GI ulcers and approximately 2000 people die from GI bleeding caused by NSAIDs

every year in the UK. COX-2 inhibitors are thought to be safer in terms of GI side-effects, but no better in terms of renal and cardiac effects. There are concerns that they may actually be more dangerous than conventional NSAIDs in patients with CHD.

GUIDANCE FROM NICE ON WHO SHOULD BE PRESCRIBED COX-2 INHIBITORS:

✓ People over 65
✓ People on coexistent drugs (but NOT aspirin) that increase risk
✓ People with a history of PUD/gastric bleeding (although COX-2 drugs should be used only with great caution in this group)

A systematic review in the *BMJ* (*BMJ 2002;325:619*) concluded that celecoxib is as effective as other NSAIDs, but shows significantly improved GI safety and tolerability (NNT to prevent an endoscopically detected ulcer = 6 for 3 months, but much larger NNT to prevent GI bleed/perforation or symptomatic ulcer). The VIGOR study (*New Engl J Med 2000;343:1520*) compared rofecoxib to naproxen in patients with rheumatoid arthritis and showed a 50% relative risk reduction with rofecoxib in terms of serious GI side-effects. However, since only RA patients were studied, the generalisability of these findings is debatable. The CLASS study (*JAMA 2000;284:1427*) found that celecoxib causes fewer ulcers than do diclofenac or ibuprofen. This study has been criticised however, in terms of its validity.

Other treatments

Intra-articular hyaluronic acid injections
This seems to reduce pain in the short-term. However, there is little evidence for its long-term use.

Surgery
There is no doubt that joint replacement is effective; hip replacement is effective for at least 10 years. However, patients over 75 or under 45 years and obese patients may have worse outcomes. Recently there has been much publicity in the lay press regarding the 'Birmingham resurfacing hip replacement', where only the arthritic joint surface is replaced, so preserving much of the femoral head. Although this has many theoretical advantages, especially in the younger patient, there is no valid long-term data as yet.

Taping of the knee joint
Australian researchers have recently shown that therapeutic taping of the knee joint reduces short-term pain and disability compared to placebo (*BMJ 2003;327:135–8*).

Autologous chondrocyte transplantation
This relatively new treatment is most useful in younger patients with a focal area of cartilage loss. Chondrocytes are harvested from the patient and multiplied in the lab, before being re-introduced arthroscopically in an attempt to correct the cartilage defect.

Physiotherapy and exercise
Non-impact physiotherapy and especially hydrotherapy not only improve symptoms, but also contribute to weight loss and ensure musculature is in optimum condition, so that the patient may make full use of any future joint replacement. Specific exercises of benefit include quadriceps strengthening for knee arthritis (eg straight leg raises sitting in a chair) and hip abductor strengthening for hip arthritis.

Weight loss
Weight loss decreases the pain felt from hip and knee arthritis and increases walking distance. Surgery for obese patients is very difficult; such patients pose a higher anaesthetic risk, are more likely to get complications from their surgery (eg DVT, wound infection) and their prostheses wear out much quicker.

Regular simple analgesia
Regular analgesia (eg paracetamol) is more effective than intermittent analgesia.

SUMMARY POINTS

✓ OA is common
✓ Glucosamine is probably beneficial
✓ According to NICE guidance, many patients with OA will be prescribed COX-2 inhibitors in the future
✓ Lifestyle factors are, as always, very important

CHAPTER 5:

OBSTETRICS AND GYNAECOLOGY

Chapter 5: Obstetrics and Gynaecology

Combined Oral Contraceptive Pill

The combined oral contraceptive pill (COCP) has been one of the most extensively researched medicines and is still providing many areas of controversy and discussion. About 80% of British women use the COCP at some time between the ages of 16 and 24 years. The pill continues to be one of the most worried and talked about drugs, regularly making newspaper headlines. Consequently, women's fears persist out of all proportion to actual risk, and in most cases women are unaware of the pill's substantial non-contraceptive health benefits.

A recent study involving over 17,000 women found that there was no harmful effect of oral contraceptive use on overall mortality (*Lancet 2003;362:185*). By contrast, however, death from all causes was more than twice as high in smokers of 15 cigarettes a day as in non-smokers.

What is the risk of deep vein thrombosis for women taking the combined oral contraceptive?

Women with a BMI of at least 35 have a fourfold increased risk of DVT when taking any type of combined oral contraceptive.

In 2002, a high court judge reviewed the available evidence and decided that the 'most compelling evidence' in the case was the Cox regression analysis carried out in the study by the Transnational Research group on Oral Contraceptives (*Human Reproduction 1999;14:1493*). This paper included full lifetime oral contraceptive exposure for over 90% of the subjects and found no association between third generation pills and any increased risk of venous thromboembolism.

A meta-analysis in the *BMJ* concluded that the risk with third-generation pills is 1.7 times that with second-generation pills (*BMJ 2001;323: 131–4*). An editorial in the same edition of the *BMJ* points out that, while debating whether the risks are one or ten in a million, it is important to remember that in most of the world the risk of death associated with pregnancy is at least 100 times greater than this.

The quoted risks of DVT per year are as follows:
Non-users   5 : 100,000
Second-generation pill   15 : 100,000
Third-generation pill   30 : 100,000
Pregnancy   60 : 100,000

In 1999 the Department of Health announced an end to the 1995 restrictions on prescribing third-generation oral contraceptive pills. The absolute risk of venous thromboembolism in women taking either second- or third-generation combined oral contraceptives remains very small and still well below the risk associated with pregnancy. Provided that the women are informed of and accept the relative risks of thromboembolism, the choice of oral contraceptive is for the woman and the prescriber to decide jointly in the light of her individual medical history and any contraindications.

A recent paper has found that the number of women prescribed the third generation pill decreased dramatically after the pill scare in 1995; the decrease was most notable for women under 25. In addition, the percentage of women prescribed a third generation oral contraceptive continued to decline over the following six years (*BMJ 2003;326:254*).

The European Agency for Evaluation of Medicinal Products published a report in October 2001 based on an ongoing review of the risk of venous thromboembolism (VTE) with the COCP. The Committee found an excess risk of VTE during the first year if a woman takes any combined oral contraceptive pill. The report concluded that if a woman uses any type of COCP for a year without suffering a clot, then her future risk of VTE is extremely low.

Should the COCP be prescribed to patients with a family history of clots?

The value of a family history of venous thromboembolism has recently been questioned, as it actually has a poor sensitivity and unsatisfactory predictive value for identifying women with thrombophilic defects (*BMJ 2001;322:1024–5*). Universal screening is not cost-effective as 8000 women need to be screened to prevent one VTE, and only screening women with a family history of VTE may miss a substantial number of women at increased risk of VTE while taking the COCP.

Is there an increased risk of myocardial infarction?

A large community-based, case-control study found no association between the use of the combined oral contraceptive and myocardial infarction, and no difference in risk between second- and third-generation pills (*BMJ 1999;318:1579–84*). However, the Transnational study demonstrated a statistically significant reduction in the risk of MI in users of third generation pills compared to second generation products. The risk of MI in women taking the combined oral contraceptive seems to increase only in association with additional risk factors (eg smoking, diabetes, obesity, hypertension). The COCP is contraindicated in women with severe or multiple risk factors for ischaemic heart disease.

Is there an increased risk of ischaemic stroke?

In women who do not smoke and do not have hypertension, the risk of ischaemic stroke is 1.5 times higher than in non-users. However, the risk rises to threefold in women with hypertension taking the combined oral contraceptive.

Does taking the combined oral contraceptive pill lead to hypertension?

There is a lack of data on the effects of the low-dose combined oral contraceptive on blood pressure. If a woman develops pill-induced hypertension she should consider an alternative method of contraception. The pill should not be used and also be stopped in patients with a sustained blood pressure above 160/95 mmHg.

Is the combined oral contraceptive pill contraindicated in women with migraine?

The incidence of ischaemic (not haemorrhagic) stroke is increased in women with migraine, particularly if they are also taking the COCP (*BMJ 1999; 318:13–18*). The combined oral contraceptive pill is contra-indicated in patients who have migraines with focal aura (migraine with focal symptoms) or classical migraine and those patients who have severe migraines lasting over 72 hours despite treatment.

What was the cervical cancer scare about?

Women with HPV who have been on the pill for five years or more could be at three times the risk of cervical cancer, or four times if they have been taking it for more than 10 years; this was according to a review of eight previously published case-control studies (*Lancet 2002; 359:1093*). Although the press had a 'field day' with this new information, the CSM concluded that the overall risk was still very small and that women on the pill should simply be encouraged to have regular smears.

What about breast cancer?

A recent large case-control study of 5000 women in America found no increase in the risk of breast cancer for current or previous use (*New Engl J Med 2002;346:2025*). However, in women who are positive for the *BRCA1* gene, it may be best avoided – smaller studies have shown that there is an increased risk in this case.

Are there benefits from taking the combined oral contraceptive pill?

It is important to remember that the pill has numerous advantages. These include:

✓ Excellent efficacy and acceptability
✓ Beneficial effects on menstrual disorders
✓ Suppression of benign breast disease

✓ Protection against endometrial and ovarian cancer
✓ Protection against pelvic inflammatory disease

Any adverse effects from taking the oral contraceptive pill are reversed after 10 years' cessation of the pill.

Newer alternatives to the COCP

EVRA
This is a new contraceptive patch releasing 20 μg per day of estradiol and 150 μg of norelgestromin (the primary active metabolite in Cilest). Women have to change their patch once a week for three weeks, then have a 'patch-free' week. A review in *JAMA* (*JAMA 2001;285:2347–54*) showed that Evra is as effective as the COCP, but compliance is better.

Cerazette
This is a new POP, containing higher dose progestogen than conventional POPs. It is thought to inhibit ovulation, and may have similar efficacy to the COCP.

SUMMARY POINTS FOR COMBINED ORAL CONTRACEPTION

✓ Very safe and effective contraception
✓ Conflicting evidence still exists regarding thrombotic risk
✓ Absolute risk of DVT very small with third-generation pill
✓ Always consider patients' risk factors for CHD
✓ COCP still has numerous advantages and is a safe contraceptive

Emergency Contraception

Emergency contraception (also called 'postcoital contraception') is a safe and highly effective way of preventing an accidental pregnancy; it is not suitable if used as a regular method of birth control. It is very popular, one-third of women aged 18–19 years and one-quarter of women aged 20–24 years have used it at least once over the preceding two years.

Levonorgestrel is the only emergency contraception pill now available. It prevents pregnancy by suppressing ovulation, impairing fallopian transport of the egg and sperm (so preventing fertilisation) and also prevents implantation of any fertilised egg. Levonorgestrel appears to be very safe and there are no contraindications for its use.

Why has levonorgestrel become available without a prescription?

A medicine must have prescription-only status: if there is a danger to health if the substance were used without medical supervision; if the product might be used incorrectly, so endangering health; or if the active ingredient, or side-effects it may cause, require further investigation. The CSM advised that levonorgestrel does not meet these criteria and so could be safely supplied by a pharmacist without medical supervision. The UK Government took this advice, and from 1 January 2001 levonorgestrel has been available, at a cost of £24, to women over 16 years of age from pharmacies without a doctor's prescription.

What are the advantages of levonorgestrel being available without prescription?

✓ Very safe medication (unlike paracetamol and ibruprofen!)
✓ Very effective medication
✓ Increases ease of access
✓ Patients may prefer anonymity
✓ Leads to reduction in unwanted pregnancies
✓ Supported by RCOG and BMA
✓ May save money by reduction in termination rates

What are the disadvantages of levonorgestrel being available over the counter?

✓ Does not address issues of ongoing contraception and sexually transmitted diseases

✓ Lost opportunity for counselling/education

✓ Patients will have to pay for it

✓ Opposition by church/anti-abortion groups

✓ Need highly motivated pharmacists

✓ Not all pharmacies will have an area available for discussing private issues

✓ Has been banned in Ireland

A qualitative study has shown that the attitudes and concerns of young women, especially those from disadvantaged backgrounds, make them less able or willing than others to take emergency contraception (*BMJ 2002;325:1393*). Those women in this study who thought it easier to avoid emergency contraception rather than face their own anxiety, sense of guilt, and concern about hat others might think were teenagers who either lived in disadvantaged areas or were homeless.

Should levonorgestrel be available free of charge over the counter?

It has been estimated that £1 spent on contraception actually saves £11 in subsequent NHS costs arising from an unplanned pregnancy; so it could be argued that offering free over-the-counter emergency contraception releases money to spend on other services.

Women still need to know how, when and where they can obtain emergency contraception free of charge through established NHS routes of supply. Emergency contraception still remains available free on prescription from GPs, family planning clinics, youth clinics, walk-in centres, some genitourinary medicine units and Emergency Departments.

It is more effective the sooner it is taken after unprotected intercourse. Results from the WHO Task Force trial are shown in Table 1. A single dose of levonorgestrel 1.5 mg is as effective as the conventional doses of 750 mcg according to a recent WHO trial in which over 4000 women in ten countries participated (*Lancet 2002;360:1830–10*). In addition, although the pregnancy rates were slightly higher among those women who took treatment more than 72 hours later, this difference was not significant.

This study has been discussed in a *BMJ* editorial which recommends that all patients should now receive levonorgestrel as 'one stat' dose (*BMJ 2003;326:775–6*). It suggests that regulatory bodies and pharmaceutical companies should consider changing the licence. It also states that the 72 h cut-off point for starting treatment seems unnecessary.

One study from London found that many young women did not take emergency contraception when they needed it because they misjudged their risk of pregnancy or had personal difficulties getting hold of emergency contraception (*BMJ 2002;325:1393*).

Finally, ongoing contraception should always be started at the same visit as emergency contraception. This will reduce the number of pregnancies conceived while waiting for the next menstruation.

The intrauterine contraceptive device (IUCD) is still available as an alternative to levonorgestrel, is effective for up to five days after unprotected intercourse and is more effective than the hormonal methods.

SUMMARY POINTS FOR EMERGENCY CONTRACEPTION

✓ Levonorgestrel is now obtainable without prescription
✓ Low incidence of side-effects
✓ Levonorgestrel should be given early to improve efficacy
✓ IUCD still more effective

Teenagers and Sexual Health

The UK has the second highest teenage pregnancy rate in the developed world. (The USA has the highest.) Many teenagers are willing to run the risk of an unplanned pregnancy or catching a sexually transmitted disease because they fear that their parents will find out if they seek advice from their GP. Reduction in teenage pregnancy was one of the targets set for improvement during the 1990s in the Health of the Nation document; however it was not met! The recently published Government document 'Tackling health inequalities – a programme for action' sets out plans to tackle health inequalities. To close the gap in infant mortality, one of the key interventions is to prevent teenage pregnancies and support teenage parents.

What are the problems?

Teenagers are often confused about where they can obtain contraceptive advice or treatment, whether it is legal, whether it will be confidential and how to actually use the different contraceptive methods. In the UK, approximately 50% of teenagers use contraception; however, this rate is much higher in Denmark, which suggests poorer access and knowledge rather than lower demand in the UK. In addition, 75% of teenage mothers admit to having had unplanned pregnancies. Amongst countries in the 'developed world', the teenage birth rate in the UK is second only to the USA and is five times higher than that of The Netherlands. In the UK in 1998, there were 30.8 births per 1000 15–19-year-olds.

In 1995–7 the rate of increase of gonorrhoea among 15–19-year-olds was 45% and chlamydia was 53%. The results of a questionnaire survey sent to 1045 children aged 13–15 years showed that 54% believed they had to be over 16 years of age to access sexual health services (*Br J Gen Pract 2000;50:550–4*).

A relatively recent landmark study has shown that risky sexual behaviour has led to a dramatic increase in sexually transmitted infections (*Lancet 2001;358:1835–54*). This study showed that among 16–24-year-olds, almost 20% of men and 15% of women have already had 10 or more sexual partners. Around one in four women and one in three men say they had sexual intercourse before the age of 16.

How should GPs be able to improve teenage sexual health?

The Fraser (previously Gillick) ruling clarifies the legal position of treating children under 16 years of age without parental consent (see Box below).

Various surveys have estimated that at least one-quarter of teenagers do not believe their consultation will be confidential. Posters or leaflets in the surgery explaining the services available and the confidentiality issue may be useful. Patients must have easy access to emergency contraception. It can be useful to advertise local family planning and youth clinics, as many patients prefer these clinics rather than seeing their own GP (many teenagers worry about running into a neighbour or friend in the waiting room). A report on teenage pregnancy from the Social Exclusion Unit in 1997 recommended more accessible services, such as lunch time sessions in schools with a nurse or doctor. Ideally, services should have suitable opening hours, eg evenings and Saturdays.

A piece of research studying teenage pregnancies found that almost all had visited a GP in the previous year, and many of them had sought contraceptive advice during the consultation (*BMJ 2000;321:486–9*). More worryingly, teenagers who had a pregnancy termination were more likely to have received emergency contraception in the past.

It is clear therefore that GPs should follow up teenage patients to ensure they are using their contraception correctly. In addition, patients who receive emergency contraception should be started on regular contraception at the same time and then have clear follow-up arrangements in place.

Unfortunately, a recent systematic review concluded that primary prevention strategies have not actually been shown to delay the time of first sexual intercourse or improve the use of contraception among teenagers (*BMJ 2002;324:1426–9*).

What is the multimedia campaign about teenage pregnancy?
This national campaign aims to give young people information about sex and contraception, including facts about the rising rates of sexually transmitted infections among teenagers and dispelling some 'urban myths' about sex. This is going to be achieved by using adverts in teen magazines, on local radio stations and through other media.

Specifically, the campaign messages are:
- ✓ You can get free, confidential advice about contraception whatever your age
- ✓ If you are sexually active, use contraception, because of the risk of pregnancy and infections

✓ You choose when to have sex, no one else

Local sexual health services are expected to see a gradual increase in demand from teenagers as a result of this campaign. To ensure the services are accessible and trusted by teenagers, best-practice guidance has been developed by the Teenage Pregnancy Unit for the commissioning and provision of effective services for young people.

CONTRACEPTION AND YOUNG PEOPLE UNDER 16 YEARS – THE FRASER GUIDELINES

A young person under 16 years may be given advice and may be prescribed contraception without parental consent if the following conditions are met:

✓ She understands the advice and is competent to consent to treatment
✓ You encourage her to inform her parent or guardian
✓ You believe she is likely to commence or continue sexual activity with or without contraception
✓ Her physical or mental health will suffer if she does not receive contraception advice or supplies
✓ Providing contraception is in her best interest

USEFUL WEBSITE

www.info.doh.gov.uk/tpu/tpu.nsf – Teenage Pregnancy Unit's website

SUMMARY POINTS FOR TEENAGERS AND SEXUAL HEALTH

✓ The UK has a high teenage pregnancy rate
✓ Most teenagers are unaware of the confidentiality and different methods
✓ Lower teenage pregnancy rates in practices having young female partners

Sexual Health and Chlamydia

The number of visits to genitourinary medicine (GUM) clinics has doubled over the past decade and the number of sexually transmitted infections diagnosed continues to rise: there were 81,680 cases diagnosed in England and Wales in 2002.

Chlamydia is now the commonest, curable, sexually transmitted disease in the industrialised world. It is currently a huge problem in young, sexually active adults; some 36% of adults diagnosed with it are aged under 20. The long-term consequences of chlamydia include increased pelvic pain, increased rate of ectopic pregnancies and increased infertility rates. This latter consequence often only becomes apparent during investigations at infertility clinics, as many patients are unaware of earlier infection with *Chlamydia* spp.

Up to 70% of women and 50% men with infections are asymptomatic. The incidence has increased by 27% in 2002 and by 106% since 1997, according to recent Public Health Service Laboratory figures (www.phls.co.uk); it has been estimated as affecting 1 in 12 women aged 16–24 years.

A recent study found that 10% of 798 male military recruits tested positive for *Chlamydia* spp (*Lancet 2003;361:1792*). The national screening pilot found 13.8% of under 16-year-olds, 10.5% of 16–19-year-olds and 7.2% of 20–24-year-olds were infected.

Why has the incidence of sexually transmitted infections, including chlamydia, increased by so much?

Some of the rise in incidence may be a reflection of improved detection and awareness. However, one of the major factors behind the recent rises in Western Europe is probably changing sexual behaviour. In addition, levels of awareness and fear of the human immunodeficiency virus (HIV) and acquired immunodeficiency syndrome (AIDS) among people have declined, and the major fear is now of unintended pregnancy rather than a sexually transmitted infection (*BMJ 2001; 322:1135–6*).

How is chlamydia detected?

Chlamydia has traditionally been diagnosed by endocervical swabs, which have a poor sensitivity. The detection of chlamydial infection in women is particularly difficult because between 5 and 30% of infected women are only infected in the urethra, which is not detected by endocervical swab culture. Taking endocervical or urethral swabs is an uncomfortable, time-consuming and relatively expensive procedure that obviously requires a pelvic examination.

New tests are emerging that are more sensitive and less invasive than previous ones. The ligase chain reaction (LCR) test can be done on a sample of urine or a vaginal swab and is more sensitive than the current ELISA tests (90% vs 65% sensitivity). Urine test kits are currently only available in some areas – cost is obviously the main consideration determining the general availability of these kits. However, with complications of chlamydia costing £50m a year, they could prove cost-effective.

It has been demonstrated that young women find urine testing more acceptable than swabs (*BMJ 2003;326:1252–5*), and that they find being tested in a contraceptive clinic less stigmatising than attending a sexual health clinic (*Sex Transm Inf 2003;79:16*).

Why not screen for chlamydia in UK?

Currently there are successful screening programmes in the USA and Sweden, which have resulted in a lower incidence of PID. Screening is currently under consideration for < 25-year-olds, patients with symptoms, women seeking termination of pregnancy and women > 25 years of age with a new partner.

However, there are many problems with introducing a successful screening programme in the UK. These are clearly documented in the report by the CMO's advisory group (see website). They include the psychological barriers of investigation, costs involved and methods of contact tracing. If contact tracing is not done effectively and efficiently then any screening programme would be wasted: treated patients would simply become reinfected and so negate any good done! Screening for chlamydia is a very sensitive area, as many women may feel 'targeted' by the introduction of this programme. A study in the *BMJ* (*BMJ 2001;322:195*) found that women were worried about the perceived stigma of this disease, were reluctant to tell their partners and were concerned about their fertility.

Before a national screening programme can be introduced, effective training and education for both staff and patients needs to be implemented, which will have huge resource implications. Many women have never heard of chlamydia, let alone its consequences, so at present it would be very difficult to expect people to be screened for a disease they have never heard of.

Ideally, for chlamydia screening to be successful, there should be a multidisciplinary, structured approach with comprehensive testing of an agreed 'at risk' population, with both effective and timely treatment of infected patients and effective tracing and treatment of sexual contacts. A primary care study (*Br J Gen Pract 2001;51:565*) found that chlamydia screening using urine testing in sexually active women under 25 was feasible and effective. Although the take-up rate was only 40%, of these, 10% were positive.

Is screening going to be implemented soon?

The Department of Health announced in the summer of 2001 that £47.5m is to be invested over the next five years as part of their First National Strategy for Sexual Health and HIV. A 'target' screening programme was phased in during 2002.

The key objectives of this strategy are to ensure that all individuals have access to the knowledge and skills necessary to achieve positive sexual health, and that services should be readily available to all who require them (*BMJ 2001;323:243–4*). The specific aims are to reduce the undiagnosed prevalence and transmission of sexually transmitted infections and HIV, to reduce unintended pregnancies and to improve social care and health for people with HIV. The proposals will increase the role of primary care and strengthen links between specialist services and other local agencies. It still looks very overambitious when considering the resources allocated to it!

Screening for chlamydia will be offered, in selected health authorities, to women attending:
- ✓ Family planning clinics
- ✓ Antenatal clinics
- ✓ For terminations of their pregnancy
- ✓ For their first smear test

Screening will also be offered to some men, such as partners of infected women. The aim will be to extend screening to GP surgeries, but careful planning is obviously needed.

Early in 2004, the government made the decision to extend its chlamydia screening pilot. This will result in 25% of PCTs in England now providing screening to at-risk groups. However, the Department of Health have not given a reason for the delay in introducing a proper screening programme, despite the huge success of the pilots. A national screening programme was recommended by the Chief Medical Officer in 1999 and highlighted as a 'matter of urgency' in June 2002 by the Commons Health Select Committee

How will the National Strategy for Sexual Health and HIV affect GPs?

This National Strategy will greatly increase the role GPs have in providing sexual healthcare. Unless they 'opt out' (as can be done under the terms of the new GMS contract), every GP will need to provide:

✓ Sexual history and risk assessment

✓ Sexually transmitted infection (STI) testing for women

✓ Pregnancy testing and referral

✓ Contraceptive information and services

✓ Assessment and referral of men with STI symptoms

✓ Cervical cytology screening and referral for hepatitis B immunisation

These services are already provided by many practices; the main change will be the introduction of screening for chlamydia. It is unclear when this is likely to be widely introduced into general practice.

How has the RCGP responded to the Strategy for Sexual Health and HIV?

The College has responded very favourably, as this is the first time there has been such a nationwide approach with the Department of Health acknowledging that sexual health and HIV are major public health problems. The College has also stated that the Government needs to ensure that adequate resources are made available for the proposals to become a reality.

USEFUL WEBSITE

www.doh.gov.uk/chlamyd.htm – report of the Chief Medical Officer's expert advisory group on chlamydia

SUMMARY POINTS FOR CHLAMYDIA

✓ Chlamydia is most prevalent sexually transmitted disease (STD) in the UK
✓ Highest rates in females aged 16–24 years
✓ Most infections are asymptomatic
✓ Screening programme needs to be properly implemented
✓ Continued lack of public awareness of chlamydia

Hormone-Replacement Therapy

Hormone-replacement therapy (HRT) is always a topical subject and, in the light of recent evidence regarding breast cancer, many doctors are now reluctant to prescribe HRT. It has always been presumed that taking HRT improves women's wellbeing and quality of life, especially during the menopause. However, this has been shown in one study not to be the case – it found that HRT had no effect on measures of depression, insomnia, sexual function or cognition (*New Engl J Med 2003; 348:1839*). HRT does certainly help with vasomotor symptoms however; and it is possible that other symptoms, eg insomnia, improve as a direct result in some women.

Does HRT protect patients from coronary heart disease?

This is still the most controversial area. Observational studies have reported that the risk of ischaemic heart disease may be reduced by up to 30–50% in women taking HRT. However, the differences may be related to selection bias and therefore interpretation of these studies is extremely difficult. Further prospective studies are planned.

The HERS (Heart and Estrogen/Progestin Replacement Study) was the first, US, randomised prospective study of postmenopausal women with established ischaemic heart disease (n = 2763). The data showed that taking combined oestrogen and progestogen had no effect on MI or coronary death after treatment for 4.1 years. This trial created a lot of debate because it reported that the overall null effect comprised what appeared to be an early adverse effect followed by a trend towards a benefit, although neither effect was actually statistically significant (*JAMA 1998;280:605–13*). The HERS-2 trial (*JAMA 2002;288:58–66*) extended the data over 6.8 years and showed no difference in the rates of CHD.

One study looked at the angiographic progression of existing coronary artery disease and found no effect of either oestrogen alone or combined oestrogen and progestogen over a three-year period (*New Engl J Med 2003;349:535–45*). However, a previous study showed that giving oestrogen alone slows thickening of the walls of the carotid artery (*Ann Intern Med 2001;135:939*).

The Women's Health Initiative (WHI) study (see below) demonstrated increased relative risks for coronary heart disease (the primary outcome) and stroke for women randomised to treatment with 0.625 µg conjugated oestrogen and 2.5 mg MPA, although the absolute risks were very small (*JAMA 2002;288:321–33*). For each 10,000 women taking HRT over a year (compared with placebo), there were an extra seven heart attacks, eight strokes and eight pulmonary embolisms. However, there were also six fewer cases of bowel cancers and five fewer hip fractures. More than 10,000 post-hysterectomy women on oestrogen alone are still being followed up; results will be reported in 2005. The findings from the WHI study only apply to this particular HRT regimen. Particularly for CHD, the dose (and possibly type) of oestrogen and the type of progesterone may well be crucial.

An interesting *BMJ* article regarding this study highlights that, given the biological effects of oestrogen on the cardiovascular system, the lack of benefit on CHD is surprising (*BMJ 2002; 325:113*).

Various other studies have shown that patients taking HRT have lower levels of LDL-cholesterol and higher levels of HDL-cholesterol compared with patients taking a placebo. Further large randomised controlled trials, including the WISDOM (Women's International Study of long Duration Oestrogen after Menopause) trial in the UK, are underway in order to clarify the association of HRT and coronary heart disease. However, these trials will not provide definitive results until about 2005.

In the meantime, the British Menopause Society suggests that the recommendations of the American Heart Association, published in April 2001, should be read and considered for patients (*Circulation 2001;104:499–503*) (see Box on p. 201).

Is HRT related to breast cancer?

The recent million-women study (*Lancet 2003;362:419–27*) showed that all types of HRT (including tibolone) are associated with a higher risk of developing breast cancer. The study was an observational one, looking at all women who were in the NHS breast-screening programme from 1996 to 2001. These women (1,084,110 in total) were asked to complete questionnaires asking about the type of HRT they had been given and how long they had taken it for; this was then compared to their general practice records to check concordance. The women were followed up for mortality and risk of cancer.

Formulation	Extra no of cases of breast cancer/1000 women over 5 years	Extra no of cases of breast cancer/1000 women over 10 years
Oestrogen alone	+1.5	+5
Oestrogen and Progesterone	+6	+19

The relative risk of breast cancer with tibolone usage was 1.45, compared to 1.3 for oestrogen alone and 2.0 for combined preparations. The relative risk declines quickly after use is stopped and returns to a never-use level within five years. The researchers estimated that the use of HRT in women aged 50–64 years, has resulted in 20,000 extra cases of breast cancer over the past decade, of which 15,000 would be associated with combined preparations. The increased risk of breast cancer became apparent within 1–2 years of starting treatment.

The Women's Health Initiative trial recruited over 16,000 women in a randomised controlled trial looking at continuous-combined HRT vs placebo (JAMA 2002;288:321–33). During monitoring, the adverse events for CHD, stroke and PE rose (within the limits), but the threshold for invasive breast cancer and also the global index of overall risk vs benefit exceeded the previously set limits. This meant that the combined HRT arm of the study was stopped early (after five years).

In this study, the combination of conjugated equine oestrogen with medroxyprogesterone acetate was used. The data cannot necessarily be extrapolated to other forms and doses of HRT. The absolute numbers of adverse events were very low (eg an extra eight cases of breast cancer per 10,000 women per year). In addition, contrary to the million-women study, up to four years' use of HRT did not seem to increase the risk of invasive breast cancer. The study did also demonstrate that HRT prevents bone fracture and that protection increases with duration of treatment (see Osteoporosis section).

Studies have shown that women using HRT after the menopause are actually more likely to have slow-growing and highly curable types of breast cancers. An American study showed that women taking HRT had no difference in risk of developing ductal carcinoma in situ, invasive ductal or lobular cancer, which together constitute 85–90% of all cases of breast cancer (JAMA 1999;281:2091–9).

Any increased risk of breast cancer only applies to women over the age of 50 years. Therefore women taking replacement HRT for premature ovarian failure (eg postoophorectomy) are at no higher risk of breast cancer until they reach the age of 50 years.

Does HRT increase the risk of ovarian cancer?

The latest US findings showed that oestrogen-only HRT increases the risk of ovarian cancer, especially if taken for more than 10 years (JAMA 2002;288:334–41). However, the increased risk is small and many women have oophorectomies at the time of their hysterectomy, so this risk would only be applicable to a small number of women in the UK. This increased risk has not been demonstrated with taking combined HRT.

Fracture prevention

See Osteoporosis section.

Do women taking HRT have a higher risk of DVT?

The excess risk of DVT in HRT users compared with non-users was estimated to be 4.1 per 1000 women in the HERS trial (*JAMA 1998;280:605–13*). The absolute risks of DVT caused by HRT are higher in older women and those with other risk factors for venous thromboembolism.

Finally, the most commonly asked question by patients

Does HRT cause women to put on weight?
Many women are worried about putting on weight when taking HRT. From many trials on HRT, however, it has been shown that all women put on weight after the menopause, but generally those taking HRT actually put on less weight than those in the placebo groups!

Has there been a change in the advice about taking HRT after the million-women study?
The CSM has advised that:

✓ For short-term use, for the relief of menopausal symptoms, the benefit outweighs the risk for many women.

✓ For longer term use, women should be aware of the increased risk of breast cancer and other adverse effects.

✓ Each decision to start HRT should be made on an individual basis and treatment should be regularly reappraised (at least once a year).

✓ For combined HRT, the benefit of the lower risk of endometrial disorders, including cancer, should be weighed against the new information about the risk of breast cancer, ie one could consider prescribing unopposed oestrogen to a woman who still had her womb. However, this is likely to lead to lots of unscheduled bleeding, necessitating unpleasant and expensive investigation.

✓ The results of the million-women study do not necessitate any urgent changes to a woman's treatment.

✓ All women over 50 should be 'breast aware' and attend for mammography.

AMERICAN HEART ASSOCIATION RECOMMENDATIONS ON HRT AND CARDIOVASCULAR DISEASE

Secondary prevention (ie in women with established CVD)

✓ HRT should not be initiated for the secondary prevention of CVD

✓ The decision to continue or stop HRT in women with CVD who have been undergoing long-term HRT should be based on established non-coronary benefits, risks and patient preference

✓ If a woman develops an acute CVD event or is immobilised while undergoing HRT, it is prudent to consider discontinuing HRT. Reinstitution of HRT should be based on established non-coronary benefits and risks, as well as patient preference

Primary prevention (ie in women without CVD)

✓ There is insufficient data to suggest that HRT should be initiated for the sole purpose of preventing CVD

SUMMARY POINTS FOR HRT

✓ Association between HRT and CHD still controversial

✓ Risk of breast cancer in HRT users higher than previously thought

✓ WHI and million-women study has provoked much anxiety in patients

✓ Osteoporosis protection only when actually taking HRT

✓ Little evidence that HRT causes weight gain

CHAPTER 6:

PAEDIATRICS

Chapter 6: Paediatrics

'Every child matters'

There has recently been much concern about child protection issues, following high-profile cases such as the tragic death of Victoria Climbie, a little girl who died of neglect and abuse, despite being known to health and social services. This and other similar cases have prompted the Government to draw up a Green Paper entitled 'Every child matters', published in September 2003, which sets out plans to reform services for young people. Its aim is to strengthen child protection services for the most vulnerable children and, rather ambitiously, to ensure that all young people have 'the best opportunities in life'!

Action is to be taken on four main areas

1. Early intervention in child protection is emphasised
A sophisticated tracking system to keep tabs on England's 11,000,000 children has been proposed, whereby every child is given a unique ID number (eg their NHS number) attached to an electronic file of personal information about their lives, including contact numbers of key professionals involved in their care. Children known to more than one agency will have a key-worker. Teachers, social workers and other professionals will work together in multidisciplinary teams based in schools and children's centres.

2. Accountability and integration
Local authority education and social services are to be amalgamated. Every council will have to set up a children's trust by 2006, bringing together health, education and social services. The trusts will include community and acute health services, such as community paediatrics, teenage pregnancy coordinators, child and adolescent mental health services and speech and language therapy. PCT's will be expected to work closely with these children's trusts, and to delegate responsibility for commissioning relevant services. Senior managers will be involved with child protection issues. A director of children's services will head the trusts and be accountable for education and social services within a local authority.

3. Supporting parents and carers

GPs and schools will take on responsibility for helping to provide parents and families with more support and advice, including parenting classes. There will be a 24 h helpline for parents.

4. Workforce reform

There will be more input from nurses, midwives and health visitors in child protection. There will be standardised training for all staff working with children.

An independent child commissioner will be appointed to protect the welfare of all young people, whose job will be to ensure that children's needs are the top priority of all public services, monitor government policy and investigate serious child protection failures. There is likely to be an NSF for children within the next couple of years.

Childhood Vaccinations

MMR vaccination

While the measles, mumps and rubella (MMR) debate persists, it appears that vaccination rates are falling. The uptake of the MMR vaccine in babies has reduced as a result of reports suggesting possible links with autism and inflammatory bowel disease. In some areas, the vaccination rates are now even below those needed to ensure herd immunity. There is concern that the incidence of measles and mumps is increasing as a result of this reduced uptake of the vaccination. As many as one in four 4-year-olds in Surrey are currently unprotected. Outbreaks of measles have occurred in London, where MMR uptake rates are among the worst in the country.

Dr Wakefield has been at the centre of the publicity surrounding the alleged link between the MMR vaccine and long-term health problems, especially inflammatory bowel disease and autism. The problem with Dr Wakefield's studies is that they were all retrospective and so subject to recall bias by the parents and carers. The original studies also involved very small numbers of children. One of the other authors has recently written to the *Lancet* to say that 'there is now unequivocal evidence that MMR is not a risk factor for autism'.

Four independent bodies have reviewed the evidence: CSM, Joint Committee on Vaccination and Immunisation, MRC expert group and CSM Working Party on MMR Vaccine. They all agreed that the information does not support the suggested causal associations or give any cause for concern about the safety of the MMR vaccine. In addition, a very large Finnish study followed an impressive 1.8 million individuals for 14 years from the start of the MMR vaccination programme, and it concluded that serious events are rare and are greatly outweighed by the risks of the disease. No cases of inflammatory bowel disease or autism were detected in this study.

The results of a new large study shows no relation between the combined MMR vaccination and the development of autism (*Paediatrics 2004;113:259–66*).

One study in London showed that many mothers are influenced by the adverse media publicity and a large percentage thought that the second dose of the MMR vaccine was unnecessary for their children. The majority of the 170 mothers said they valued their own GP's opinion the most when deciding whether to have their child vaccinated or not (*Br J Gen Pract 2000;50:969–71*). This is quite worrying as another study, which was based on 500 healthcare professionals, showed that almost half of GPs, health visitors and practice nurses felt very uneasy about giving the second dose of the MMR vaccine (*BMJ 2001;322:82–5*). In addition, one-third of the practice nurses thought that the link of the vaccine with Crohn's disease was either very likely or possible. This wide variation in knowledge regarding the vaccine may be influencing the advice given to parents.

Is there any place for single-antigen vaccines?

Some parents and professionals still feel reticent about the MMR vaccine and would prefer the use of single vaccines. When single measles vaccine was used in the UK before 1988, there were regular epidemics of measles with 10–20 deaths each year. There is no research evidence or experience of a regimen giving measles, mumps and rubella vaccine separately to preschool children. A link between the single vaccine and autism and bowel disease has never been investigated. It is not known what the optimum time interval between doses should be, or even if it provides adequate protection against the diseases. Children would need to have many more injections.

All single measles and mumps vaccines available in the UK are unlicensed and therefore could be unreliable. Finally, no country in the world recommends the use of single measles, mumps and rubella vaccines as an alternative to the combined MMR vaccine.

 USEFUL WEBSITES

www.doh.gov.uk/mmr/index.html – Department of Health site on MMR vaccination
www.immunisation.org.uk – NHS Health Promotion England immunisation website

SUMMARY POINTS ON MMR VACCINE

✓ Reduced uptake of vaccination
✓ MMR vaccine is very safe
✓ Wide variation in knowledge and attitudes amongst healthcare professionals
✓ Numerous incorrect media reports

Meningococcal C Vaccination

The incidence of group C meningococcal infection has increased to account for approximately 40% of meningococcal disease. This rise is particularly prominent in teenagers, in whom mortality rates have been as high as 20% in those infected. It has been estimated that between July 1998 and June 1999 more than 1500 cases of group-C disease occurred in the UK, leading to 150 deaths.

The vaccine has an excellent safety profile in all ages and has been given to babies, young children, schoolchildren and students. The meningococcal group-C conjugate vaccines were introduced into the UK primary immunisation schedule in November 1999. The impact of this immunisation campaign has been significant, with substantial reductions in meningococcal group-C disease in both children and young people.

The Chief Medical Officer announced in January 2002 that people aged 20–24 years should also be immunised against meningitis C. The vaccine has a good safety profile, and good primary antibody responses have been shown in all age groups following immunisation (*Arch Dis Child 2001;84:383–6*).

A meningitis B vaccine is currently undergoing trials, but is realistically several years away from obtaining a licence.

Haemophilus influenzae b vaccination
Recently, there has been a HiB catch-up programme for under-5's, due to a resurgence in the incidence of cases of HiB. This ran from May 2003 until September 2003.

CHAPTER 7:

CANCER

Chapter 7: Cancer

The NHS Cancer Plan

The NHS Cancer Plan was introduced in September 2000. It is the first comprehensive national cancer programme and aims to improve the way in which cancer care is organised in the UK. It aims to:

- ✓ Save more lives
- ✓ Ensure cancer patients receive correct professional support and care
- ✓ Ensure patients receive the best available treatments
- ✓ Tackle the inequalities in cancer healthcare

The plan includes new targets for how quickly treatment should begin after patients see a consultant, and how soon treatment should begin after referral by a GP.

The Government believes that the targets can be met because it is proposing the creation of almost 1000 new cancer consultant posts by 2006. The Government is also planning to increase investment in palliative care services and hospices by £50m and provide more treatment equipment and 250 new scanners.

Cancer specialists have expressed doubts about whether the NHS will be able to achieve the set targets (*BMJ 2000;321:850*). They have welcomed the increased funding for cancer services, but have said it is doubtful whether some of the targets could be met. For example, the target of a maximum two-month wait from urgent GP referral to treatment for colorectal cancer may be unrealistic because presently the investigations necessary for a definite diagnosis can often take a month or more.

Targets set out in plan

✓ Maximum 1-month wait from urgent GP referral to treatment guaranteed for children's and testicular cancers and acute leukaemia by 2001

✓ Maximum 1-month wait from diagnosis to treatment for breast cancer by 2001

✓ Maximum 1-month wait from diagnosis to treatment for all cancers by 2005

✓ Maximum 2-months' wait from urgent GP referral to treatment for breast cancer by 2002

✓ Maximum 2-months' wait from urgent GP referral to treatment for all cancers by 2005

How does the cancer plan affect GPs?

All primary care trusts are expected to review their cancer screening coverage and improve the uptake, especially by ethnic minorities and deprived patient groups. A national system of cancer networks is being set up which aims to plan cancer services to meet individual needs and coordinate cancer plan initiatives at a local level. A lead clinician for cancer should have been appointed for each primary care trust (PCT); this is a GP who has dedicated time to work for the cancer network and help to improve clinical standards. They will also help to improve communication across primary, secondary and tertiary services.

Cancer registers have also been established for each PCT, and GPs have to contribute to these. The UK Association of Cancer Registers have found that the most reliable and consistent data on cancers are obtained at the time of diagnosis from histopathology departments. Patients must be given clear details on how the information from their disease may be used, and they must have access to that information in order to be assured of its validity. If patients refuse to let their details go to the cancer registries then the epidemiological picture of the disease is obviously going to be distorted.

The GMC recommends that informed consent be obtained from patients before they are placed on the cancer register. However, an amendment to the Health and Social Care Bill was passed by Parliament in May 2001 (*BMJ 2001;322:1199*), which should clear the way for health registries in the UK to continue collecting data on public health without the patient's consent. A new body is being set up under the Health and

Social Care Bill, called the 'Patient Information Advisory Group'. Individual registries who want to be exempt from the GMC's guidance on informed consent will be able to appeal to this group, who will decide whether to recommend to the Secretary of State that exemption be given.

What role should GPs play in cancer diagnosis and treatment?

General practitioners are gradually becoming more involved in managing patients with cancer. They are concerned with the comprehensive, coordinated and continuous care of individuals, families and, increasingly, populations. General practitioners have an important role in cancer and the British Government's desire to improve cancer outcomes relies heavily on GPs playing their part.

Diagnosing cancer in primary care is often difficult. Many cancers present with common symptoms such as persistent cough or non-specific abdominal pain, yet few patients with such symptoms turn out to have cancer. Primary care clinicians need to be able to discriminate which patients within a relatively unselected population have a higher likelihood of malignant disease. The Government has produced guidelines regarding urgent referrals of patients with suspected malignancies, and most hospital departments have created referral forms for GPs to complete as a consequence of these guidelines.

What are the problems with the GP referral guidelines?

The guidelines have been criticised as they are based on poor-quality evidence; the evidence used was obtained from patients seen in secondary and tertiary care and then applied to primary care. As many of the guidelines are quite general, the system could become overloaded very quickly, which would then be detrimental to cancer patients.

An editorial in the *BMJ* has highlighted that the two-week rule for cancer referrals does not appear to be working well (*BMJ 2001; 322:1555–6*). The two-week standard is often being met at the expense of a substantial increase in waiting times for routine referrals. A retrospective study of patients with colorectal cancer found that about 30% of cases would not actually have met the referral criteria for an urgent referral (*Gut 2001;48(Suppl):A53*).

USEFUL WEBSITE

www.doh.gov.uk/cancer

SUMMARY POINTS FOR CANCER

✓ Overambitious targets in NHS Cancer Plan
✓ Lead clinician to be appointed for each PCT
✓ GPs have a crucial role in both cancer and cancer screening
✓ Two-week cancer referrals are not working well

Prostate Cancer

Prostate cancer is the second most common cause of male cancer deaths in the UK – and the incidence is rising as a result of earlier detection of the disease and an ageing population. Men (with no family history of the disease) have a 1 in 12 lifetime risk (*Br J Urol 2000; 85:588–598*). Death rates from prostate cancer have doubled over the last 20 years and 9000 men in the UK died from it in 2001.

Prostate cancer is increasingly detected at an earlier stage by serum measurement of PSA. However, it is still highly debatable as to whether screening for prostate cancer is worthwhile; we have no evidence that screening will lead to a reduction in cancer-specific mortality. It has been estimated that anything from 29% (*J Natl Cancer Inst 2002;94:981–90*) to 80% (*Can Med Assoc J 1998; 159:1368–72*) of PSA screen-detected cancers would, even without treatment, never become symptomatic, represents a huge over-diagnosis of the disease (the incidence–mortality ratio for the year 2000 in the USA was 6.3).

What are the benefits of measuring PSA levels in patients?

PSA is probably the best available blood test for detecting any cancer, although it still has somewhat limited specificity. Its value has been improved by techniques such as monitoring change in concentration with time (velocity), assessing concentration in relation to prostate volume (density), using age-adjusted upper limits and, most recently, measuring the free to total prostate-specific antigen ratio (the lower the free PSA, the greater the chance of prostate cancer being detected by biopsy).

What are the problems with measuring PSA levels in patients?

Poor specificity
About 10% of men aged 50–69 years will have raised PSA levels, but only about 25% of those with a PSA between 4 and 10 will be confirmed to have prostate cancer (this increases to 60% if the PSA > 10). Certain events can result in a transient change in the serum PSA level. For example, it can fall after a long period of recumbency and can increase with BPH, prostatic biopsy, transrectal ultrasound and vigorous prostatic

massage. However, a digital rectal examination alone does not appear to have any significant effect on the serum PSA level.

Poor sensitivity

Indeed, a recent American study concluded that if the current cut-off for PSA of 4.0 is used, a staggering 82% of men under 60 who go on to be diagnosed with prostate cancer will be missed (*New Engl J Med 2003;349:335–42*). It has been suggested that the following age-specific, cut-off values of PSA are used (although for patients on finasteride, any measured PSA should be doubled to reflect a true PSA, as this drug artificially lowers PSA):

Age	Normal PSA result
40–49	0–2.5
50–59	0–3.5
60–69	0–4.5
70–79	0–6.5

Controversy exists about the treatment of apparently localised prostate cancer (*BMJ 2000;320:69–70*). Some prostate cancers develop slowly and may never cause problems in the patient's lifetime; 50% of men aged 80 have prostatic cancer, but only 4% die of it. However, other cancers evolve rapidly and are fatal within a few years. Approximately 60% of men have metastases at the time of diagnosis. When the treatment of prostate cancer is so unclear, it is difficult to justify screening for it in order to pick it up earlier.

What is the optimal treatment for prostate cancer?

This is an area of great debate and there is still no clear agreement (*BMJ 1999;318:299–300*). A Government-funded trial, the ProtecT study (Prostate testing for Cancer and Treatment) has commenced, which will investigate the best treatment option for men who are diagnosed with prostate cancer – watchful waiting, radical surgery or radiotherapy. Men aged 50–69 years with at least ten years life expectancy are being offered PSA testing after full counselling of the implications of a raised PSA. Those with PSA > 3.0 ng/ml (but < 20 ng/ml) undergo biopsies. If they are shown to have localised prostate cancer, they are offered a choice of radical prostatectomy, radical radiotherapy or active surveillance. Recruitment closes in mid 2006 and the main endpoints will be survival at 5, 10 and 15 years, disease progression and treatment complications. Its results are eagerly awaited!

In a recent Swedish RCT (*New Engl J Med 2002;347:781*), men with early prostate cancer were randomised to conservative treatment ('watch and wait') or radical prostatectomy. Over six years of follow-up, 4.6% of men who had the surgery died from prostate cancer compared to 9% of the men who had conservative treatment. Interestingly however, there was no overall difference in survival, perhaps due to an effect of having had the surgery in the first place. Other studies have also failed to find a difference in survival between radical versus conservative treatment.

A recent American study examined the outcome over 14 years of men diagnosed with localised prostate cancer, and found that for men with palpable but non-metastatic prostate cancer the mean time to death was 11.7 years (*BJU Int 2000;85:1063–6*). The authors of this study actually propose an upper age limit of 62 years for a screening programme when the intent is to cure. The difficulty obviously remains that some men in their seventies and eighties will present with metastatic bone disease and will leave us wondering whether this could have been prevented by screening.

Who should get radical treatment?

Only patients with a life expectancy of over 10 years should be considered for radical treatment, since prostatic cancer does not usually kill men in less than 10 years from diagnosis. Radical treatment is generally not justified for patients with a PSA concentration over 20 µg/l, as the tumour will often extend beyond the prostatic capsule and there may be micrometastases or lymph node deposits.

Patients with well-differentiated tumours may do well without radical surgery, whereas those with poorly differentiated tumours usually do badly. Most men have moderately well-differentiated tumours and are likely to benefit from radical treatment if they have a life expectancy of more than 10 years.

Each of the main treatments – radical prostatectomy, radical radiotherapy, brachytherapy, cryosurgery (freeze/thawing to destroy tissue, this is gaining in popularity) and monitoring – has risks. Radical treatment offers the potential for cure, but can have serious side-effects, including pain, hospitalisation, varying levels of incontinence and impotence and, rarely, death. With monitoring, men will have to live with the knowledge that they have untreated cancer and with the risk of progression, which in a few cases may be fatal.

Can we prevent prostate cancer?

Finasteride (an α-reductase inhibitor) may decrease the incidence of prostate cancer. However, men who do develop prostate cancer while on finasteride, may have more aggressive, poorly differentiated tumours than those who are not taking it (*New Engl J Med 2003;349:213–22*).

Should prostate cancer be screened for?

Media publicity and a heightened public awareness of prostate cancer have increased the profile of PSA screening. The question of whether screening should be implemented is still extremely debatable. First of all, only a minority of cancers spread beyond the gland to cause disease and shorten life expectancy. In addition, curative treatments have major side- effects (eg impotence and incontinence). At present, PSA testing for prostate cancer does not fulfil all of Wilson's criteria for screening (refer to the section on Screening on p. 150).

The National Screening Committee has advised against screening, as:
- ✓ Many subclinical cases would be detected
- ✓ Excess anxiety would result
- ✓ In many cases there would be no change in the overall outcome
- ✓ The PSA level can not predict whether the cancer is indolent or aggressive
- ✓ PSA has a poor specificity
- ✓ There is still a lack of consensus regarding treatment for early disease
- ✓ Physical harm caused by prostate biopsies
- ✓ Some cancers detected would never present clinically

Despite the widespread use of PSA in the USA, and apparent incidence rates of three times that in the UK, mortality in the USA has for many years been almost the same as the UK and other European countries.

There are also strong arguments towards introducing a screening programme including:
- ✓ Men's autonomy
- ✓ PSA is a cheap and readily available test
- ✓ Screening may possibly be beneficial (lack of evidence of effectiveness does not prove ineffectiveness)
- ✓ May lead to detection of early, potentially curable cancers

A recent American study has demonstrated that screening men for prostate cancer has no impact on death rates from the disease (*J Clin Epidemiol 2002;55:603*). This study examined the outcomes of more than 1000 men with prostate cancer. Half of the patients had been screened using PSA testing alone or in combination with a rectal examination. The other half had not been screened at all. The patients were followed up for four to nine years, and the conclusion was that PSA screening did not improve survival in men under 70 years.

The argument is neatly summarised by the following quote from a recent issue of the *Lancet* (*Lancet 2003;361:1122–8*): 'The balance of proof must be high to justify exposing men older than 50 years to a process where, of 1 million men, about 110,000 with raised PSAs will face anxiety over possible cancer, about 90,000 will undergo biopsy, and 20,000 will be diagnosed with cancer. If 10,000 of these men underwent surgery, about ten would die of the operation, 300 would develop severe urinary incontinence, and even in the best hands 4000 would become impotent.   The number of men whose prostate cancer would have impinged on their lives is unknown.'

What are the NHS Prostate Cancer Screening Policy recommendations?

These were implemented in July 2001 and recommend that when a patient requests a PSA test, he should be given full information on the advantages and disadvantages of testing. The National Electronic Library for Health has produced patient information leaflets – available online – these vary from a one-page summary to a detailed five-page leaflet, so can supposedly be 'tailored' to the patient's level of interest.

Under the policy, the NHS will not be inviting men for PSA testing and does not expect GPs to raise the subject of PSA testing with their asymptomatic patients. However, the Government policy states that 'any man considering a PSA test will be given detailed information to enable him to make an informed choice about whether to proceed with a test or not'. This therefore implies that asymptomatic men may have the test if they want, so there is now ambiguity about whether screening is supported and confusion about what this policy means in everyday practice.

An assumption has been made that most men will not want to be tested once they are informed of the uncertainties. However, in the feasibility study for the ProtecT trial, around 90% of men given detailed information about the implications of PSA testing and the lack of evidence about treatment consented to a test!

The proof of the ability of PSA testing to reduce the disease-specific mortality of prostate cancer will be provided by randomised controlled trials, which are currently underway in both the USA and Europe. Unfortunately, it will be many years before these results are available and, in the interim, doctors must act on the information that is currently available in the best interests of their patients. Patients must be informed of the pros and cons of PSA testing and also the implications of a positive result before having a PSA test performed.

USEFUL WEBSITE

www.cancerscreeningnhs.uk/prostate/index.html – NHS prostate cancer screening policy

SUMMARY POINTS FOR PROSTATE CANCER

✓ Incidence of prostate cancer is rising
✓ Screening may occur in future
✓ Controversial treatment options exist

Bowel Cancer Screening

The Government is considering the introduction of a national programme of bowel cancer screening. The problem lies with which method to chose for screening: FOB (faecal occult blood) testing or flexible sigmoidoscopy.

Faecal occult blood testing

The media has been printing stories of how many thousands of lives could be saved if FOB testing were to be universally introduced. These stories are based on the findings of the UK Colorectal Cancer Screening Pilot Evaluation Team, set up by the Government's National Screening Committee in 1999. Their report was published in July 2003. Everyone aged between 50 and 69 years from Tayside, Grampian, Fife and the West Midlands was offered testing. Some 60% took up the offer (less in the South-Asian population, in Scotland and in socially deprived groups); these people were then sent home-testing kits, 1 in 50 tested positive and were offered colonoscopy. The take-up rate was considered high enough to warrant a national screening programme.

What is the evidence for FOB testing?
The sensitivity of FOB testing is about 60–70%. There is some evidence that it reduces mortality from colorectal cancer; with a 60% uptake rate, it is projected that approximately 1200 lives would be saved every year.

A systematic review (*BMJ 1998;317:559*) showed a fall in mortality of 23% in those who accepted screening. Other studies have shown that screening by FOB every two years reduces mortality by 20%.

Advantages of FOB testing
✓ Cheap and easy to perform at home
✓ Acceptable
✓ Non-invasive.

Disadvantages of FOB testing
✓ Has to be repeated every two years
✓ Poor sensitivity (60-70%)
✓ Poor specificity (5% false-positives)
✓ Results in large numbers of colonoscopies; the NHS currently have

does not the resources to cope with this. There can be significant adverse events associated with colonoscopy

Flexible sigmoidoscopy

Dr Wendy Atkins, director of Cancer Research UK, is in favour of flexible sigmoidoscopy as a screening test. She has said that it would be at least as effective as FOB testing and that it would only need to be done once. It has a 70% uptake rate in northern California, where it is offered routinely. In the UK Flexible Sigmoidoscopy Screening Trial (*Lancet 2002;359:1291*), patients have been offered a one-off flexible sigmoidoscopy around 60 years of age. The trial is still ongoing (it is due to finish in 2005), but data so far suggest that for every 1000 people screened, three cancers are detected and 120 adenomas. These figures suggest that screening with flexible sigmoidoscopy will reduce the incidence of colorectal cancer. Right-sided tumours, however, cannot be detected with flexible sigmoidoscopy.

Any screening programme will probably take at least five years to set up and will inevitably have huge cost-implications.

Mammography

Mammography is currently offered to all women between the ages of 50 and 64 in the UK, although women up to and including the age of 70 will receive routine invitations for screening by the end of 2004. There is much controversy about whether routine mammography has helped to increase survival from breast cancer, and if so, by how much. Some experts claim that increased survival is due to better treatments and earlier diagnosis, although the majority view is that mammography has also played a part.

Arguments against mammography

Mammography is about 90% sensitive in women over 50 who are not on HRT, so 10% of cancers are missed; and probably more in women on HRT. It is not particularly specific: 10% of women will have an abnormal mammogram, but of these, only about 5% will truly have breast cancer. DCIS (ductal carcinoma in situ) accounts for about 20% of mammographically detected cancers. This localised cancer has an uncertain natural history, and early detection may lead to unnecessary mastectomies; particularly in older women with coexisting morbidity whose life expectancy is limited anyway (this is similar to the prostate cancer treatment argument). It is an uncomfortable and potentially embarrassing procedure.

A Cochrane review re-analysed all the existing trial data supporting mammography in 2001, and concluded that there was no evidence to prove a survival benefit of mass screening for breast cancer. The methodological quality of the major trials evaluating mammography was criticised in this review. This was preceded by a similar review in the *Lancet*, which came to the same conclusions (*Lancet 2000;355:129–34*).

Arguments for mammography

Experts from the WHO have concluded that mammography helps to cut death rates from breast cancer by about a third and have directly refuted the reviews quoted above. These experts re-examined the original studies and found that they were indeed reliable (*BMJ 2002;324:695*).

Of the 21% fall in breast cancer mortality since 1991, 6% is estimated as being due to screening, and 15% due to better treatment (*BMJ 2000;321:665*).

A large Swedish meta-analysis (*Lancet 2002;359:909*) showed a significant reduction in mortality in screened vs non-screened women. There may be fewer mastectomies and more breast-conserving surgery in screened women (*BMJ 2002;325:418*) who are diagnosed earlier.

What constitutes a significant family history?

✓ One first-degree relative (ie mother or sister) diagnosed with breast cancer < 40 years of age

✓ One 1st or 2nd degree relative with bilateral breast cancer < 60

✓ One 1st degree male relative with breast cancer diagnosed < 60

✓ One 1st or 2nd degree relative diagnosed with ovarian cancer at any age and breast cancer < 50

✓ One 1st or 2nd degree relative with ovarian cancer and another with breast cancer < 50, or two others with breast cancer < 60

✓ Two 1st or 2nd degree relatives < 60

✓ Three 1st or 2nd degree relatives < 70

✓ Four 1st or 2nd degree relatives at any age

The lifetime risk of breast cancer is 7.8% for women with no affected first-degree relatives, 13.3% for those with one and 21.1% for those with two (*Lancet 2001;358:1389–99*).

Screening

A screening procedure is one that is applied to a population to select people at risk of an unfavourable health outcome for further investigation, monitoring or advice and treatment. Informed choice with regard to screening is essential; as, although screening programmes may benefit populations, not all participants will benefit and some will even be harmed by participation (*BMJ 2002;325:78–80*).

What is informed choice?

Informed choice has two core characteristics – it should be based on relevant, good-quality information and the resulting choice should reflect the decision-maker's values. The GMC has produced guidance on the information that should be provided to people offered screening.

How do GPs contribute to cancer screening?

General practitioners occupy a critical position in ensuring the effectiveness of national cancer screening programmes, as well as providing effective and cost-effective advice on specific primary-prevention strategies. In the United Kingdom's breast and cervical cancer screening programmes, primary healthcare team members have both developed and been delegated important roles in providing information and advice to women at all stages of the screening process (*BMJ 2000;320:1090–1*).

Patients often do not understand the rationale for screening or the inevitability of some false-positive and false-negative results. General practitioners thus have an important and expanding role in ensuring their patients truly understand these issues and the need for continuing vigilance about new symptoms.

What are Wilson's criteria for screening?

These well-established criteria should ideally be met before implementing a screening programme. They are important to know and can be applied to other screening programmes as well as to different types of cancer. There are, however, very few conditions for which all the criteria can be met.

They state that:
- ✓ The condition should be common and important
- ✓ There must be a latent period or early symptomatic stage during which effective treatment is possible
- ✓ There must be acceptable and available treatment for the disease
- ✓ The untreated natural history of the disease must be known
- ✓ The screening tests must be acceptable, cost-effective, safe and reliable
- ✓ The screening test should be highly sensitive and specific
- ✓ The screening should be continuous (not just a 'one off' test)

What are the ethics of screening?

The four main principles of ethics should be applied here (they are very useful to know for the viva exam!):

1. Beneficence (do good)
The benefit of screening must outweigh any potential harm to an individual.

2. Non-maleficence (do no harm)
Personal costs include problems with false-positive results, which can lead to distress and possible unnecessary treatment. False-negatives can also occur as no test is 100% sensitive, which can then lead to false reassurance by both patients and doctors. This may even dissuade patients from returning for future screening tests.

Misinterpretation of results can lead to a false sense of security, for example patients with normal cholesterol or normal blood pressure may continue to smoke. There are also the costs to society, the actual costs of equipment, services, treatment, etc and also the time taken off work to attend for the screening test and the treatment.

Finally, psychological costs are involved. One article showed that false-positive results of screening tests can have undesirable effects (*J Public Health Med 2001;23:292–300*). Women who had been given the 'all clear' after having had abnormal mammography results three years previously remained significantly more anxious than those who had normal results. This was actually sufficient to deter 15% of them from attending for mammography the next time round.

3. Autonomy

Some people have different health beliefs and cultures and object to being screened. These factors need to be appreciated when considering individual autonomy.

4. Justice

Implementing screening tests may mean that funds are diverted away from other services, for example cancer treatments. The correct allocation of limited resources is very important, especially in the current climate.

 USEFUL WEBSITE

www.gmc-uk.org – GMC website

CHAPTER 8:

ANTIBIOTICS

Chapter 8:
Antibiotics

Antibiotic Resistance

Resistance to antibiotics and other antimicrobial agents. House of Lords Select Committee Seventh Report, 17 March 1998

USEFUL WEBSITE

www.parliament.uk

- ✓ Highlighted the problem of increasing resistance to antibiotics
- ✓ It stated that most antibiotic use is in two areas: in humans in the community; and in animals as growth promoters and for prophylaxis
- ✓ In the UK, most antimicrobials used in human medicine are prescribed by GPs
- ✓ Antibiotic misuse is common, and studies have suggested up to 70% of treatment courses are unnecessary or inappropriate
- ✓ Therapy is often unnecessarily prolonged, and prophylaxis is often inappropriate or given at the wrong time
- ✓ One major factor affecting the prescribing behaviour of GPs is the expectations of their patients
- ✓ Increasing resistance problems are probably related to the use of broad-spectrum agents, such as cephalosporins, and crowding of susceptible people in institutions like nursing homes
- ✓ Veterinary and agriculture practices were also analysed and are expected to change

The Standing Medical Advisory Committee (SMAC) Report

USEFUL WEBSITE

www.doh.gov.uk/smac1.htm – full report available

Recommendations for treatment:

✓ No prescribing of antibiotics for simple coughs and colds

✓ No prescribing of antibiotics for viral sore throats

✓ Limit prescribing for uncomplicated cystitis to three days in otherwise fit women

✓ Limit prescribing of antibiotic agents over the telephone to exceptional cases

Further recommendations

✓ Support for appropriate prescribing in primary care to be provided by developing and promulgating evidence-based national guidelines for the management of certain infections, under the aegis of NICE

✓ Guidelines would aim to minimise unnecessary use of antimicrobial agents and that, when needed, the most appropriate antimicrobial agent and regimen are used to ensure the best possible clinical outcome and to reduce the risk of resistance developing

✓ National guidelines are adapted for local use during the development of Health Improvement Plans

✓ The best of guidelines are of no value if they are not used; so to incorporate the guidelines into everyday practice as effortlessly as possible, they recommended that these should be integrated within computerised decision-support systems as soon as possible

✓ A national campaign should be launched to increase public and health professionals' understanding of the problem

The national campaign mentioned above was launched shortly afterwards, and you may recall featured leaflets with a character called 'Andy Biotic'. It was a public education exercise and also provided support to doctors to encourage more appropriate prescribing. In addition, it promoted advice-seeking from community pharmacists.

Following the campaign's introduction an update report was issued in March 2001 by SMAC. It stated that the 'antibiotic resistance campaign may be in part responsible for antibiotic prescribing by GPs falling by 19% in England between 1997 and 1999'. Inevitably, the results were taken to show that the campaign was a huge success. However, it has been commented that awareness of practitioners to the problem of resistance and increased media coverage may also be responsible for the improving trend.

SUMMARY POINTS FOR ANTIBIOTIC RESISTANCE

✓ 5% of antibiotic use in the UK is in humans, 50% in animals
✓ 80% of human use is in the community
✓ 50% of community use is for respiratory tract infections, 15% for urinary tract infections
✓ Considerable local and regional variation exists in the levels of community prescribing
✓ In hospitals, antimicrobial agents account for 10–30% of the drugs' budget

Papers

1. Antibacterial prescribing and antibacterial resistance in English general practice – cross-sectional study

(*P. Priest, et al, BMJ 2001;323:1037–41*)

✓ 405 practices in SW and NW England (38 groups)

✓ Design: Cross-sectional study of antibacterial prescribing and antibacterial resistance of routine isolates within individual practices and primary care groups

✓ Objective: To quantify the relationship between community-based antibacterial prescribing and antibacterial resistance in community-acquired disease

✓ Main outcome measures: Correlation between antibacterial prescribing and resistance for urinary coliforms and *Streptococcus pneumoniae*

✓ Looked at resistance to urinary coliforms and *S. pneumoniae*

✓ Prescribing 20% less ampicillin/amoxicillin would lead to 1% reduction in resistant coliforms (95% confidence interval, 0.02–1.85).

✓ Resistance of *S. pneumoniae* to both penicillin and erythromycin remains uncommon, and no clear relationship with prescribing was found

✓ Although antibacterial resistance in urinary coliform isolates is common, the correlation with prescribing rates was relatively low for individual practices and primary care groups

✓ Concluded that routine microbiological isolates should not be used for surveillance of antibacterial resistance in the community or for monitoring the outcome of any change in antibacterial prescribing by GPs, and that improved methods of assessing national antimicrobial resistance are required

✓ Controversially stated that trying to reduce the overall level of antibiotic prescribing in UK general practice may not be the most effective strategy for reducing resistance in the community

Commentary discussed the future of resistance

✓ Strategies in Europe and North America are based on the belief that the process can be reversed (or at least held in check) by using antibiotics more prudently

✓ Differing conclusions can be drawn from the study, eg the minimal variation in ampicillin and trimethoprim resistance between practices with differing rates of prescribing (and various criteria for submitting specimens to a laboratory) does not necessarily imply that a change in prescribing would not affect resistance

✓ The dynamics between prescribing and resistance are exceedingly complicated.

✓ Mathematical modelling gives some insights:
  • Generally, resistance rates are low after a new antimicrobial drug is introduced into a community
  • Resistance then appears and increases steadily until it reaches a steady-state level
  • The rate of increase in resistance depends on the drug and how much is used, the bacteria and the nature of the community, eg the opportunity for cross-infection
  • If ampicillin and trimethoprim are at steady-state levels in the UK, we would expect little interpractice variation
  • Such models also predict that the decline in resistance after the withdrawal of antibiotic selection pressure will be uncomfortably slow

Urinary Tract Infections

SUMMARY POINTS FOR CYSTITIS (BY SMAC)

✓ Each year about 1 woman in 20 will present to her GP with symptoms of cystitis

✓ About half of these women will have an infection (defined by the presence of a significant number of bacteria in the urine)

✓ Most of these infections in otherwise healthy women are caused by coliforms

✓ Uncomplicated cystitis can be treated empirically with trimethoprim

✓ If resistance is common locally, the medical microbiologist can advise on an appropriate alternative

✓ Several studies have shown that a 3-day course of treatment is as effective as a 5- or 7-day course

✓ Limiting the prescription of antibiotics for uncomplicated cystitis in otherwise healthy women to 3 days reduces selection pressure for resistance

Acute Sinusitis

SUMMARY POINTS FOR SINUSITIS (SMAC)

✓ There are conflicting results from trials. Several studies, including RCTs, have shown antibiotics to be effective in proven acute sinusitis

✓ Most of these studies have used 10-day courses of antibiotics

✓ One comparative study showed that three days of antibiotics were as effective as 10 days

✓ Recent overviews of the treatment of acute sinusitis-like symptoms in adults in the primary care setting suggest there is no benefit from antibiotic treatment

✓ A recent RCT (*Arch Intern Med 2003;163:1793–8*) showed that co-amoxiclav was no faster than placebo at relieving symptoms in 252 patients diagnosed with acute sinusitis in general practice; they all had symptoms of maxillary/frontal pain and purulent discharge for at least 48 hours. One patient in the placebo group did, however, die from a brain abscess

✓ Adults with 'sinusitis-like symptoms' in primary care do not need immediate antibiotics

✓ In proven cases of acute sinusitis, three days of antibiotics are as effective as 10 days' treatment

Acute Bronchitis

Reducing antibiotic use for acute bronchitis in primary care: blinded, randomised controlled trial of patient information leaflet
(*J. Macfarlane, et al, BMJ 2002;324:91–4*)

✓ This RCT from Nottingham looked at whether the use of written and verbal explanations as to the uncertainty of the value of antibiotics made any difference to the likelihood of patients taking them

✓ Acute bronchitis is a common condition that results in nearly two million consultations in England and Wales each year

✓ Defined as a 'new, acute lower respiratory tract illness in a previously well adult' (LRTI of 21 days or less, cough as the main symptom and at least one other lower respiratory tract symptom: sputum production, dyspnoea, wheeze, chest discomfort or pain)

✓ 75% of such GP consultations result in an antibiotic script

✓ 259 previously well people presenting with acute bronchitis were recruited from three practices in Nottingham

✓ 212 formed Group A, where the GP judged them not to need antibiotics that day, but were given a prescription to use if they got worse and standard verbal reassurance. Half of them (106) were randomised to be given an information leaflet detailing the advantages/disadvantages of antibiotics and history of an LRTI

✓ Group B comprised 47 patients who were judged to need antibiotics and were given a prescription and encouraged to use it

✓ The primary endpoint was whether the patient took the antibiotics (in the first two weeks) they had been prescribed, and the second was the re-consultation rate in the next month

✓ In Group A, fewer patients who received the information leaflet took antibiotics compared with those who only received verbal reassurance (49 vs 63, risk ratio 0.76, 95% confidence interval 0.59–0.97, $p = 0.04$)

✓ Numbers re-consulting were similar (11 vs 14)

✓ In Group B, 44/47 patients took the antibiotics

✓ In conclusion, most previously well adults with acute bronchitis were judged not to need antibiotics. Reassuring these patients and sharing the uncertainty about prescribing in an information leaflet supported by verbal advice is a safe strategy and reduces antibiotic use

✓ The use of the patient information leaflet reduced the use of antibiotics by nearly one-quarter

✓ This may underestimate the true efficacy of the leaflet as all patients were also reassured verbally by their GP

✓ Rates of re-consultation were no higher in the leaflet group and no patients required referral to hospital

✓ These practices were used to research this topic, which may make the doctors and patients unrepresentative

In his commentary, Professor Weel, from The Netherlands, argued that patients influence prescribing, and there is a strong perception among practitioners that, in general, patients value a prescription. He also stated that about half the patients still used the antibiotics their GP thought they could do without.

The message 'antibiotics are not required' was accompanied by the handing out of a prescription that implied a totally different message. This may trigger doubt and lack of confidence, particularly in patients who value medical as opposed to self-treatment.

Sore Throat

When should we use antibiotics?

Antibiotics have been used in the past to:
- ✓ Reduce the severity or shorten the duration of symptoms
- ✓ Reduce the risk of complications, suppurative (quinsy, otitis media, sinusitis) and non-suppurative (rheumatic fever, nephritis)
- ✓ Satisfy non-clinical purposes, eg perceived patient demand terminating consultation

But:
- ✓ At least 70% of sore throats are caused by viruses
- ✓ We now have evidence to help us select those patients who probably have a bacterial infection and may benefit from penicillin (Centor criteria; patients with high fever, purulent tonsillitis, cervical lymphadenopathy and no concurrent cough are more likely to have bacterial infection)

SUMMARY POINTS FOR SORE THROAT (BY SMAC)

✓ Most are viral and can be left to run their course without resort to antibiotics

✓ Indeed, recurrence and relapse may be more common in those who have had early treatment with antibiotics

✓ A recent study showed that patients with sore throats were more likely to leave the consultation satisfied if they received a prescription

✓ However, they were no more likely to be satisfied at the end of the illness

✓ Those who received antibiotics were more likely to return for treatment in future attacks and were more likely to believe in the efficacy of antibiotics

✓ A minority of sore throats are caused by a bacterium, *Streptococcus pyogenes*

✓ *S. pyogenes* can lead to local abscesses and, rarely, to kidney problems and rheumatic fever

✓ Therefore, many doctors prescribe antibiotics for a sore throat with the intention of preventing the consequences of *S. pyogenes* infection

✓ Sore throats should not be treated with antibiotics, unless there is good evidence they are caused by *S. pyogenes*

Papers

1. Penicillin for acute sore throat: randomised double blind trial of 7 days vs 3 days treatment or placebo in adults

(S. Zwart, et al, BMJ 2000;320:150–4)

✓ GP-based study from The Netherlands

✓ Randomised to three groups: phenoxymethylpenicillin (penicillin V; pen V) for seven days; pen V for three days followed by placebo for four days; or placebo for seven days

✓ Sore throats for less than seven days and with three of the four 'Centor' criteria:
  • Fever
  • No cough
  • Tonsillar exudate
  • Swollen, tender, anterior cervical nodes

Showed that penicillin V for seven days resulted in:
✓ Two days' shorter duration of symptoms

✓ Reduced the incidence of complications (quinsy)

✓ Supports the use of penicillin V in patients with three of the four Centor criteria

Arguments against using an antibiotic:
✓ Benefit shown is so modest that one can dispute its clinical importance

✓ Actual benefit is marginal/modest at best

✓ Harms may outweigh benefits. Bacterial resistance, can cause allergic reactions (rashes/anaphylaxis 2–4/10,000 and death 2/100,000)

✓ Diarrhoea, candidiasis, unplanned pregnancy if on combined oral contraceptive pill can ensue

✓ Costs to NHS

✓ Increased patient dependence, expectation and future demands

2. Open randomised trial of prescribing strategies in managing sore throat

(P. Little, et al, BMJ 1997;314:722–7)

✓ Designed to test three different prescribing strategies in terms of: duration of symptoms; satisfaction and compliance with treatment; and time off school or work

✓ Group 1: 10 days' prescription for antibiotics; Group 2: no prescription; Group 3: prescription if symptoms did not settle in three days

✓ No significant difference found in the proportion of patients better in three days, duration of illness, time to return to work or satisfaction

✓ More people in the first group thought antibiotics were effective and intended coming to the doctor in future attacks

✓ 69% of patients in the delayed prescription group did not use their prescriptions

✓ Concluded that antibiotics had a marginal clinical effect

✓ Prescription resulted in enhanced belief and intention to re-consult when compared to other groups

3. Antibiotics for symptoms and complications of sore throat

(C. D. Del Mar, et al, Cochrane Systematic Review 2000; (4) CD000023)

✓ Found that prescribing antibiotics reduced the symptoms of sore throat, fever and headache by 50% in the short term, but 90% of all patients were symptom-free by one week anyway

✓ Pooling of data (large number of patients) allowed rarer complication rates to be elicited

✓ Risk of rheumatic fever reduced by 30%, but authors were unable to assess whether treatment offered protection against glomerulonephritis as numbers were still too small

✓ Effect of antibiotics on suppurative complications: acute otitis media reduced by 25%, acute sinusitis by 30% and quinsy by 20%

✓ Concluded that antibiotics offer a modest clinical benefit

✓ In the Western world, it was not thought to be worth recommending the routine use of antibiotics to treat sore throats for the small reduction in the number of cases of rheumatic fever and glomerulonephritis

Acute Otitis Media

- ✓ Acute otitis media is a common condition with a high morbidity and low mortality
- ✓ In the UK, about 30% of children aged under three years are taken to their GP with acute otitis media each year
- ✓ 97% receive antimicrobial treatment
- ✓ 1 in 10 children will have an episode of acute otitis media by three months of age
- ✓ Most common bacterial causes for acute otitis media are *Streptococcus pneumoniae*, *Haemophilus influenzae* and *Moraxella catarrhalis*
- ✓ Risk factors for poor outcome are young age and attendance at day-care centres such as nursery schools
- ✓ Others risks include White race, male sex and history of enlarged adenoids, tonsillitis and asthma
- ✓ Factors predisposing to poor outcome: multiple previous episodes, bottle feeding, history of ear infections in parents or siblings and use of a soother/pacifier (dummy)
- ✓ Evidence for the effect of environmental tobacco smoke is controversial
- ✓ In 80% of children the condition resolves without antibiotic treatment in about three days
- ✓ Complications are rare, but include hearing loss, mastoiditis, meningitis and recurrent attacks
- ✓ In the developed world, the majority of children with AOM are treated with antibiotics
- ✓ In The Netherlands only a minority are treated with antibiotics, but the outcome seems no worse
- ✓ Antibiotics give limited benefits
- ✓ Most children can be treated without antibiotics
- ✓ Pain lasts no more than 24 hours in 80% of children
- ✓ Benefits of withholding antibiotics include reduced cost, reduced side-effects and reduced antibiotic resistance

'Clinical Evidence' published by the BMJ Publishing Group included a review of the effects of treatment for otitis media and of the effects of preventive interventions. This particular section also appeared in the BMJ (25 September 1999).

KEY POINTS FOR ACUTE OTITIS MEDIA

✓ Limited evidence from one RCT that non-steroidal anti-inflammatory drugs are more effective than placebo in relieving pain in children with acute otitis media

✓ Effectiveness of antibiotics is conflicting

✓ The review found no clear evidence favouring a particular antibiotic for treating acute otitis media

✓ One systematic review of RCTs found greater immediate benefit but no difference in long-term outcome with short (≤ 5 days) rather than longer courses of antibiotics

✓ One systematic review of RCTs found that long-term antibiotic prophylaxis has a modest effect in preventing recurrences of AOM; however, which antibiotic to use, for how long and how many episodes of AOM justify treatment have not been adequately evaluated

SUMMARY POINTS FOR AOM (BY SMAC)

✓ Reviews on AOM suggest that the benefit of routine antimicrobial use is unproved or modest

✓ A proportion of children do benefit, but it is difficult to predict which ones

✓ Countries with lower rates of antibiotic prescribing for AOM show no increase in the number of complications compared with those where a prescription is usual

✓ Even if antibiotics are prescribed, there is debate about the appropriate length of treatment: 3- and 10-day courses were equally effective in one study

✓ Antibiotics are probably unnecessary in AOM

✓ Reassurance, time and adequate pain relief are required

✓ If antibiotics are prescribed, the course should be limited to three days

SUGGESTED EVIDENCE-BASED MANAGEMENT

Explain that:

✓ Most patients get better within 24 hours without antibiotics

✓ Most cases are due to viruses, which are not killed by antibiotics

✓ Withhold antibiotics in mild cases

✓ Advise paracetamol every 4 hours in correct doses

✓ Offer to review the child in 24–72 hours if parental/doctor concern

✓ Consider giving information leaflets

✓ Consider deferred prescription of antibiotic, only to be used if the child is no better after 24–48 hours

✓ Consider an antibiotic at the outset if the child is unduly ill, toxic or has a high fever

Papers

1. Are antibiotics indicated as initial treatment for children with acute otitis media? A meta-analysis

(*C. Del Mar, et al, BMJ 1997;314:1526–9*)

Meta-analysis of controlled trials (antibiotics versus placebo):

✓ Early use of antibiotics conferred marginal benefit, with 17 patients requiring immediate treatment to prevent one getting pain at 2–7 days

✓ Antibiotics benefit only those 14% still in pain 24 hours after presentation

✓ Antibiotics double the risk of vomiting, diarrhoea and rashes

2. Pragmatic randomised controlled trial of two prescribing strategies for childhood acute otitis media

(*P. Little, et al, BMJ 2001;322:336–42*)

✓ This clinically useful, large RCT study looked at the rationale behind delayed prescriptions in general practice

✓ 315 children aged between six months and 10 years were recruited from practices in SW England

✓ They were randomised to receive immediate treatment or delayed treatment with support from standardised advice sheets (antibiotic prescription to be collected at parents' discretion after 72 hours if child still not improving)

✓ Outcome measures were symptom resolution, absence from school or nursery and paracetamol consumption

✓ On average, symptoms resolved after three days

✓ Children in the immediately prescribed antibiotic group had a shorter duration of illness (–1.1 days), fewer disturbed nights (–0.72 days) and slightly less paracetamol consumption (–0.52 spoons/day).

✓ There were no differences in school absence or pain or distress scores, since the benefits of antibiotics occurred mainly after the first 24 hours when distress was less severe

✓ Parents of 36/150 of the children given delayed prescriptions used antibiotics, and 77% were very satisfied

✓ Fewer children in the delayed group had diarrhoea (14/150 (9%) vs 25/135 (19%)).

✓ Fewer parents in the delayed group believed in the effectiveness of antibiotics and in the need to see the doctor with future episodes

✓ In conclusion, immediate antibiotic prescription provided symptomatic benefit mainly after the first 24 hours, when symptoms were already resolving

✓ For children who are not very unwell systemically, a wait-and-see approach seems feasible and acceptable to parents, and should substantially reduce the use of antibiotics for acute otitis media

3. Selecting persistent glue ear for referral in general practice: a risk factor approach
(*Medical Research Council Multi-centre Otitis Media Study Group, Br J Gen Pract 2001 52;480:549–54*)

✓ This study tried to establish a set of risk factors that would allow glue ear to be predicted and to ensure the appropriateness of referral

✓ Glue ear (otitis media with effusion) is the most common reason for surgery in children

✓ It is also the most common cause of hearing loss in children

✓ Resolution occurs in about 50% of cases after 12 weeks and 75% after 24 weeks

✓ Most prevalent between the ages of 2 and 5 years, and in most instances it begins to regress between 6 and 7 years of age

✓ A set of risk factors for persistence of glue ear would be useful in helping GPs to decide which children might benefit from referral and possible subsequent specialist intervention

✓ This nested case-control study involved 16 ENT departments in the UK

✓ With the aid of audiometry and tympanometry, diagnostic information was collected on 548 children after referral by their GP

✓ Using cases and controls, children were classified as either having or not having persistent glue ear

✓ From the results, after adjustment for time spent waiting to be seen from GP referral and age at referral, four main significant factors emerged for the persistence of glue ear. These were:

- Referral between July and December
- Having a mother who smokes 10 or more cigarettes per day
- Multiple upper airway symptoms
- Siblings with a history of glue ear

✓ They concluded that for a child who is referred between July and December with two or more upper airway symptoms, with a sibling who has had glue ear and a mother who smokes 10 or more cigarettes per day, the odds of having persistent glue ear are over 10 times that of a child without these adverse factors

Syphilis

Education and debate, Syphilis: old problem, new strategy

(L. Doherty, et al, BMJ 2002;325:153–6)

This article outlines recent changes in the epidemiology of infectious syphilis in England.

✓ Syphilis is on the increase again

✓ Syphilis is most infectious through sexual contact during the primary or secondary stages, but transmission can also occur during the early latent stage

✓ Syphilis is preventable, and treatable with effective and inexpensive antibiotics

✓ Recently, there has been an upward trend in incidence, partly due to several localised outbreaks affecting homosexual men and heterosexual men and women

✓ Between the 1960s and the late 1970s cases of homosexually acquired syphilitic infection increased, in keeping with the liberalisation of attitudes towards homosexual behaviour

✓ Changes in behaviour in response to HIV/AIDS, particularly among homosexual men, may have contributed to dramatic reductions in the number of cases of syphilis in the 1980s

✓ During the 1990s, until 1998, the number of diagnosed cases of infectious syphilis remained stable among both sexes in England

✓ But it more than doubled between 1998 and 2000 (from 172 to 372) in men and rose by 53% (102 to 156) in women

✓ In 2000, 48% of syphilis infections in men were homosexually acquired, rates being highest in London and NW England

✓ Investigations into the outbreaks showed a number of common features:
- Infection from unprotected intercourse
- Cases linked to high-risk social and sexual networks
- High rates of change of partners and of anonymous contacts
- Unprotected oral sex reported as the sole high-risk sexual practice

- Illicit drug use during sexual intercourse
- Concomitant HIV infection
- One-third of cases presented with primary syphilis. But more than one-third presented with symptoms of secondary syphilis, such as fever, malaise and pharyngitis, and with skin rashes and lymphadenopathy.
- The remainder were diagnosed as early latent syphilis on the basis of positive serology in the absence of clinical signs

KEY MESSAGES FOR HEALTH PROFESSIONALS

Explain that:

✓ 'Safer sex' messages need continual reinforcement among the sexually active population

✓ Unprotected oral sex is a risk factor for the transmission of sexually transmitted infections, including syphilis

✓ Healthcare professionals, particularly GPs, should refer those suspected of having syphilis to specialist genitourinary medicine services for investigation and treatment

Clinical presentation of syphilis

✓ **Primary syphilis:**
- Presents 9–90 days after exposure
- One or more chancres (ulcers): 'any anogenital ulcer is syphilis until proven otherwise'
- Regional lymphadenopathy

✓ **Secondary syphilis:**
- Presents six weeks to six months after exposure
- Localised or diffuse mucocutaneous ulcers
- Generalised lymphadenopathy
- Rash may affect palms and soles, and may be itchy
- Condylomata lata
- Less commonly seen alopecia, iritis, uveitis, meningitis, hepatitis, cranial nerve palsies, splenomegaly

✓ **Tertiary syphilis**
- Follows 2–20 years' latency
- Can develop gummas (granulomas occurring in the skin, mucosa, bone)

✓ **Quaternary syphilis**
- Can present with cardiovascular (eg aortic aneurysm) and neurological complications (eg cranial nerve palsies, CVA, tabes dorsalis, dementia, Charcot's joints)

Detection

The mainstay of diagnosis is serological testing. Cardiolipin antibody (eg VDRL) indicates active disease and becomes negative after treatment. It is detectable in primary disease but wanes in late syphilis. Treponeme specific antibody (eg TPHA) is positive in primary disease and remains so after treatment.

USEFUL WEBSITE

www.phls.org.uk/topics_az/hiv_and_sti/guidelines/managing_outbrea ks_of_sti.htm – Communicable Disease Surveillance Centre. Draft for consultation. Guidelines for managing local outbreaks of sexually transmitted infections. July 2001

CHAPTER 9:

CLINICAL
GOVERNANCE

Chapter 9: Clinical Governance

Definition: *'A system through which NHS organisations are accountable for continuously improving the quality of their services and safeguarding high standards of care and creating an environment in which excellence in clinical care will flourish.'*

USEFUL WEBSITE

www.doh.gov.uk/newnhs/quality.htm – From 'A first class service – Quality in the New NHS'

What are the components of clinical quality?

✓ Professional performance (technical quality)
✓ Resource use (efficiency)
✓ Risk management (risk of injury or illness associated with the service)
✓ Patient satisfaction

What can we do to improve?

✓ Audit
✓ Review complaints
✓ Critical incident reporting
✓ Routine surveillance

Why is it needed?

✓ GP quality is too variable

✓ Patients have a right to expect greater consistency in access to, and quality of, primary care services

✓ Patients need to be assured that their treatment is up to date and effective, and is provided by 'up to date' doctors

In reality

✓ Doctors must take part in audit

✓ Leadership skills must be developed within clinical teams

✓ Evidence-based medicine must be practised

✓ Good practice must be disseminated

✓ Risk management procedures must be in place

✓ Adverse events must be detected and investigated

✓ Lessons learnt must be applied to clinical practice

✓ Poor performance must be recognised early and tackled promptly

How will it work in primary care trusts (PCTs)?

✓ Each PCT has to nominate a senior professional to lead on clinical standards and professional development

✓ Each practice must have a named clinical governance lead, responsible for liaising with the rest of the primary healthcare team (PHCT), and with the PCT

✓ Information on quality (audits) may become public and identifiable as lay members of the PCT may demand it and other doctors may want it

Conclusions

✓ The advent of clinical governance is a watershed in the history of general practice

✓ Each GP is to be responsible for providing high-quality care, auditing care, auditing their own standards and those of their colleagues in the PCT

✓ Clinical governance is a powerful tool for improving quality of care in general practice

✓ Clinical governance is hence a means of maintaining quality assurance and accountability to the public

✓ It may be our last chance for self-regulation

National Institute for Clinical Excellence (NICE)

NICE gives guidance by:
✓ Appraisal of evidence
✓ Development and dissemination of audit methods
✓ Development and dissemination of guidelines
✓ Effectiveness bulletins

Commission for Health Improvement:
✓ Looks at clinical governance at PCT level
✓ Visits a random selection of practices
✓ Provides a collaborative approach with poorly performing PCTs
✓ Can report underperforming health bodies to the Health Secretary
✓ Tells us whether we are following guidance by:
   • Provider and service reviews
   • Performance indicators
   • Troubleshooting problem areas

Papers

The following papers, although not essential to the exam, would provide you with a more in-depth understanding of the practical problems facing general practice in the current political climate. They were part of a series of five papers written to encompass clinical governance in practice. A few key points are summarised for those who, understandably, would find it tedious to venture further.

1. Clinical governance in primary care – knowledge and information for clinical governance
(*A. McColl and M. Roland, BMJ 2000;321:871–4*)

This paper discussed the additional knowledge that will be needed by all staff working in primary care and the challenges faced by leaders of primary care groups and trusts. They suggested where relevant information could be found. Everyone in primary care needs to be familiar with these sources if clinical governance is to succeed as a way of improving the quality of healthcare.

SUMMARY POINTS

✓ Everyone in primary care needs to be familiar with the requirements of clinical governance if it is to succeed as a way of improving the quality of care

✓ Although producing, collecting and analysing primary care information is difficult, but some practices have already overcome these barriers

✓ Individuals and primary care group and trust leaders can do much to promote clinical governance, but problems remain

✓ The version of this paper on the BMJ's website includes numerous URLs to show what information is available

2. Clinical governance in primary care: participating in clinical governance
(M. Pringle, BMJ 2000;321:737–40)

Emphasised the need for clinicians to find information that will improve their own practice and aid learning in the primary care team as a whole. Such work is likely to go a long way towards fulfilling the General Medical Council's requirements for revalidation.

✓ NeLH (The National electronic Library for Health) will eventually help to improve access to information in the practice. In one English region only 20% of GPs had access to bibliographic databases in their surgeries and 17% to the World Wide Web

✓ Primary care groups and trusts will need to invest in adequate information technology hardware, software and training

✓ To avoid duplication of effort, relevant information should be coordinated at a national level and facilitated locally through postgraduate libraries

✓ Computerised clinical-decision support systems used during consultations can help to improve performance and patient outcomes

✓ In England and Wales, Prodigy software is available free of charge on 85% of computer systems; it can offer advice during consultations on what to do in over 150 conditions commonly seen in primary care

✓ The MIQUEST project is one of the national facilitating projects within the NHS information management and technology strategy. It aims to help practices standardise their data entry and provides software to help with data extraction, including data required for national performance indicators

3. Accountability for clinical governance: developing collective responsibility for quality in primary care
(A. Allen, BMJ 2000;321:608–11)

This paper discusses how the notion of accountability in clinical governance could be understood and used within primary care.

✓ It would use the clinical governance work of a London PCG as a case study to illustrate mechanisms and different forms of accountability between health professionals

✓ Clinical governance will extend the primary healthcare professionals' accountability beyond current forms of legal and professional accountability

✓ Clinical governance in primary care is aimed at enhancing the collective responsibility and accountability of professionals in primary care groups or trusts

✓ It is mainly concerned with increasing the accountability of primary health professionals to their local communities (downwards accountability), the NHS hierarchy (upwards accountability) and their peers (horizontal accountability)

✓ Primary care groups and trusts may find that, in addition to encouraging a culture of accountability, financial incentives are useful for achieving greater accountability

4. Using clinical evidence
(S. Barton, editor for 'Clinical Evidence', BMJ 2001;322:503–4)

Points raised:
✓ Most health carers want to base their practice on evidence and feel that this will improve patient care

✓ It has proved too difficult, alongside the competing demands of clinical practice, to implement the original idea that each health professional should: formulate questions themselves; search, appraise and summarise the literature; and apply the evidence to patients

✓ Over 90% of British GPs believe that learning evidence-handling skills is not a priority, and even when resources are available, doctors rarely search for evidence

✓ However, 72% often use evidence-based summaries generated by others, which can be accessed by busy clinicians in seconds

✓ The NHS will now be providing many of its clinicians with one of those sources – Clinical Evidence

✓ Clinical Evidence is a compendium of summaries of the best available evidence about what works and what doesn't work in healthcare

✓ It is constructed by transparent methods and updated regularly (so earlier issues should be discarded)

✓ In addition, NHS professionals in England, Scotland and Wales can access Clinical Evidence through the National electronic Library for Health (NeLH) or through one of the 14,000 paper copies being distributed to NHS institutions

✓ Will the distribution of Clinical Evidence improve patient care? Sadly, there are no large studies of the results of distributing similar printed materials

✓ One systematic review (nine studies) found that the passive distribution of printed educational materials compared with no distribution produced only small effects of uncertain clinical importance

✓ Printed materials may be necessary to transmit knowledge, but they are probably insufficient to change practice

✓ No study explored why printed materials were ineffective

✓ It is not surprising that passive distribution of printed materials does not automatically change behaviour:
  • Information may have been difficult to access when it was needed
  • May have been difficult to understand or be irrelevant
  • May have lacked credibility without a method of checking that the information is rigorous and complete
  • Too much paper information tends to get 'filed' as circulars – better to have one person allocated to distribute the information verbally during a meeting of all practice members once every two weeks or once a month

Clinical Evidence presents the evidence, but does not tell doctors or patients what to do because evidence is only part of making a clinical decision. Clinical expertise to evaluate each patient's circumstances and personal preferences is also important. Even the best available evidence may need adapting for individual patients. Thus a valid, relevant and accessible source of detailed clinical evidence is a necessary, but not sufficient, precursor of innovation to achieve evidence-based healthcare. Additional professional, educational and operational support for clinical innovation will probably accelerate the use of clinical evidence. Clinical Evidence will provide access to evidence in the way the *BNF* provides access to prescribing information, and earn as welcome a place in the consulting room.

CHAPTER 10:

REVALIDATION

Chapter 10: Revalidation

Self-regulation

✓ Self-regulation is whereby a profession determines its own training, qualifications and codes of ethics and behaviour
✓ This has been threatened by recent events such as:
  * Loss of confidence by public
  * Perception that the profession closes ranks to protect its own interests
  * Demands for greater transparency and accountability
  * Being undermined by a less deferential and better-informed public

Arguments for self-regulation

✓ A doctor's performance can only be adequately judged by someone doing the same job
✓ Self-regulation engenders self-respect and motivation to perform well
✓ Self-regulation helps to maintain professionalism and gives doctors a direct interest in maintaining standards
✓ Without self-regulation, doctors would cease to be members of a profession

Organisation of self-regulation

✓ GMC is currently consulting with the profession, the public and the Government
✓ Specialists' place on the Specialist Register may be made dependent on revalidation

✓ GMC may create a 'Generalists Register' for GPs, with inclusion dependent on revalidation

✓ Mechanism of revalidation to be supportive, not punitive, and largely by peer review, not examination

✓ Poor performance must be recognised early, and intervention must be sympathetic but decisive

✓ Support/retraining for any underperforming doctor must be available

✓ Removal from the Register to be used as last resort, only for those beyond help

✓ Overall, self-regulation must be robust and open to scrutiny, to avoid accusations of professional protectionism

The 'Council for the regulation of Healthcare Professionals' is a new overarching body, established as a result of the Kennedy report into heart surgery at Bristol Royal Infirmary. Its function is to regulate all the health professions and will exercise independent oversight of the GMC, although it is not in itself a regulatory body. Its principal concern is the interest of patients, and it can question a GMC judgement if it feels it has been too lenient.

Latest arrangements for revalidation

✓ Revalidation will mean that all doctors will have to demonstrate regularly to the GMC that they are up to date and fit to practise medicine

✓ It will also enable doctors to identify and correct any weaknesses they may have

✓ Doctors who are successful will be granted a licence to practise

✓ Doctors who choose not to participate in revalidation will be able to stay on the register without the entitlement to exercise the privileges currently associated with registration

✓ If concerns are raised about a doctor's 'Fitness to Practise' during the revalidation process, they will be referred to the GMC's Fitness to Practise procedures

There will be three stages to revalidation: collection of information; 5-year assessment; GMC decision.

1. Collecting information and yearly appraisal

Doctors will have to collect evidence, which will be considered against the seven headings set out in the GMC guidance 'Good Medical Practice':
1. Good clinical care
2. Maintaining good medical practice
3. Teaching and training, appraising and assessing
4. Relationships with patients
5. Working with colleagues
6. Probity
7. Health

✓ These headings have also been used to structure the annual appraisal

✓ Sufficient information for headings 1–5 should be available from the documentation summaries of the appraisals

✓ Doctors will be asked to sign declarations about their health and their probity (including past criminal convictions)

✓ During the appraisal, evidence being collected should help to identify any shortcomings in the doctor's performance, which can be addressed

✓ However, if there is serious concern that the doctor poses a risk to themselves or to patients they should be referred to the GMC immediately

2. 5-year assessment

✓ This is the second stage and is led by the GMC

✓ Applies to NHS and non-NHS doctors

✓ It is an assessment to check that the doctor is fit to practise

✓ Both doctors and members of the public will be used to help consider the evidence

✓ It is expected that the majority of doctors will be recommended for revalidation

✓ But if necessary the GMC will invoke the Fitness to Practise procedures

3. The GMC decision

✓ The third and final stage is the GMC decision

✓ It is expected that most doctors will be granted a licence to practise

✓ However, if, as a result of the revalidation process a doctor is considered under the Fitness to Practise procedures, then a number of outcomes are possible, including conditions placed on their practice or suspension

✓ Effective action will be taken to protect patients

Implementation

✓ In May 2001, the GMC agreed to take the next steps towards implementing revalidation

✓ This included working with the BMA/Academy of Medical Royal Colleges and the Council for the Heads of Medical Schools to ensure the mechanisms are in place

✓ GMC is now in the process of working with the Government to obtain the legislation

✓ Revalidation is likely to start no sooner than 2005; the legislation backing revalidation was passed in December 2002.

USEFUL WEBSITE

The above information and latest developments on appraisal and revalidation can be found at:
www.gm-uk.org/revalidation/index.htm – this is a joint website by the Department of Health and the GMC

Risks

✓ Further controls lead to reduced morale

✓ Maintaining standards becomes 'following fashion'

✓ Possible deterioration into an empty chore, therefore diverting doctors' time and energy from care of patients

Paper

Assuring the Quality of Medical Practice, Implementing 'Supporting doctors, protecting patients', January 2001

This report from the DoH discusses revalidation.

KEY CHANGES

✓ A new National Clinical Assessment Authority to assess poorly performing doctors by practice visits
✓ Annual appraisals for all GPs to started in 2001
✓ A revised national disciplinary procedure for GPs
✓ Pre-employment checks introduced in 2001
✓ Guidance for a new occupational health service in 2001
✓ New independent patient advocacy service to help patients with complaints against doctors

Patient power

✓ New national network of patient forums to monitor health organisations, supported by a Patient Advocacy and Liaison Service (PALS)
✓ Separate independent patient advocacy service to help with complaints
✓ NHS organisations to produce patient prospectuses to report action on patients' comments
✓ Local authority scrutiny committees to monitor health authorities (HAs)
✓ Annual appraisal already in place

Discipline and the GMC

✓ Revised disciplinary action
✓ Revised suspension action
✓ Alert letters to warn about bad doctors
✓ GMC future rests with governments
✓ GMC civil burden of proof to make it easier to strike doctors off the Register
✓ GMC to become part of the UK Council for the regulation of Health Care Professionals

Performance

✓ Annual appraisal for all doctors including locums to begin in 2002
✓ All doctors to carry out medical audits
✓ New systems for reporting adverse incidents, feeding into a national register
✓ National Clinical Assessment Authority to deal with poor and underperforming doctors

Other key points

✓ National Clinical Governance Support Team set up in 1999 to become part of the Modernisation Agency
✓ Information technology implications of NHS plan; all GP practices now connected to Internet. Plans for broadband connections underway.

Statutory changes

✓ GPs to declare criminal convictions
✓ Mandatory exclusion from HA lists for a conviction of murder; other convictions at HA discretion
✓ Has to keep list of locums, deputies and assistants
✓ Immediate suspension from HA list if there are fears for patient safety
✓ Only GPs on the HA list can practise
✓ Deaths in surgery to be reported
✓ GPs to declare all gifts

National Clinical Assessment Authority (NCAA)

- ✓ The NCAA offers a rapid performance assessment and support service for doctors
- ✓ Will recommend monitoring, education, retraining, medical treatment or referral to the GMC
- ✓ Has special HA status
- ✓ Health authority can refer doctors for advice and assessment
- ✓ Assessment carried out via practice visits
- ✓ Health authority will still be able to refer to GMC or deal with a doctor itself
- ✓ Assessors will be lay and medical
- ✓ GPs will be able to self-refer
- ✓ NHS pays for assessment
- ✓ GPs will have input
- ✓ Links with postgraduate deans and tutors
- ✓ Disciplinary action if GPs refuse to cooperate

Practice And Personal Development Plans (PPDPs)

Aims

✓ To combine personal self-directed learning with organisational development framework
✓ To predispose to, enable and reinforce change, ie deliver information, rehearse behaviours and to provide reminders and feedback
✓ To require learning portfolios for all members of the practice team (doctors, nurses, managers), taking into account the development needs of both individuals and the working unit
✓ To involve the shift away from an individual performance to organisational performance as measure of quality
✓ To involve patients, which should ensure local responsiveness and prevent loss of personal care

Ask yourself

✓ What do we need to do to improve our own practice?
✓ How have we identified what we need to do?:
   • Discussions
   • Surveys
   • Audits
   • Significant event analysis
✓ Are these needs specific to our own practice, or do they reflect priorities in our PCT or the wider NHS?
✓ How are we going to address these needs?
✓ How will we judge our success?
✓ What do I need to improve the quality of care I provide? ('Reflection')
✓ How can I achieve these aims? ('Education')
✓ You choose your education on the basis of what you need to learn (Continuous professional development (CPD))

A personal development plan (PDP) is part of the PPDP, as the team (practice) may require an individual to learn new skills in order to develop services.

Thus:

✓ There is a lot in common between Clinical Governance (CG) and PPDPs/PDPs

✓ Education should help you maintain and improve the quality of your care

The learning portfolio

Contains:

✓ All past significant sources and experiences of learning

✓ May include a description of your work and practice

✓ A summary of all your learning experiences

✓ A description of how you would like to develop professionally in the future

✓ Personal development plan would be at the heart of the learning portfolio

✓ Portfolio would act as a more long-term record of past experience and future aspirations

Could include:

✓ Workload logs

✓ Case descriptions

✓ Videos

✓ Audits

✓ Patient surveys

✓ Research projects

✓ Accounts of change or innovations

✓ Reflective diaries on study and ongoing education

CHAPTER 11:

THE FUTURE OF GENERAL PRACTICE

Chapter 11:
The Future of
General Practice

Current problems

✓ Job satisfaction
✓ Morale
✓ Autonomy
✓ Workload
✓ Bureaucracy
✓ Recruitment
✓ Retention

GP numbers threatened by:

✓ More early retirement
✓ More part-time principals, women principals (career breaks)
✓ More doctors needed in secondary care
✓ Reduced immigration from outside the European Union (EU)

Possible solutions

✓ Increased medical school intake
✓ Increased resources for staff premises and technology
✓ Increased delegation to practice nurses (nurse practitioners)
✓ Limiting expansion of GPs' workload, especially from secondary to primary care
✓ Core contract changed to ensure GPs retain control of workload (variable, flexible, minimal, practice- rather than individual-based)

✓ Appropriate funding for care transferred from secondary to primary care

✓ Easier re-entry arrangements after a career break

✓ Flexible working arrangements

✓ Increased linking of practices through PCGs, PCTs and cooperatives

✓ Other healthcare professionals working in surgeries; eg: pharmacists, physiotherapists, chiropractors, osteopaths, social workers, optometrists

✓ GPs employed by Community Trusts

✓ Initial triage by nurse practitioners – GP becomes specialist in family medicine (ie team leader) to be called upon only when needed

✓ Split contract – day and night elements

The NHS Plan

When it came out, the Labour party's 'NHS plan' was very radical; in 1998, after 20 years of Conservative Government, the UK had the lowest %GDP spending on health in Western Europe.

Investment

- ✓ 7000 extra beds in hospitals and intermediate care
- ✓ Over 100 new hospitals to be built by 2010 and 500 new one-stop primary care centres
- ✓ Over 3000 GP premises modernised and 250 new scanners
- ✓ Clean wards – overseen by 'modern matrons' – and better hospital food
- ✓ Modern IT systems in every hospital and GP surgery
- ✓ 7500 more consultants and 2000 more GPs
- ✓ 20,000 extra nurses and 6500 extra therapists
- ✓ 1000 more medical school places
- ✓ Childcare support for NHS staff with 100 on-site nurseries

Reform

- ✓ New relationship between the DoH and the NHS to enshrine the trust that patients have in front-line staff
- ✓ A new system of earned autonomy will devolve power from the Government to the local health service as modernisation takes hold
- ✓ DoH will set national standards, matched by the regular inspection of every local health body by an independent inspectorate, the Commission for Health Improvement (CHI)
- ✓ NICE will ensure that the availability of cost-effective drugs, like those for cancer, is not dependent on where you live
- ✓ The Modernisation Agency will be set up to spread best practice
- ✓ Local NHS organisations that perform well for patients will have more freedom to run their own affairs
- ✓ There will also be a £500m performance fund

✓ But the Government will intervene more rapidly in those parts of the NHS that fail their patients

Integration

✓ Social services and the NHS will come together with new agreements to pool resources
✓ New Primary Care Trusts (PCTs) to commission health and social care in a single organisation
✓ Modern contracts for both GPs and hospital doctors
✓ Extension of quality-based contracts for GPs in general, and for single-handed practices in particular
✓ If consultants are entitled to additional discretionary payments, these will rise from half to two-thirds, but in return they will be expected to increase their productivity while working for the NHS

Extended roles

✓ By the end of 2004 over 50% of nurses will be able to supply medicines. Some £280m is being set aside to develop staff skills.
✓ All support staff will have an Individual Learning Account worth £150 per year
✓ The number of nurse consultants will increase to 1000 and a new role of consultant therapist will be introduced
✓ A Leadership Centre will be set up to develop a new generation of managerial and clinical leaders, including 'modern matrons' with authority to get the basics right on the ward

Patient power

✓ Letters about an individual patient's care will be copied to the patient
✓ Patients' views on local health services will help to decide how much cash the services get
✓ Patient advocates will be set up in every hospital
✓ If operations are cancelled on the day they are due to take place the

patient will be able to choose another date within 28 days, or the hospital will pay for it to be carried out at another hospital of the patient's choosing

✓ Patients' surveys and forums will be set up to help services become more patient-centred

Recruitment

✓ By 2004, patients will be able to have a GP appointment within 48 hours; this so-called 'advanced access' has already been implemented in many practices

✓ Up to 1000 specialist GPs taking referrals from fellow GPs

✓ Long waits in Emergency Departments will be ended

✓ By the end of 2005, the maximum waiting time for an outpatient appointment will be three months and for inpatients, six months

Chronic diseases

✓ A big expansion in cancer screening programmes

✓ End to the 'postcode lottery' in the prescribing of cancer drugs

✓ Rapid-access to chest pain clinics have been established through much of the UK

✓ Shorter waits for heart operations

✓ Hundreds of mental health teams to provide an immediate response to crises

Elderly

✓ Nursing care in nursing homes will be free

✓ By 2004, a £900m package of new intermediate care services to allow older people to live more independent lives

✓ National standards for caring for older people to ensure that ageism is not tolerated

✓ Breast screening to cover all women aged 65 to 70 years

✓ Personal care plans for elderly people and their carers

National inequalities target

✓ Increase and improve primary care in deprived areas
✓ Introduce screening programmes for women and children
✓ Step up smoking cessation services
✓ Improve the diet of young children by making fruit freely available in schools for 4–6-year-olds

'Tackling health inequalities – A Programme for action' was recently published by the Government and set out plans to tackle health inequalities over the next three years (until 2006), in order to 'establish the foundations' required to meet the national targets of reducing the gap in infant mortality across the social groups and increasing the life expectancy in the most disadvantaged areas faster than anywhere else, by 2010. Currently, a man born in Manchester can expect to live 10 years less than one born in Dorset, and a woman born in Manchester can expect to live seven years less than one born in Somerset. Health inequalities have actually increased over the last 20 years. It is known that deprivation leads to many health problems, including a substantially higher risk of CHD (approximately double), cancer-related death and chronic disease. Tackling deprivation is therefore a top priority. The programme for action is organised around four themes:

1. Supporting families, mothers and children to ensure the best possible start in life (eg with schemes such as 'sure start')

2. Engaging communities and individuals to ensure that policies are relevant
3. Preventing illness and providing effective treatment

4. Addressing the underlying causes of health inequalities, eg smoking, poor diet, poor housing, etc

USEFUL WEBSITE

www.nhs.uk/nhsplan – Summary of the NHS Plan and full document

Shaping Tomorrow: Issues Facing General Practice in the New Millennium, GPC 2000

This was a discussion document issued by the General Practitioners Committee (GPC) of the BMA; it gathered views from the profession, politicians and patients. Each subheading below is an area discussed by the three parties, the salient points of which are summarised.

My doctor or any doctor quickly?

✓ Two apparent patient groups exist. The first group are essentially well and value easy access to healthcare with staff able to deal with their problem. The other comprises the chronically ill (elderly, poor) who place a high value on seeing their doctor

✓ Divisions exist between GPs

✓ Some feel that GPs overinvest in the notion of personal doctoring, like a psychological comfort blanket

✓ However, the personal relationship is something that many patients do rate very highly

✓ Many GPs see the personal relationship as central to what they do

✓ Others see it as a fading asset in a world of portfolio careers and part-time working

✓ A small minority think the concept is dead and the profession should be honest that the future is increasingly likely to be about 'one hit' consultations

✓ Advocates of personal lists point out that knowledge of the patient reduces expenditure (less investigation, etc)

Professor Mike Pringle admits that in reality doctors are unable to provide continuity of care in their practice. GPs are increasingly being asked to do things that the Government (and some doctors) think is valuable, such as sit on PCT boards, organise education and do research, all of which means they are not seeing patients. Other doctors (and the Government) feel that continuity of care is not as an important issue as the continuity of patient record.

Some consensus exists that a core group of chronically ill patients benefit from having their own doctor and that this should always be a priority.

The demands of the well population must not be allowed to overshadow the demands and needs of the chronically unwell.

Is there still a role for the GP as gate-keeper?

Gone are the days when anyone with any minor illness went straight along to see their family GP. With the expansion of nursing roles, NHS Direct, Walk in Centres, etc, there are many options for patients these days. Studies show that most patients are happy to see a nurse for triage/treatment of minor illnesses. The number of 'GP Specialists' is increasing. Many people feel that the role of the future GP will be of a 'Community specialist', supervising the management of difficult problems and leaving more trivial illness to others. This view was put forward in the Wanless report; according to this key report commissioned by the Government, the future GP will spend double the time they currently do on clinical governance, lose their gate-keeper role, manage chronic disease, focus on disease prevention and work in multidisciplinary teams with paediatricians and psychiatrists.

However:
- ✓ Some fear that giving up seeing some patients will reduce the quality of care, status or even pay
- ✓ Some say that there is no such thing as a minor illness or a trivial consultation
- ✓ Each consultation is an opportunity for identifying the hidden agenda and that only someone sufficiently trained (GPs) will be able to uncover it
- ✓ Evidence is scanty that enormous increases in nurse care will reduce the utilisation of doctors (as in the USA)
- ✓ Further research into the cost-effectiveness of nurse practitioners is needed to see if they do indeed reduce the doctor's workload

Independent contractor (IC) status versus salaried service: phoney war or real debate?

The arguments are for and against overlap, but essentially could be summed up as philosophical, clinical and financial – a heady enough mix to fuel any debate.

Pros to IC status:
- ✓ Allows GPs greater control of their jobs, ie ways of working, hours, staff, etc
- ✓ Allows GPs to believe themselves to be other than 'mere employees of the state'
- ✓ Allows us to be independent advocates on behalf of our patients
- ✓ Allows innovation, promotes entrepreneurial spirit, encourages change and efficiency
- ✓ Leads to the development of vocational training, primary care teams, out-of-hours care and models of commissioning
- ✓ It is a cheap service
- ✓ If all GPs were salaried and employed and therefore clocked on at 9 a.m. and off 36 hours later we would need far more GPs

Cons:
- ✓ Young doctors don't want to buy into partnerships
- ✓ Young doctors want a more flexible way of working
- ✓ Perverse financial incentives, whereby a high list size and lack of investment in facilities and staff produces a better income than services provided by more conscientious GPs
- ✓ Researchers and academics complain of a data 'black hole' in general practice
- ✓ Much of the independence is illusory, and will become more so in the future in a world of clinical governance, CHI, NSF, PCTs
- ✓ A salaried system might stop GPs worrying about money and allow them to get on with doctoring
- ✓ At its heart, independent contractor status has a lack of revalidation and supervision

A job for life or portfolio careers

It isn't just changing patient expectations that will affect the shape of tomorrow's primary care – it's changing expectations among tomorrow's GPs. If young doctors do want part-time working, flexible careers, the chance to move practices every few years and the opportunity to mix general practice with other kinds of employment, then ultimately these desires need to be accommodated. It is undoubtedly tempting for an older generation of GPs to complain about 'Generation X slackers'. There is a growing feminisation of the workforce, which raises issues around career breaks for motherhood and part-time working, and perhaps leads to wider questions about public and political perceptions of general practice in the future.

This way of working will be better accommodated under a salaried partnership, rather than a premises-owning, IC partnership. Personal medical services (PSM) pilot schemes explore different ways of providing primary care – and are heavily supported in the NHS Plan/Government.

NHS Direct and walk-ins: will they change the game?

✓ More access points now exist – NHS Direct, walk-in centres.

✓ Direct access to specialist care is expensive (but specialist GPs may be cheaper?)

Those supporting NHS Direct and walk-ins believe they will work to reduce trivial demands on the time of GPs. Replacing phone calls to a surgery with a more systematic service, with quality-assurance protocols, doesn't seem to pose a threat to general practice. It seems to be potentially of considerable benefit. This Government is encouraging self-care, and this potentially benefits GPs.

There's an unreasonable fear and paranoia about walk-in centres. If 100 centres treated 100,000 people a year, then that would be 10 million consultations. But there are 300 million patient contacts a year in general practice. Nurses are also convinced that the service can help to reduce unnecessary work for GPs, without undermining their position in primary care.

Clinical autonomy, does it have any place anymore?

In a world of NICE, NSF, guidelines and protocols, Prodigy and Evidence-based Medicine (EBM), clinical governance as well as CHI, does the concept of clinical autonomy still have any real meaning? Does this mean that GPs will lose the ability to mould care and treatment to individual patients? Many GPs take the view that guidelines and protocols are counsels of perfection, which are unobtainable under current resources. Yet doctors, rather than politicians, will be held to account, when it is not possible to deliver services to such standards.

Revalidation, poor performance, Bristol, are all saying to doctors 'you had better conform to the written standards otherwise you are out'. But if they do this it will produce huge cost pressures on the NHS. It's only because we use our generally excellent clinical judgement to flout almost every guideline going that this hasn't happened. Politicians are getting away with the rhetoric of perfection, and doctors are being held to account for not delivering it.

Primary care trusts: working together or professional straitjacket?

Will primary care trusts encourage GPs to work together in a more collective and cooperative way, or will they emerge as a new bureaucracy imposing a deadening uniformity and thereby extinguishing innovation and diversity?

Alongside new structures, a new public mood is emerging, which is demanding greater accountability from doctors, and a more transparent understanding of how they arrive at the judgements they do and what yardsticks are used in these decisions. In a narrow sense, it isn't immediately clear to whom PCTs will be accountable: Strategic Health Authorities? The NHS Executive? Ultimately to the Secretary of State, of course, but what will that mean for democracy on the ground?

In the wider sense of accountability, how will family doctors make it clear they want a genuine partnership with patients, and are they prepared to explain, and justify, what they do?

Promoting quality – what makes a good GP?

Is it possible that doctors, patients and politicians have different visions of what constitutes a quality service and, if so, how can these be reconciled? Among the mechanisms due to be launched in 2005 to shore up quality, revalidation is the profession's own answer to charges that self-regulation is no longer up to the job of protecting the public. But will it work, or just be another burden GPs have to attend to every five years then forget about? If it's not to be too onerous and time-consuming, diverting resources from patient care, revalidation must judge with a fairly light hand, but will the public believe it has any validity?

Amongst many questions about how general practice develops in the future is the issue of the generalist versus the subspecialist. The generalist role is very dear to the heart of most GPs, and is perhaps gaining increasing importance with the demise of the generalist hospital physician.

But many GPs also have special interests, and some would argue that such interests increase intellectual stimulation and allow GPs to better serve their patients. Should such interests and expertise be further formalised, and made available not just within a practice but also between practices or even across a PCT?

What do patients want?

It's an old joke, but it still raises a smile at every medical retirement party: When asked what was the best part of the job, the GP always says 'the patients'. Asked next what was the worst thing about the job, the GP always replies 'the patients'.

If GPs obtain intellectual stimulation from solving medical jigsaw puzzles, or boost their inner psyche by feeling that they are contributing to a kinder world or making a difference, or even saving life, that's fine. But the patient just wants to get better. So what should the relationship of the future be between GPs and patients? Everyone talks of partnership and the end of benign paternalism, and patient autonomy and shared care, sometimes, however, it is not hard to feel that the profession looks over its shoulder and rather wishes that 'doctor knows best' was still a politically correct option.

If we are moving into a more honest and sharing relationship with patients, when doctors are advisers and guides and not gurus and wizards, there still seem few clear mechanisms to listen to what patients actually want, as opposed to doctors assuming they know what patients want.

If patients become clients, or even customers, does that make doctors into therapists and shopkeepers? And if it does, is that any bad thing? What do patients want?

Claire Rayner, of the Patients' Association, believes firmly that the way forward is for the profession to see that patients are part of the health team and are as much involved with the provision, design, delivery and cost of healthcare as anyone else. She also recognises that because patients are recipients it doesn't alter the fact they have responsibilities to the service. But better ways of listening are needed. Patients' liaison groups, citizens' juries and patient advisory panels – this is the road we are going down. We do need much better mechanisms to hear the voice of the patient. GPs can't carry on being paternalistic. The days of a submissive, subdued, semiliterate, lumpen proletariat, people who were underfed and had rotten lives of quiet desperation, are over.

Funding and rationing – how is it all going to be paid for?

Most GPs would welcome a system that takes them out of the rationing front-line, be it a national rationing council, the Department of Health or NICE. At the very least, many would welcome a little more political honesty about the current situation. Proponents of the co-payment system argue that it would not only boost income for the health service, but also reduce workload. The counter-argument, of course, is that if people pay they become more demanding.

Primary Care Trusts

Health authorities were abolished in 2002 and funding and commissioning of health services were devolved to PCOs (Primary Care Organisations) or Trusts. PCOs are overseen by the Strategic Health Authorities; SHAs might get involved if, for example, an acute trust (hospital) was in serious debt. There are 5 Strategic Health Authorities in London and 35 in the UK. Each PCT has a board, responsible for vision and values, strategies and planning. The board comprises a Professional Executive Committee (made up of five GPs, two or three nurses, one or two allied health professionals, the Director of Public Health, the Head of Social Services, the Director of Finance and the Chief Executive of the PCT, as well as pharmacists and dentists) and an executive committee.

Personal Medical Services' (PMS) Pilots

As a result of the NHS (Primary Care) Act 1997, PMS schemes were designed to allow experimental schemes to test alternative models for delivering primary and community care.

British GPs have traditionally been self-employed, the contract under which they perform work for the NHS is elaborate and is perceived as being inflexible and bureaucratic. This is termed 'General Medical Services' (GMS), arrangements of which are set out in the 'Red Book'.

Although the PMS scheme has sometimes been called the 'salaried doctors' scheme (to contrast with the normal self-employment arrangements), this has not been its defining characteristic.

The PMS scheme has been well received, and a third wave of successful applicants is due to be announced and wave 5B was announced in October 2003. The reasons for its popularity are several.

The scheme has generally succeeded in giving those taking part a perception of self-determination and relative freedom from the constraints of NHS bureaucracy. How much this perception is based on the active attitudes of the health authorities who hold the personal medical services contracts and how much on the fact that these authorities have often not had the capacity to manage the scheme at all remains a moot point. Schemes in deprived areas were more likely to attract extra resources that were not generally available to practices working under the old regime, since GMS allocations are not usually linked to population needs.

These resources have been used to create new services, liberate practitioners for professional development and improve facilities, especially for disadvantaged groups such as homeless and mentally ill people.

Aims

✓ To attract GPs to areas with recruitment problems
✓ To get GPs and community nurses to work more closely together
✓ To tackle inequalities and health problems of deprivation

PMS Models

From 94 begun in April 1998, approximately one-third of all primary care is now PMS. Different models exist:
- ✓ Traditional, profit-sharing partners
- ✓ Salaried partners
- ✓ Salaried GPs and nurses providing primary care to homeless people
- ✓ Partnership of GP and nurse with joint responsibility for running a single practice
- ✓ Nurse practitioners act as team leaders in a practice and/or employ their own salaried GPs
- ✓ Local practice to run a cottage hospital as a primary care and minor injuries unit
- ✓ NHS trusts to employ salaried GPs to provide primary care under the same roof as other community health services

Significance and implications

- ✓ All practices have an individual contract negotiated directly with their PCT, dispensing with the 'Red Book' and all its restrictions and limitations
- ✓ Breaks the monopoly of the single national contract
- ✓ Allows GPs to switch to salaried status, pass management responsibilities to others and concentrate on clinical work
- ✓ Gives primary care trusts a new tool for discharging their local responsibilities to provide primary care
- ✓ Offers great potential for innovation and service development, eg drug misuse clinics, minor surgery, commuter surgeries

However

- ✓ PMS budgets are not guaranteed; the terms could change if PCTs run out of money
- ✓ Externally imposed targets
- ✓ Weakens GP IC role

✓ Could potentially create a two-tiered system of salaried GPs and GP partners, with the latter receiving better remuneration and having greater autonomy

With the New Contract, the boundaries between PMS and GMS may become blurred. For example, there are also many externally imposed targets in the new GMS contract, and salaried status is encouraged.

The New Contract

The proposals for the new national contract were announced on 19th April, 2002, jointly by the NHS confederation and the British Medical Association.

The contract was voted in, in July 2003, by a comfortable margin; a relief to the Government and the BMA after the rejection of the Consultant contract.

Current problems

✓ The 'Red Book' as discussed previously has long been criticised as being bureaucratic and inflexible
✓ The PMS pilots in 1998 were an acknowledgement by the Government for a need for change
✓ Currently, resource allocation poorly reflects patient need
✓ The GMS contract is focused on the individual practitioner and fails to recognise the role of the practice team
✓ The perverse incentive for GPs to manage large lists with a limited range of services, for high income
✓ Quality measures are poor and crudely implemented
✓ A recent BMA survey of the profession showed:
  - Devastatingly and unacceptably low morale – a profession in poor heart
  - Consequential intentions to retire early or to leave general practice
  - Excessive workload, and the need to control that workload in the future
  - The perception that the role of general practice within the NHS is undervalued
  - A commitment to quality and to better services for patients, delivered in part through lower average list sizes and through longer consultations, which the research evidence shows are the best available markers for high-quality care

USEFUL WEBSITE

www.bma.org.uk/ap.nsf/Content/annrep2002%5Cannrep2002+-+survey
– You will need to be a BMA member to access this site.

The New Contract

This will be between the individual practice and the PCO, not the GP. There will be five different types of services, which each practice will have to provide some or all of the following:

1. Essential services

These are mandatory and cover the provision of health care to everyone who is sick or 'believes themselves to be sick'; ie seeing patients in the traditional way. This covers emergency care and care for patients with chronic diseases.

Practices can either opt in or out of the following services, depending on staffing issues, training, etc. Also, if a practice feels they are not being paid enough to provide a particular service, they could decide not to provide it.

2. Additional services

This comprises services such as child health surveillance, contraception, cervical screening, childhood immunisations, antenatal and postnatal care, ie services which most GPs routinely provide at present. Accordingly, under the new contract, most practices are expected to provide these services.

3. Directed enhanced services

These services are more specialised. The PCT is expected to ensure provision of these services somehow, but not all practices will offer everything. These services comprise things like care of violent patients, minor surgery (not cryo and curettage which are 'additional services') and flu immunisations.

4. National enhanced services

The PCT itself will decide whether to provide these services. This category covers services that are needed throughout the UK, eg drug misuse services, anticoagulant services, intrapartum care.

5. Local enhanced services

These services are tailored to local needs, eg care of refugees. This is obviously more of an issue in some regions of the UK than others. Although there should be ring-fenced sums of money that go towards paying for enhanced services, there has been some concern about PCTs re-badging many types of expenditure as 'enhanced services', thus reducing the amount of money that will go to GPs.

Payment

All practices will receive a 'Global sum' and money for quality payments. This is paid by the Government to the PCT and is ring-fenced so that practices are guaranteed to receive it. The Global sum makes up two-thirds of GPs' payments and comprises payments for essential and additional/enhanced services. Quality payments make up the other third.

Quality payments are not paid via the PCT and are separate from the Global sum. There are six 'quality domains', all offering a potential 1000 points: clinical (eg chronic disease such as asthma, mental health, CHD, diabetes); organisational (education and training, record keeping, practice and medicines management); patient experience (eg length of consultation, patient satisfaction); additional service quality payments (eg achieving a certain percentage uptake of smears); holistic (for achieving across the clinical domain); and quality practice payments (for achieving across the other three domains). Achieving the 48 h access target can make the practice an additional 50 points. Carr-Hill does not apply to quality payments.

The Carr-Hill formula and MPIG

The exact figure for the Global sum is calculated using the controversial 'Carr-Hill formula'. This is calculated according to a weighted patient-needs basis rather than per GP as under the old GMS contract. The projected patient numbers are based on census figures, which is more accurate in certain parts of the country than others. The figures for London seem to be particularly skewed. Each practice has a 'notional list size', with a fixed sum per notional patient, taking into account such factors as deprivation, rurality, the number of nursing homes in the area, etc. The notional list size is based on the assumption that every practice has 'ghost' patients who do not exist. Practices who regularly update their patient records are therefore penalised. There has been a huge uproar about the Carr-Hill formula, which often grossly underestimates the true population of practices. To save the new contract, the 'MPIG' (minimum practice income guarantee) was introduced. This guarantees that practices will not lose out under the new contract. There is a commitment to phasing out Carr-Hill altogether, to achieve a more equitable method of payment.

Problem with quality payments

Originally, it was proposed that quality payments would be made according to the percent of target outcomes achieved, eg HbA_{1c} targets. This, however, fails to take into account disease prevalence. For example, a GP practice in the East End of London whose population has a high prevalence of diabetes would have to work much harder to get their quality payment than a practice serving an affluent population with a low prevalence of diabetes. This issue is being urgently addressed and it is likely that disease prevalence will be introduced into the quality and outcomes framework as a basis for weighting quality payments for the clinical domains from 2004/5.

Other important points in the new contract

It will be possible to 'opt out' of 24 h responsibility. This will cost 6% of the Global sum, which is approximately £6000/GP/year.

✓ Seniority payments will start earlier and increase year by year. They will be based on the date of GMC registration, not the number of years worked as a GP

✓ The PCT will purchase and own all IT equipment; there may therefore be issues around control of and access to data

✓ Pensions will improve; all NHS work will now be pensionable, eg extra locums worked by a salaried doctor, teaching students, etc

✓ There will be a more flexible career structure, with salaried options; the Government seems to ultimately want more salaried GPs

---

SOURCES

NHS Confederation 2000. *The new GMS contract – delivering the benefits for GPs and their patients.* London, NHS Confederation.

General Practice Committee 2002. *Your contract your future.* London, British Medical Association.

Editorial. A fresh new contract for general practitioners. *BMJ 2002 (4 May).*

Freedom of Information Act

The Freedom of Information Act received Royal Assent in 2000 and replaces the Open Government Code of Practice, which has been in operation since 1994. It puts a legal requirement on all NHS organisations (and those contracted to supply NHS services, such as GPs) to publish and share certain information with members of the public. Since October 2003, it has been compulsory for GPs to have such a publication scheme in place.

Information which must be made public includes basic data on practice staff, opening hours, out-of-hours cover arrangements, ancillary services offered, practice policies on health and safety, contact information, language services offered and, most controversially, the annual income of the practice and the practice drug expenditure. Unsurprisingly, not all GPs are happy about this.

In addition, there are plans to make measures of GPs' performance available to the public from Spring 2005. This includes treatment of common chronic illnesses such as diabetes and hypertension. GPs will be graded according to outcome and also on adherence to good practice. It is planned that new software will automatically compile most of the data needed.

There are concerns that these types of outcome measure do not necessarily correlate with how good a doctor is, in terms of holistic individual patient care. Publishing this data might undermine patients' confidence in their GP and change the doctor–patient relationship. To a large extent, these plans mirror the changes occurring in secondary care, with publication of league tables. In the same way that surgeons might be less willing to take on high-risk operative cases, there is a danger that GPs might be reluctant to take on patients with multiple co-morbidities, who may thus adversely affect their performance statistics.

Rationing

Know examples of scenarios where rationing may affect your practice, moral obligations, duty of care, postcode prescribing, etc. For example, sildenafil (Viagra) and donepezil (Aricept).

✓ What in your practice do you not prescribe to certain patients because of cost and not doubt over clinical efficacy?

✓ Rationing is regarded by many as the only method open if the NHS is to survive while delivering an apparently high standard of publicly funded quality care to the masses

✓ Can we continue to offer 'gold standard' publicly funded care as well as comprehensive care, or are the two subject to financial forces?

✓ With rationing you could either deliver the 'best to most' or the 'average to all'; what choice would you make?

✓ The general consensus is that the 'best to most' strategy is the best solution, while still maintaining honesty and transparency to the public

✓ Politicians are unlikely to make this a public issue while trying to win elections, the stark reality that widespread rationing exists has rarely been admitted to, and hence would ruffle many a feather

This problem has been actively explored in other countries. In 1993, 'The Oregon Experiment' took place in the USA; discussed in detail in an Education and Debate article in the BMJ (*BMJ 1998;316:1965*). A decade ago, the state of Oregon attracted worldwide interest when it began an ambitious attempt to set priorities for healthcare on a systematic basis.

Stimulated by the death of a 7-year-old boy who had been waiting for a bone marrow transplant operation, and led by John Kitzhaber, a doctor turned politician, Oregon passed legislation in 1989 designed to provide access to health insurance for all residents. This was a huge market research exercise, which gathered opinions from a broad public base, treatments were explained and justified and a list was compiled according to priority. Compilation of the list included a weighting to clinical effectiveness, social values and emphasis on primary/preventive care. The difference was that the information gathered was used; a cut-off line for conditions to be funded was decided according to available resources, but it remained dynamic with regular review.

In New Zealand, a government-appointed committee made a broad assessment of treatment priorities, as in the USA involving the public. It initiated a programme to devise guidelines for the provision of services. Criteria were written to determine access to publicly funded elective surgery. Treatment is given on the ability of patients to benefit (clinical and social): those with highest need would go first and those with little need may be refused.

The obvious disadvantage of either system is that the wealthy could by-pass it altogether and hence a two-tier system would be (and has been) created. The poor do not have that option. Means testing may be an alternative to 'all care'.

Would a modest charge, say, to see a GP help?
The answer is 'Yes'. Evidence shows this leads to a reduction in help-seeking behaviour to raise income tax and/or NI contributions.

Hopefully, evidence-based practice and guidelines from NICE will help avoid implicit rationing.

Out-of-Hours Care and 24 h Responsibility

Risks of split contract (day and night)

✓ Rolling, renewable contract could result in insecurity
✓ Other primary care providers may bid for out-of-hours work, eg community trusts, Emergency Departments and BUPA
✓ Further threatens integrity of GPs' role, already at risk from hospital outreach, community paediatricians, community psychiatric teams, midwives, etc
✓ Dilution and fragmentation of GPs' work
✓ Loss of control of care outside hospitals

Advantages

✓ Satisfaction from personal service
✓ Educational benefits
✓ Financial reward
✓ Prevention of erosion of GPs' role by other providers

Disadvantages

✓ Heavy workload – demand increased fivefold in last 25 years
✓ Stress – may result in: impaired quality of care at the time; impaired quality of care the next day; burn out
✓ Risk of violence

Deputising services

✓ Surveys show high degree of patient satisfaction
✓ Quality must be maintained
✓ Deputies must be well paid and well supported

Paper

A qualitative study of older people's views of out-of-hours services
(J. Foster, et al, Br J Gen Pract 2001 51(470):719–23)

✓ This study looked to ascertain the views of the elderly in relation to their use of various models of out-of-hours care
✓ While older people are more likely to have increased needs for such services, evidence suggests they are reluctant users of GP out-of-hours services
✓ A total of 30 people aged between 65 and 81 years from community groups based in SE London attended focus-group sessions of 90 minutes and comprising between 5 and 12 participants
✓ The study was conducted in Lambeth, Southwark and Lewisham, a socially deprived, multi-ethnic area of south London
✓ The session was audiotape-recorded with consent and then transcribed verbatim
✓ Two related themes were identified:
  1. Attitudes to health and healthcare professionals with reference to the use of health services prior to the establishment of the NHS, a stoical attitude towards health, and not wanting to make excessive demands on health services
  2. The experience of out-of-hours care and the perceived barriers to its use, including the use of the telephone and travelling at night. Participants preferred contact with a familiar doctor and were distrustful of telephone advice, particularly from nurses
✓ They concluded that older people appear reluctant to make use of out-of-hours services and are critical of the trend away from out-of-hours care being delivered by a familiar GP

✓ With increasing numbers of older people in the population it is important to consider steps to address their reluctance to use out-of-hours and telephone-advice services, particularly those based around less personal models of care

NHS Direct

Nurse-led, 24 h telephone helpline has been available throughout England and Wales since the end of 2000.

In response to:

✓ Growth of the 24 h society
✓ Increasing demand for primary and emergency care
✓ Problems in recruiting and retaining nurses and general practitioners

Aims to:

✓ Reduce workload
✓ Provide easy access to an appropriate level of expertise
✓ Empower patients with knowledge and thus foster self-care

Long-term aims

✓ Health promotion
✓ Information centres
✓ Health guides
✓ Internet services

Concerns

✓ It will uncover unmet demand, so fuelling workload
✓ Will threaten continuity of care
✓ Telephone contact by nurses rather than a consultation with a GP may mean that important diagnoses are missed
✓ It will not be integrated with the rest of gateway services such as GP cooperatives
✓ Would result in waste of resources and patient confusion

Criticisms

- ✓ Service needs to be equally accessible to those without English as a first language, mentally ill people and elderly – they are less likely to use a telephone service
- ✓ Money for NHS Direct was not offered to existing primary care services to update the existing service arrangements
- ✓ Not enough liaison with GPs
- ✓ Lack of consistent advise in clinically identical cases

Papers

1. Evaluation of NHS direct first wave sites: First interim report to the Department of Health
(*J.Munro, 1998. London, The Stationery Office*)

Looked at three aspects of the service in the first three pilot sites:
1. Descriptive account of the organisation and users of NHS Direct
2. Caller satisfaction
3. 'Before and after' assessment of its effects on other services

Showed that in the first eight months:
- ✓ Demand was only one-third of that expected (expected to rise)
- ✓ Essentially used as an out-of-hours service, with 72% of calls being out-of-hours
- ✓ Demographics reflected patterns for GP services, except that the elderly were underrepresented
- ✓ Caller satisfaction rates were high
- ✓ Significant differences in the percentage of callers advised to attend the Emergency Department and/or their GP between the three sites
- ✓ Significantly different advice given to 120 dummy cases (clinically identical) between the three sites

A follow-up study by J. Munro et al. (*BMJ 2000;321:150–3*) showed:

Same three pilot sites studied over 24 months, in summary:

✓ No significant changes in uses of ambulance services and A&E departments

✓ Changes in use of GP out-of-hours cooperatives were small but significant (increase of 2% per month to a decrease of 0.8%)

✓ May have restrained increasing demand

✓ Overall, in the first year did not reduce pressure on the NHS

✓ No evidence that it had uncovered extra demand

✓ Apparently is still popular with the public

2. *National Audit Office Report published January 2002*

✓ Stated – NHS Direct is used less by ethnic minorities, people aged over 65 years and disadvantaged groups than by the general population

✓ Report stated that these groups had 'as much need as others and perhaps an even greater one'

✓ Service is nevertheless operating safely and effectively

✓ Details only 29 cases of adverse events between its inception in 1998 and 2001 (less than one in every 220,000 calls)

✓ Service has also reduced demand on healthcare services that are provided outside normal working hours, eg GPs

✓ One GP cooperative providing out-of-hours services saw an 18% fall in the number of calls received when callers were transferred to NHS Direct first

✓ However, NHS Direct is underperforming in some areas

✓ Only 64% of callers managed to speak to a nurse within five minutes

✓ Target set by the Government was 90%

✓ One in five callers had to wait more than 30 minutes for a nurse to call them back

Walk-in Centres

✓ Announced in April 1999
✓ Offer people the opportunity to see a healthcare professional face to face on a walk-in basis
✓ Open from 0700 h to 2200 h weekdays and weekends to provide information and treatment for minor conditions
✓ With or without appointments
✓ Sited in convenient locations, mainly in large towns
✓ Consultations mainly provided by nurses, using clinical assessment software
✓ These nurse-led centres provide advice and treatment for minor illnesses and also direct people to the most appropriate healthcare provider for their needs
✓ Centres will be funded initially for three years, but concerns have been voiced about subsequent funding
✓ Same concerns voiced over NHS Direct have been discussed with regard to walk-in centres
✓ Run by cooperatives, GPs and NHS Trusts

Objections

✓ Diversion of funds from other parts of primary care
✓ May generate additional demands
✓ Cause fragmentation of primary care and erosion of Family Doctor Service which has:
  • Comprehensive medical record
  • Continuity of care at its core
  • Gatekeeper role

Benefits

✓ May reduce workload of GPs (especially trivial)
✓ Responds to demand for wider access

✓ NHS Direct may help the public make more appropriate use of health and social services

Papers

1. An observational study comparing quality of care in walk-in centres with general practice and NHS Direct using standardised patients

(*C. Grant, et al, BMJ 2002;324:1556*)

The UK Government, as part of a bid to modernise health services and make them more convenient to use, has introduced NHS walk-in centres and commissioned their evaluation by an independent team.

This study forms one component of that evaluation.

✓ They directly compared the quality of clinical care in walk-in centres with that provided in general practice and by NHS Direct

✓ It was an observational study involving assessment of clinicians by standardised patients

✓ It involved 20 walk-in centres, 20 general practices and 11 NHS Direct sites

✓ 297 consultations with standardised patients were analysed, 99 in each setting, carried out by professional role players who had been trained to play five clinical scenarios (postcoital contraception, chest pain, sinusitis, headache and asthma)

✓ Outcome measures were mean scores on consensus-derived checklists of essential items for the management of the clinical scenarios

✓ Data were also collected on access to and referral by walk-in centres, general practices and NHS Direct

✓ Walk-in centres achieved a significantly greater mean score for all scenarios combined than general practices (difference between groups = 8.2) and NHS Direct (10.8)

✓ Walk-in centres performed particularly well on postcoital contraception and asthma scenarios. In contrast to general practices, walk-in centres and NHS Direct referred a higher proportion of patients (26% and 82%, respectively)

✓ They performed significantly less well than general practice in examination of chest pain and the diagnosis, advice and treatment of sinusitis

✓ The authors state that these inadequacies do not necessarily provide evidence of poor quality care

✓ Examination may be of secondary importance in the overall management of musculoskeletal chest pain

✓ Significantly lower antibiotic use by walk-in centres for sinusitis may reflect acknowledged difficulties identifying patients who will benefit from antibiotics

✓ Walk-in centres' better performance was particularly noticeable for history taking, perhaps owing to the longer consultations undertaken in this setting

✓ The authors concluded that walk-in centres perform adequately and safely compared with general practices and NHS Direct for the range of conditions under study, but the impact of referrals on workload of other healthcare providers requires further research

✓ Although walk-in centres may provide a comparable quality of care, both the centres and NHS Direct referred a proportion of standardised patients elsewhere. Some of the referrals were to emergency departments, which may not be appropriate for the conditions studied and raises questions about the impact on workload of other providers

Problems

✓ Non-random sampling of participating sites

✓ Use of a limited number of scenarios, some of which are more discriminating than others

✓ Participating sites, particularly general practices, were likely to be more interested in the research question and may have provided a higher quality of care, possibly attenuating the study findings

✓ Scenarios were chosen as typical of those seen in walk-in centres and because they were appropriate for portrayal by standardised patients

✓ Scenarios necessitating the presence of abnormal findings or potentially involving certain types of physical examination or referral to third parties could not be included

2. Questionnaire survey of users of NHS walk-in centres: observational study

(C. Salisbury, et al, Br J Gen Pract 2002;52:554–61)

✓ The principal aim of NHS walk-in centres is to improve access to primary healthcare

✓ This study attempted, through a questionnaire, to ascertain the client group that attended and their satisfaction

✓ The survey was also conducted among people who attended general practices close to a walk-in centre on a 'same-day' basis; that is, by attending without an appointment booked before the day of their consultation

✓ For this group of people, attending a nearby walk-in centre would be a realistic alternative source of care

✓ The survey was conducted at all walk-in centres that were open by March 2001

✓ The general practice nearest to each walk-in centre was approached to act as a control site; if this practice declined the invitation, they approached the next nearest practice and so on

✓ The questionnaire was divided into two sections. The first was designed to be completed before the consultation and included questions about sociodemographic characteristics, convenience of location and opening hours, reasons for consulting, expectations, recent use of health services and attitudes to continuity of care. The second section, completed after the consultation, included questions about waiting times, satisfaction, treatment, referrals and enablement

✓ 38 walk-in centres and 34 neighbouring general practices took part

✓ The results showed that walk-in centre visitors were more likely to be:
- Owner-occupiers (55% vs 49%)
- To have further education (25% vs 19%) and
- To be Caucasian (88% vs 84%) than GP visitors

✓ Therefore the authors stated that visitors to walk-in centres in the UK were younger, better educated and more affluent than those attending general practice

✓ Main reasons for attending a walk-in centre were speed of access and convenience

✓ They also found that walk-in centre visitors were more likely to attend on the first day of illness (28% vs 10%)

✓ Walk-in centre visitors were less likely to expect a prescription (38% vs 70%) and placed less importance on continuity

✓ People were more satisfied with walk-in centres

✓ Enablement scores were slightly higher in general practice

✓ Following the consultation, 13% of walk-in centre visitors were re-referred to their GP, but 32% intended to make an appointment

✓ They concluded that NHS walk-in centres improve access to care, but not necessarily for those people with the greatest health needs

✓ It then has to be argued whether they are a justified use of scarce resources for a patient group in least need

3. Editorial: NHS Direct audited. Customer satisfaction, but at what price?

(*BMJ 2002;324:558–9*)

This editorial was written by a board member of an NHS Direct site and gives a surprisingly unbiased view as to the evaluation of the service. In summary:

✓ Three NHS Direct pilot sites were launched in March 1998 and sites now cover the whole of England and Wales

✓ While not the first telephone health service in the world, it promised something more than triage of emergency calls

✓ It is now set to become the hub of out-of-hours care

✓ In January 2002, the National Audit Office, an independent body that scrutinises public spending on behalf of Parliament, published its report on NHS Direct in England and Wales

✓ Generally, the report is positive but there are problems

✓ In addition to difficulty with meeting call-handling targets, there has been no visible effect on demand for NHS services overall

✓ The hoped for reduction in demand for other services might be achieved by the proposed integration of NHS Direct with existing out-of-hours general practice cooperatives and ambulance services

✓ Where such integration has taken place, demand for general practice consultation has fallen, especially for telephone consultation

✓ Despite its shortcomings, customer satisfaction with NHS Direct is high, that is among those who use it

✓ Evidence indicates they are the same people who use existing health services

✓ It is underused by older people, ethnic minorities and other disadvantaged groups

✓ Rather than reach people who are currently failed by the health system, NHS Direct may have discovered previously unexpressed demand among the worried well of the middle classes

✓ The Internet version of the telephone service makes only a brief appearance in the report, but its use is clearly limited to those with access to the Internet and money to pay for it

✓ When callers reach a nurse the advice they get may vary, usually on the side of caution

✓ This is predictable, but has inevitable consequences. For every caller with a serious condition detected by NHS Direct, many more with self-limiting conditions will be directed into the health system

✓ Consistently to err on the side of safety might seem logical, but the effect of doing so is to fill a health system with people who do not need to be there

✓ However, is it worth the money? The report suggests that half of the £90m annual cost of NHS Direct has been offset by encouraging more appropriate use of NHS services

✓ Is £45m, the theoretical additional cost of NHS Direct, worth it for a system that eventually might work as a coordinator of access to healthcare? It seems unlikely that NHS Direct will do anything to address health inequality, and it may even serve to widen existing differences

✓ If you had £45m a year to spend on improving health, empowering the socially disadvantaged and reducing health inequality what would you spend it on?

 KEY SOURCES

Department of Health 2000. *Raising standards for patients: new partnerships in out-of-hours care.* London, Stationery Office.

The Comptroller and Auditor General 2002. *NHS Direct in England.* London, Stationery Office.

Diagnostic and Treatment Centres

The Government is planning to commission certain services to private clinics, which will be staffed by local or foreign doctors. 140,000 operations such as cataract extraction and hip and knee surgery are planned each year. The stated aim is to take the pressure off NHS facilities, reduce waiting times and allow hospitals to 'focus their expertise' on complicated elective work. However, there has been concern regarding the following points:

These centres may not be cost-effective

Many hospitals have already spent money to try and cut waiting times by increasing staff and facilities. If patients are diverted away to private clinics, there may have to be job-losses. Often, routine operations such as cataract extraction help hospitals to subsidise more specialised work, eg in chronic eye disease. Posts which do not offer enough experience for surgical trainees will be taken away, potentially leaving consultants without junior staff. Surgical trainees may get insufficient experience of routine surgery. Also follow-up arrangements for patients may not be comparable.

Public–private partnerships appear to be generally popular with this Government. For example, hospitals are being built under 'PFIs' (private finance initiatives). The LIFT scheme (Local Improvement Finance Trust) is a PFI and is going to put £1 billion into building new premises in deprived areas; PCTs bid for pots of money, which go into local schemes. There are obviously concerns about the motivation of the private companies involved and about long-term consequences and costs to the NHS.

Specialist GPs

In January 2004, there were 1250 specialist GPs practising in the UK (the NHS plan stated that there should be 1000 in place by 2004). Key points regarding the benefits and threats of the new grade were raised in a joint report by the RCGP and RCP in May 2001.

Potential benefits

✓ Getting high-quality care more rapidly and closer to home offers patients considerable advantages

✓ Increased communication between local GPs may enhance team working and continuity

✓ Clinical care outside general practice also offers interest, personal development, and heightened self-esteem for GPs

✓ Advantages for GPs may include enhanced retention, delayed burn-out and increased job satisfaction

✓ Increased working with consultants will also help to break down barriers

Potential threats

✓ The creation of GPs with special interests may degrade the discipline of general practice and the value of generalism

✓ Fragmentation of general practice, with the devaluing and eventual loss of generalism to the detriment of patient care, as occurred to the general physicians

✓ Adverse effects on resources: 'For every session done by a GP with a clinical special interest, there will be one session less of clinical care in other environments. Many of these sessions will come from clinical general practice. Some may be a direct transfer of a general practitioner from a clinical assistantship in the hospital setting. Whatever the source, the new sessions will remove capacity from elsewhere in the NHS'

✓ Specialist GPs may become a second-class service designed to ease the pressure on hospital outpatient clinics, reducing clinical standards while denying patient access

USEFUL WEBSITE

'General Practitioners With Special Interests' is accessible at www.rcgp.org.uk

Nurse Practitioners

What work might they do?

✓ Prevention, immunisation, smears, contraception, review, BP, asthma, diabetes, etc
✓ Medical triage, independent management of minor illness with limited prescribing rights, referring to GP only when necessary
✓ Social triage – guiding patients needing social or financial help

How would GPs benefit?

✓ Overtrained for much of what we do – less time spent on trivia would mean that more time is available for patients with more serious problems
✓ Skills learnt during training need no longer atrophy through disuse
✓ Potential for GPs to specialise in aspects of primary care
✓ Increased job satisfaction
✓ Improved morale .
✓ Increased income through larger lists, eg 4000 patients per doctor

What are the possible problems?

✓ Dilution of continuity of care and of personal care
✓ GPs may feel themselves redundant
✓ Nurses may fail to diagnose rare but life-threatening conditions, or to spot unusual presentations
✓ More specialisation by GPs may lead to loss of 'generalist role'
✓ Cost of training programmes and salaries to be borne by health authorities
✓ Legal responsibility – nurses are responsible for own actions but GPs still have 'vicarious liability'

✓ Nurse practitioners need to protect themselves by writing evidence-based protocols for delegated tasks

✓ Patients must be informed that they are not seeing a doctor so they don't consent to procedures believing a doctor – not a nurse – will perform them

What do the studies show? Nurse practitioners are:

✓ Safe
✓ Effective
✓ Popular with patients
✓ Good at listening, understanding and explaining
✓ Good at following protocols
✓ Less likely to prescribe
✓ More likely to use non-prescription approaches
✓ Likely to advise on prevention
✓ Good at using drug formularies

How can they act as point of first contact?

✓ Triage
✓ Telephone advice
✓ Same-day appointments
✓ Home visits

Effect on GPs GPs report:

✓ Reduced workload
✓ Increased satisfaction
✓ Improved standards of care
✓ More patients seen

What are the pitfalls?

(This is food for thought, not necessarily the authors' views)
- ✓ The title 'Nurse Practitioner' is not regulated, the courses they go on are neither externally assessed nor regulated
- ✓ Are we therefore allowing non-medically trained people to practise as doctors?
- ✓ Having to access a GP only via a nurse, is it acceptable that patients do not have a choice to see a doctor first
- ✓ Introduction of a two-tier service with nurses providing much of the care in those areas where it is difficult to recruit GPs, whereas leafy suburbs where GPs want to work are well staffed but patients have the least need
- ✓ What effect would it have on the nature of general practice?
- ✓ Ability to distinguish self-limiting from serious disease and the opportunity to develop a close rapport with patients are key skills of GPs, would these be compromised?

What does a practice need before appointing a nurse practitioner?

- ✓ Job description to clarify role, responsibilities, accountability and liability
- ✓ Protocols and guidelines
- ✓ Formulary
- ✓ Education of staff on role of nurse practitioner
- ✓ Education of patients on role of nurse practitioner

What will the nurse practitioner need?

- ✓ Mechanisms of support, supervision, professional development, ie a mentor
- ✓ Mechanisms of problem resolution
- ✓ Training in protected time
- ✓ Accreditation scheme in addition to the Nurse Practitioner degree
- ✓ Education funded by health authority
- ✓ Fewer prescribing restrictions

Papers

1. Nurse management of patients with minor illnesses in general practice: a multicentre RCT

(*C. Shum, et al, BMJ 2000;320:1038*)

Taken from a themed issue, this explored the changing roles of nurses in the NHS. Four trials of nurse impact on primary care were published.

✓ Practice nurses attended a degree-level course on managing minor illness for half a day a week for three months, they also observed GPs in surgeries twice a week. Two sessions equates to one day or two surgery lists. Two-month pilot period after the nurses were recruited

✓ Patients asking for same-day appointments with minor illness were randomly distributed between a GP and practice nurse

Outcomes

✓ High satisfaction for both doctor and nurse consultations (but significantly higher for nurses)

✓ Consultations with nurses took and average of 10 minutes, with doctors eight minutes

✓ Similar prescription rates for a similar number of patients

✓ 73% of patients seen by nurses required no input from doctors

✓ Conclusion – practice nurses offer an effective service for people with minor illness

2. Randomised controlled trial comparing cost effectiveness of general practitioners and nurse practitioners in primary care

(*P. Venning et al, BMJ 2000;320:1048–53*)

This further RCT in the same issue as Paper 2 looked at cost-effectiveness. It showed that:

✓ Nurse consultations were significantly longer than those of doctors

✓ They carried out more tests and asked patients to return more often

✓ There was no significant difference in patterns of prescribing or outcome

✓ Patients were more satisfied with the nurse consultations (allowing for time difference)

✓ No significant difference in health service costs between the two groups

✓ Conclusions were that costs were similar, but that if nurses could maintain the benefits whilst reducing their return consultation rates or shortening consultation times then they could be more cost-effective than general practitioners

3. Systematic review of whether nurse practitioners working in primary care can provide equivalent care to doctors
(S. Horrocks, et al, BMJ 2002;324:819–23)

✓ This study asked the question 'can nurse practitioners provide care at first point of contact equivalent to doctors in a primary care'

✓ Nurse practitioners have existed in North America for many years

✓ An increasing number are being employed in the UK in general practice, emergency departments and other primary care settings

✓ This was a systematic review of RCTs and prospective observational studies comparing nurse practitioners and doctors providing care of undifferentiated health problems in primary care

✓ Outcome measures were patient satisfaction, health status, costs and process of care

✓ 11 trials and 23 observational studies met all the inclusion criteria

✓ They found that patients were more satisfied with care by a nurse practitioner

✓ No differences in health status were found

✓ Nurse practitioners gave longer consultations and performed more investigations than did doctors

✓ No differences were found in the number of prescriptions, return consultations or referrals

✓ Quality of care was in some ways better for nurse practitioner consultations

✓ They concluded that:
- Increasing availability of nurse practitioners in primary care is likely to lead to high levels of patient satisfaction and high-quality care
- Patients are more satisfied with the care from a nurse practitioner than from a doctor, with no difference in health outcomes
- Nurse practitioners provide longer consultations and carry out more investigations than doctors
- Most recent research has related to patients requesting same-day appointments for minor illness, which is only a limited part of a doctor's role
- Further research is still needed to confirm that nurse practitioner care is safe in terms of detecting rare but important health problems

Outreach Clinics

Advantages

✓ Improved communication between GP and consultant
✓ Increased range of services in general practice
✓ Fewer non-attending patients
✓ Reduced and more appropriate referral to hospital
✓ Patient convenience
✓ Better management
✓ GP education

Disadvantages

✓ Widens divide between progressive and inert practices
✓ Inefficient use of consultant time
✓ Inadequate facilities
✓ No hospital records available
✓ No diagnostic services available
✓ Reduced consultant cover, teaching and research at hospital
✓ Increased referral waiting time for those patients of non-participating practices
✓ Unnecessary referrals

The above are theoretical points as no evidence is available. As such, more evaluation is needed.

Q. What are the costs to the patient, GP and hospital?
Q. How would they impact on referral, prescribing and on junior training (lack of consultant cover)?

Practice Formulary

Aim

To improve the quality of care through rational, cost-effective prescribing

Criteria for inclusion

Drugs must be: necessary, safe, effective and economic

Method

✓ Develop own formulary
✓ Participate in development of district formulary
✓ Take over and amend established formulary

Benefits

✓ Education
✓ Generic prescribing increased
✓ Prescribing costs reduced
✓ Influence of drug companies reduced
✓ Prescribing policies/management policies agreed
✓ Self-audit
✓ Peer review

Problems

✓ Patients reluctant to change
✓ Doctors feel restricted
✓ Hospital-initiated therapy with non-formulary drug

Q. How would you instigate a practice formulary?

Post 'Shipman': What are the Long-Term Effects?

Alan Milburn ordered a wide-ranging inquiry into the issues raised by the case. Following the publication of the inquiry into the Shipman case it appears that Harold Shipman murdered at least 215 of his patients (171 women and 44 men): 45 other cases are possibly suspicious.

The head of the inquiry, High Court Judge, Dame Janet Smith, also speculated that Shipman may have been hoping to get caught when he altered the will of his last victim, Kathleen Grundy, aged 81 years. The forgery was described as 'crude' and 'made detection inevitable'.

The report 'Death Disguised' examined a total of 888 cases in its 2000 pages.

Harold Shipman committed suicide in January 2004 and admitted guilt in a letter to his wife before he died. It appears that he murdered at least 215 of his patients (171 women and 44 men). Dame Janet Smith is heading the Shipman inquiry. The inquiry has to consider the following:

✓ Death and cremation certification, in particular reporting and investigation of sudden deaths. Dame Janet Smith recommended changes to the current systems, in a report published in July 2003. She heavily criticised the current system of death certification, in that it relies too much on the integrity of a single doctor. She has proposed that all deaths be referred to a coroner's service – a combination of medical coroners, judicial coroners and coroner's investigators. Where a doctor has been able to give an opinion on the cause of death, a coroner's investigator will look into the case and certify death. If not, the medical coroners will look into the case in more detail. In all cases, the investigator will talk to the family of the deceased to find possible inconsistencies in the GP's story. GPs will have to complete a new form 2, giving an account of the circumstances leading up to death, a brief medical history and details of nursing care. They will no longer certify death and there will be no separate cremation form. Dame Janet wants the GMC to impose an ethical professional duty on doctors to cooperate. The BMA has welcomed Dame Smith's proposals, but there is serious concern about time and staffing issues.

✓ Controlled drugs; procedures for prescribing, dispensing and storing controlled drugs
✓ It is charged with the task of recommending what steps, if any, should be taken to protect patients in the future. A document entitled 'Safeguarding patients' was published in November 2003, which formed the basis for discussion about possible ways of monitoring doctors and disciplinary systems; a series of seminars took place in January 2004, covering the topics of whistle-blowing, complaints, and monitoring and regulation of General Practitioners.

Issues raised in 'Safeguarding patients' include:
✓ Whether the current system of annual appraisal is sufficient, or whether there needs to be a more objective type of GP appraisal, including assessment of consultation skills and random reviews of medical records.
✓ Whether there should be a central repository for information about doctors, so that PCTs can make all necessary checks simultaneously.
✓ Whether patients should be provided with more information about their GPs so that they can make an informed choice, eg any previous convictions or disciplinary findings.
✓ Whether patients should direct complaints to the PCT rather than to the GP practice.
✓ Whether GPs should be required to list all complaints received by them to the PCT
✓ Whether there should be a helpline where staff could bring forward concerns about the doctor employing them
✓ Whether there should be new disciplinary procedures for 'unacceptable professional practice' which 'falls short of the GMC threshold, but is nevertheless significant'

A report is expected on the basis of this seminar.

USEFUL WEBSITE

www.the-shipman-inquiry.org.uk/reports.asp – Shipman inquiry reports

Possible effects of the case on single-handed/small practices

An editorial in the *Br J Gen Pract* by Mike Pringle (May 2000) looked at the implications of the Shipman case:

✓ Profession should be defending single-handed practices

✓ Professional isolation should be the focus

✓ Restore patient confidence by professional development, revalidation and appraisal

✓ Death rates, although crude, may become part of any clinical governance monitoring system

✓ Stricter control of use and storage of controlled drugs

Papers

1. Do single-handed practices offer poorer care?
Cross sectional survey of processes and outcomes
(*J. Hippisley-Cox, et al, BMJ 2001;323:320–3*)

This study, published at the height of the Shipman fallout in general practice, looked at whether there are important differences in performance between group practices and single-handed GPs, and the extent to which any differences are explained by practice characteristics such as deprivation.

We already know that:

✓ 10% of all GPs are single-handed

✓ Single-handed general practitioners tend to work in areas of high deprivation and need

✓ Patients like single-handed practices because they are offer good communication, rapport and continuity

✓ Concerns have been expressed about professional isolation and quality of single-handers, on the basis of little evidence

✓ NHS Plan will have an impact on single-handed GPs, through either a negotiated change to the 'Red Book' or the new national contract into which all single-handed GPs were transferred in 2004

The study

✓ Cross-sectional survey design

✓ 206 single-handed practices and 606 partnerships in the Trent region were analysed

✓ Routinely collected data on hospital admissions and target payments for single-handed practices and partnerships were studied, as well as confounding effects of general practice characteristics such as deprivation, percentage of Asian residents, percentage of Black residents, proportion of men over 75 years, proportion of women over 75 years, rurality, presence of a female general practitioner and vocational training status

✓ They found no difference in achievement of immunisation and cytology targets after adjustment made for other general practice characteristics

✓ No significant differences for three types of hospital admission seen on initial observation after adjustment for other practice characteristics

✓ They concluded that there was, 'no evidence that single handed general practitioners are under performing clinically. Our results offer insight into the structural difference between the two types of practice and underline the importance of the effect of other practice characteristics on process and outcome measures'

Limitations

✓ Largely based on routinely collected data on hospital admissions and target payments (small selective part of general practice)

✓ They were unable to adjust for more subtle population characteristics, such as smoking habits

✓ Private referrals were excluded

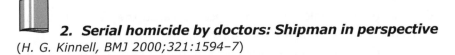 ***2. Serial homicide by doctors: Shipman in perspective***
(*H. G. Kinnell, BMJ 2000;321:1594–7*)

A somewhat stranger perspective on the whole tragic affair appears in this next article. The author, Kinnell, who is a retired psychiatrist, discussed serial homicide by the medical profession.

Kinnell discussed that, as a profession, worldwide we account for more notorious murderers than any other profession. He gives a historical perspective over the decades of other such cases. Listed below are a few points of interest:

Needless to say, this will not be a 'Hot Topic', but a snippet from the article has nonetheless been included. This is partly because I was surprised to find it was published at all, in such volatile times.

For those of you who are interested please feel free to read the full article, otherwise I have quoted a few points:

✓ The previous BMA chairman, among others, is on record as saying that Harold Shipman is unique, yet medicine has arguably thrown up more serial killers than all the other professions put together

✓ Nursing comes a close second

✓ Dentistry too has had its notorious characters

✓ Among veterinarians, homicide seems to be almost unknown

✓ The medical profession seems to attract some people with a pathological interest in the power of life and death

✓ Doctors have been responsible for killing not only patients and strangers but members of their own family

✓ The political killers par excellence were the Nazi doctors and the Japanese doctors engaged in biological warfare comparative over the decade of cancer such cases. Listed below are new joint statements.

The doctors say this will result in a major policy swing to see from the country has nonetheless been resisted. This is partly because it is not surprised to find a way bypassed at all in which these cases arise.

Reference: If you think this intervention connected with a read log from a verbal emphysema I have quoted a few pts at 43%.

The previous BMA resolutions on one other law on record as saying that Harold Shipman is a difficult one matters has emphasis the way information concludes that all the patients' missions still repeated, but not forced a close shave.

- children is forced that is more common among
- young infirm and on more severe cases older actually
- the methods and not to seem to be attract of the people whose religion is mixed in the power of... and death.
- Doctors have been persuaded the voting for only patients and families of the effect of their own death.
- The culture which some reflects a perhaps the true culture such as physician is one improved death; he says.

CHAPTER 12:

MEDICINE AND THE INTERNET

Chapter 12: Medicine and the Internet

Typing the word 'health' into a well-known search engine will throw up almost 54 million relevant websites!

Increasingly, patients are now using the Internet to search for detailed information about their medical condition; they can obtain a second opinion from a 'cyberdoc' and can also check with various patient support groups about their best treatment options. The knowledge gained can then be used to challenge their doctor during subsequent consultations, which may then affect the doctor–patient relationship.

What makes the Internet attractive?

As part of their everyday work, doctors and other healthcare professionals need to access information. The Internet accelerates and broadens such provision. Patients, too, often want more information and they can search for remedies on the Internet.

It has been estimated that more than 25 million people use the Internet to search for health information. Medical information is thought to be one of the most retrieved types of information on the Web. More Internet users have sought medical information on the Web than have shopped online, looked up share prices or checked sports scores (*BMJ 2002;324:567*)! Recent surveys have shown that 40–54% of patients access medical information via the Internet, and that this information affects their choice of treatment.

Through the Internet, patients not only have access to almost as much information as clinicians, but they are also starting to provide advice to other patients through websites that they host and manage. Even children can provide information to their peers, their parents and clinicians.

Is there any regulation of the information available on the Internet?

A major concern is the reliability of the information accessed, opinions offered, claims made and materials supplied by the Internet. The NHS Plan sets out its intention for patients to have 'greater access to authoritative information about how they can care for themselves', including the quality of information of governmental related websites. In addition, the European Commission has introduced a kitemark to validate the quality of information on health websites (www.medcertain. org). This will contain a set of criteria for quality, and is part of a wider programme to clarify the legal aspects of online information and promote best practice.

Along with the rapid growth of healthcare websites came a number of initiatives, both academic and commercial, that generated criteria by which to ensure or judge the quality of websites offering health information. Some of these rating instruments took the form of logos resembling 'awards' or 'seals of approval' and appeared prominently on some websites. A recent paper reviewed the instruments used to assess the quality of information available on the Internet (*BMJ 2002;324: 569–73*). This is interesting because it found that, although 51 rating instruments had been developed in the past five years, only five actually provided some information by which they could be evaluated! It also showed that many incompletely developed rating instruments continue to appear on websites providing health information, even when the organisations that gave rise to them no longer exist.

A recent study found that providing references to scientific publications or prescribing information was significantly associated with high quality (*Br J Clin Pharmacol. 2004;57:80*). Another study found that most sites on back pain can be classified more as advertising sites and are of very variable quality (*Spine 2001;26:545*).

However, the exact purpose of controlling the quality of information on the Internet remains unclear and debatable. Health information in other media has received nowhere near the amount of attention, even though the public is exposed to misleading and inaccurate information from a variety of sources (TV, radio, magazines, etc).

What is the Health on the Net Foundation?

Health on the Net Foundation (see website) is an international, non-profit-making organisation based in Geneva. It provides a database of evaluated health materials, and also promotes the use of the HON code as a self-governance initiative to help unify the quality of medical and health information available. Users of website health information displaying the HON logo can be assured that the material has been developed in accordance with these guidelines. This is the oldest, and probably best known, quality label and is currently used by over 3000 websites.

What problems may the Internet pose to healthcare professionals?

The biggest problem with obtaining health information from the Internet is that it is not always easy to decide what is reliable. As an example, one website has apparently reported the mortality rate from a certain type of bone cancer as 5%, while in reality it is closer to 75%! Only about half of medical sites are estimated to have their content reviewed by doctors. In addition, many of the sites are American where the investigations and treatments for diseases are very different to those in UK, which often adds confusion to patients.

Although data are not yet available, it is evident that clinicians can find themselves upstaged by and ill-prepared to cope with those patients who bring along information downloaded from the Internet.

More resources are needed to study the implications of the Internet for the role of patients and clinicians, and also to ensure that the clinician–patient relationship is strengthened rather than undermined.

It has been proposed that public health practitioners and healthcare professionals should be involved in the design, dissemination and evaluation of web-based health and medical information (*Health Promot Int 2003;18:381*).

What is the NHS Net?

All GP practices should now be connected to the NHS Net. It has been proposed that Networked Electronic Health Records will be developed which will be available to all healthcare professionals 24 hours a day. All appointments and laboratory requests will be booked via the NHS Net and community prescribing will also go electronic, with pharmacists accepting prescriptions via the Net. An electronic library with health information for both the public and professionals will be available on the NHS Net.

The main concern of all this is confidentiality. It is, however, likely to take far longer to be running smoothly than the time proposed by the Government!

What are the problems with e-mail consultations?

The GPs' Committee has recently produced a guide to online consulting (*Consulting in the Modern World*). This warns practices that electronic communications systems could seriously damage the consultation process, may increase workload and also leave GPs open to legal action. It states that e-mail exchanges are best suited to arranging repeat prescriptions or booking appointments. In addition, GPs are warned to always be wary of responding to patients who are abroad as this could potentially cause conflicts between overseas regulatory bodies and the General Medical Council.

The GMC recently found two doctors guilty of serious professional misconduct through their provision of services over the Internet. The first involved a private doctor who recommended weekly testosterone injections through an e-mail consultation without seeing the patient or any medical records.

The GMC's *Good Medical Practice* clearly states that all doctors who provide advice to patients who are not registered with them should endeavour to provide the patient's GP with any information necessary for the continuing care of that patient. Doctors who do not tell the patient's GP, before or after providing treatment, will be responsible for providing or arranging all necessary aftercare until another doctor agrees to take over.

Are there any problems with writing for medical websites?

Doctors are less likely to face criticism for placing medical information on a website, providing it does not refer to specific cases. It is recommended that a statement be added stating that the medical advice provided is as accurate as possible, but should not be used as a substitute for advice that patients can obtain from their own doctors.

Technology is increasingly becoming integrated into modern clinical practice, so it is therefore important that all users are fully aware of any of its potential pitfalls.

USEFUL WEBSITES

www.hon.ch/ – Health on the Net Foundation
www.medcertain.org – MedCERTAIN Network

SUMMARY POINTS ON MEDICINE AND THE INTERNET

✓ Medical information is very commonly searched for over the Internet
✓ Downloaded information is often very challenging to doctors
✓ Information is often inaccurate
✓ HON code is a self-governance initiative for health sites
✓ Confidentiality is still a concern
✓ Consultations via e-mail are not encouraged by the GPs' Committee

CHAPTER 13:

COMPLEMENTARY MEDICINE

Chapter 13: Complementary Medicine

Many more people are now using complementary and alternative medicine; up to 10% of NHS physiotherapists are currently using acupuncture. It has been estimated that alternative medicine is used by about 30% of the population in the UK, which is actually much less than in Germany and the USA. Currently, it is legal for anyone in the UK to practise alternative medicine without any training (except chiropractic and osteopathy).

Many complementary practitioners claim that their treatments are more cost-effective and safer than conventional medicine; however, the evidence for this is still very scanty and weak. Most people quite rightly accept that neither safety nor efficiency can be assumed; any alternative treatment must now be supported by hard evidence. Good design of RCTs would avoid invalid results and misrepresentation of the holistic essence of complementary medicine – this is discussed in a recent *BMJ* paper (*BMJ 2002;325:832*).

A widespread lack of interest in interactions between herbal products and prescribed medicines is putting the public at risk. A study found that most pharmaceutical and herbal companies had never conducted research regarding herb–drug interactions (*Arch Int Med 2003;163: 1371*).

Many patients believe that doctors prescribe too many medicines. Some also suspect that medicines are either addictive or lose some of their efficacy with regular use. Patients also fear the safety of medicines; especially with scares about adverse effects and withdrawal of some medicines from the market. Patients perceive treatments containing herbal agents to be 'natural' and therefore safe.

There is a huge variation in the quality of different herbal medicinal preparations. Herbal remedies are sold as food supplements in the UK and so evade any regulation of their quality and safety. In addition, any evidence of efficacy does not match the standards imposed upon other synthetic chemicals or modern biological remedies. The Medical and Healthcare products Regulatory Agency has produced a report that gives an overview of the safety problems arising with herbal medicinal products.

Practitioners of traditional Chinese medicine have agreed to cooperate with the Department of Health to improve the safety of traditional medicines after concerns that they may contain potentially toxic or carcinogenic ingredients.

The Committee on Safety of Medicines (CSM) have found banned substances such as mercury and arsenic in traditional Chinese medicines sold in the UK, despite previous warnings. Some medicines also contained steroids, even though the label did not declare it. Banned products containing the herb aristolochia, which has been associated with two cases of kidney disease in the UK, are also still being offered for sale.

St John's wort

St John's wort (*Hypericum perforatum*) is an increasingly popular choice for the treatment of depression, and there is plenty of evidence which shows that hypericum is as effective as imipramine in the treatment of mild to moderate depression (*BMJ 2000;321:536–9*). In addition, the side-effects are less when compared with imipramine, but as yet there have been no randomised controlled trials comparing SSRIs with St John's wort. The use of St John's wort is more limited than initially thought as it is a liver inducer and therefore reduces levels of digoxin, carbamazepine, warfarin and the oral contraceptive pill. It has numerous interactions with other drugs, which patients should be warned of before starting it.

However, a randomised controlled trial involving 200 adults has actually shown St John's wort to be ineffective against major depression (*JAMA 2001;285:1978–86*). This obviously highlights the need for further RCTs before St John's wort can confidently be recommended for patients with depression.

Ginkgo biloba

The published evidence suggests that ginkgo is of questionable use for treating memory loss and tinnitus, but, that it has some effect on both dementia and intermittent claudication (*Ann Int Med 2002;136:42–53*). It is, however, also a potent inhibitor of platelet-activating factor, so increasing the risk of intracerebral haemorrhage in those people taking aspirin and warfarin. The recommended dosage for use in dementia is 120–240 mg standardised extract of ginkgo three times a day (equivalent to 200–250 mg ginkgo leaf tds). Tablets need to be taken for 4–6 weeks before any positive effect is noted.

Phytoestogens

Phytoestrogen supplements have been topical recently in view of the adverse publicity regarding hormone-replacement therapy. Although dietary supplements containing isoflavones are widely used as alternatives to hormonal therapies for hot flashes, there is still a paucity of data supporting their efficacy. One study compared the efficacy and safety of two dietary supplements derived from red clover with placebo in symptomatic menopausal women (*JAMA 2003; 290:207*). Neither supplement was found to have had a clinically important effect on hot flashes or other symptoms of the menopause.

Butterbur

This has been found to be as effective as cetirizine for treating hayfever but with fewer side-effects (*BMJ 2002;324:144–6*).

Saw Palmetto

This seems to be about as effective as finasteride for symptoms of benign prostatic hyperplasia.

Agnus castus

This is effective for treating PMS; 50% of women show improvement (*BMJ 2001;322:134–7*).

Other herbal remedies

There is an excellent Bandolier review of herbal medicines, available on their website. Other herbal treatments that seem to be effective include feverfew for treating migraine, ginger as an anti-emetic (particularly useful in pregnancy) and garlic for cholesterol and BP reduction.

Is there any good evidence available to support homoeopathy?

There is currently insufficient evidence that homeopathy is clearly efficacious for the treatment of any single clinical condition. Randomised trials have not been independently replicated for many of the conditions treated in homeopathic practice, such as depression, fatigue and eczema. However, many people have reported numerous benefits from homeopathy.

A recent study carried out by the NHS Centre for Reviews and Dissemination (based at York University) reviewed data from over 200 randomised clinical trials of homeopathy, but the data that did exist were of poor quality and came from trials that were often deeply flawed. Common problems included under-powered studies, failure to analyse by intention to treat and failure to use allocation concealment. Some of the published systematic reviews are criticised for pooling clinically heterogenous data.

Despite many longstanding doubts, homeopathic remedies remain widely used in the NHS. There are five homeopathic hospitals and it has been estimated that 20% of GP practices provide access to homeopathy (*BMJ 2002;324:565*). A BBC telephone survey in 1999 suggested that 470,000 people take homeopathic remedies in the United Kingdom each year.

Results of a small randomised controlled trial failed to show that homeopathic arnica had any advantage compared with placebo in reducing postoperative pain, bruising and swelling in patients having elective hand surgery. (*J R Soc Med 2003;96:60*).

Most trials of homeopathic medicines do not individualise treatment, which is obviously the hallmark of homeopathic practice. Moreover, randomisation and blinding of participants substantially distorts the context of homeopathic prescribing, thus potentially weakening its effect. There is much debate that a lack of supporting evidence does not mean these treatments are ineffective.

The Medical and Healthcare products Regulatory Agency has launched the website 'Herbal Safety News', which provides a convenient reference source by bringing together the latest issues about complementary medicine. This website also includes information on possible interactions with herbal remedies.

It is unlikely that complementary therapies will become more available within the NHS as further studies are done and the therapies evaluated properly.

USEFUL WEBSITES

www.medical-acupuncture.co.uk – British Medical Acupuncture Society
www.acupuncture.org.uk – British Acupuncture Council
www.bsmdh.org – British Society of Medical and Dental Hypnosis
www.osteopathy.org.uk – Osteopathic Information Service
www.mca.gov.uk/ourwork/licensingmeds/herbalmeds/herbalsafety.htm
– Medicines Control Agency website
www.york.ac.uk/inst/crd – homoeopathy report

SUMMARY POINTS FOR COMPLEMENTARY MEDICINE

✓ 30% of the UK population use complementary medicine
✓ Lack of good supportive RCTs
✓ Contents of herbal remedies vary widely
✓ Need to consider implications on doctor–patient relationship

CHAPTER 14:

MEDICOLEGAL ISSUES AND GUIDELINES

Chapter 14: Medicolegal Issues and Guidelines

General Medical Council

The General Medical Council (GMC) was established in 1858, and licenses doctors to practise in the UK under the provisions of the Medical Act 1983.

The GMC's core functions are:
- ✓ Maintaining an up-to-date register of qualified doctors
- ✓ Fostering good medical practice
- ✓ Promoting high standards of medical education
- ✓ Protecting the public from doctors whose fitness to practise is in doubt

The GMC produces a number of booklets setting out the standards which the Council expects individual doctors to follow. Of particular interest and relevance to general practice (and especially the MRCGP) are:
- ✓ *Good Medical Practice*
- ✓ *Confidentiality*
- ✓ *Consent: the ethical and legal issues*

What is 'Good Medical Practice'?

In 1995 the GMC published a comprehensive statement (or code) setting out the principles of 'Good Medical Practice', at the core of which it listed the 'Duties of a Doctor' – which should be read carefully, for the exam as well as for good clinical practice! 'Good Medical Practice' now sets the framework of the professional standards within which doctors must practise in this country. Doctors accepting GMC registration are therefore making a commitment to their patients and to their profession to practise accordingly.

The GMC has recently set out a proposed third edition of *Good Medical Practice* with the intention of preparing doctors for revalidation checks.

What are the 'Duties of a Doctor'?

Doctors as a profession have a duty to maintain a good standard of practice and care and also show respect for human life. The guidelines emphasise what is expected of a doctor in practice today; they state a doctor must, among other things:

- ✓ Make the patients their first concern
- ✓ Treat patients politely and considerately and respect their dignity and privacy
- ✓ Listen to patients and respect their views
- ✓ Give patients information in a way they can understand
- ✓ Respect the rights of patients to be fully involved in decisions about their care
- ✓ Keep their professional knowledge and skills up to date
- ✓ Recognise the limits of their professional competence
- ✓ Be honest and trustworthy
- ✓ Respect and protect confidential information
- ✓ Make sure that their personal beliefs do not prejudice their patient's care
- ✓ Act quickly to protect patients from risk if the doctor has good reason to believe himself or herself or a colleague may not be fit to practise
- ✓ Avoid abusing their position as a doctor
- ✓ Work with colleagues in the ways that best serve patients' interests

In all these matters, doctors must never discriminate unfairly against their patients or colleagues and they must always be prepared to justify their actions to them.

 USEFUL WEBSITE

www.gmc-uk.org - General Medical Council

SUMMARY POINTS FOR GENERAL MEDICAL COUNCIL

✓ GMC gives doctors licences to practise
✓ *Good Medical Practice* provides framework of professional standards
✓ *Duties of a Doctor* are very important

Complaints

Complaints are a fact of life; the best approach is to manage them quickly and efficiently. Failure to satisfy a complainant at an early stage often results in the entrenchment of positions, and therefore ultimately demands a much greater investment of time in resolving the conflict. Complaints in general practice are increasing, and have been estimated to have increased threefold over the past 10 years. It is difficult to obtain exact figures because the majority of complaints are dealt with 'in-house' so are only recorded in the practice records.

The GMC guidance regarding complaints states that: 'Patients who complain about the care or treatment they have received have a right to expect a prompt, open, constructive and honest response. This will include an explanation of what has happened, and where appropriate, an apology. You must not allow a patient's complaint to prejudice the care or treatment you provide or arrange for that patient.'

What are common complaints in primary care?

The majority of complaints in primary care are dealt with promptly and efficiently, with minimal repercussions.

Common complaints include:
- ✓ Complications of requests for visits
- ✓ Prescribing errors
- ✓ Delay or missed diagnosis
- ✓ Delay in referral
- ✓ Failure to explain investigation or treatment plans
- ✓ Breach of confidentiality
- ✓ Failure to seek consent
- ✓ Unacceptable attitude on the part of professionals

What is the complaints procedure?

The new NHS patient complaints procedures were introduced in April 1996 and have certain key objectives:
- ✓ Ease of access for patients and complainants
- ✓ A thorough and local resolution phase
- ✓ Fairness for both complainants and staff
- ✓ Investigation of complaints entirely separately from any subsequent disciplinary proceedings

The process for dealing with complaints is relatively simple:
- ✓ The first stage is local resolution, to resolve the issue within the practice
- ✓ The second stage is an independent review
- ✓ The third stage is review by the Health Service Commissioner (Ombudsman) if requested by either the complainant or the doctor

How are complaints dealt with in primary care?

All GPs are now required under the terms of service to operate a practice-based complaints procedure. A complaints manager should be appointed within each practice (usually the practice manager). The in-house procedure must be:
- ✓ Practice-owned and supported by all staff
- ✓ Adequately publicised with detailed written information

When are complaints dealt with?

All complaints must:
- ✓ Be dealt with at the time, if a verbal complaint
- ✓ Be acknowledged within two working days
- ✓ Br given a full written response and explanation within 10 working days

Complainants should always be invited to discuss the matter in an attempt to resolve it at an early stage.

USEFUL WEBSITE

www.doh.gov.uk/NHScomplaintsreform

SUMMARY POINTS FOR COMPLAINTS

✓ Complaints are common
✓ They should be resolved promptly
✓ Complaints procedure is simple to follow
✓ Most complaints are dealt with 'in-house'

Confidentiality

Confidentiality is both a legal and ethical principle and is the cornerstone of medical practice. Confidentiality is, in theory, a very straightforward issue; however, translating it into practice often proves problematic. Confidentiality issues are far the commonest reason for doctors to contact medicolegal advisers for independent expert advice.

Practitioners have a professional obligation to protect confidentiality and the presumption should always be made that all information is confidential. It is only under extreme circumstances (eg legal or moral duty) that confidentiality can be breached.

When can doctors disclose information without consent?

This question often crops up in the oral examination.

Disclosure of personal information without consent, or against a patient's wishes, should only occur in the most exceptional circumstances; it may be justified when failure to do so may expose the patient or others to a risk of death or serious harm. Consent should be sought prior to disclosure where third parties are exposed to a risk so serious that it outweighs the patient's privacy interest. However, if this is not practicable, the information should be disclosed promptly to an appropriate person or authority.

This can occur in the following circumstances:
- ✓ Patient with an illness that is placing others at substantial risk (eg HIV infection)
- ✓ Patients continuing to drive against medical advice (see later)
- ✓ Where disclosure may assist in the prevention, detection or prosecution of a serious crime
- ✓ Death certificates
- ✓ Statutory requirement (eg the notification of communicable diseases)
- ✓ Following an order by a judge or presiding officer of a court
- ✓ When the patient is unable to give consent and it is in the patient's best interests (eg to relatives)

The GMC clearly states: 'Doctors who decide to disclose confidential information must be prepared to explain and justify their decision to the patient, if appropriate, and to the GMC and the courts, if called on to do so.'

Under which circumstances can doctors disclose information to the DVLA?

The Driver and Vehicle Licencing Agency (DVLA) is legally responsible for deciding if a person if medically unfit to drive, and patients have a legal duty to inform the DVLA of any medical condition that affects their ability to drive. The patient's doctor must make sure the patient understands that their medical condition may impair their ability to drive.

If patients are incapable of understanding the advice (eg dementia) the DVLA must be informed immediately.

If a patient refuses to inform the DVLA the doctor should make every reasonable effort to persuade the person to stop driving, which may even include telling the next of kin. If the patient cannot be persuaded to stop driving the doctor should then disclose the relevant medical information immediately, in confidence, to the medical advisor of the DVLA. Before giving the information to the DVLA, the patient should be informed of the doctor's decision to do so. Once the DVLA has been informed, a letter should be written to the patient confirming that the disclosure has been made.

What is the Data Protection Act 1998?

This Act came into force in March 2000 and has significant implications for all healthcare professionals, and it is important to be aware of the main provisions of this Act.

The Act means that:
- ✓ Patients are entitled to see all their manual and computer medical records
- ✓ All health records are now disclosable (previous deadline of 1 November 1991 under the Access to Health Records Act no longer applies)
- ✓ Application to do this should be made by written request

- ✓ Applicants can inspect his/her own record or can request a readable copy
- ✓ The data must be disclosed within 40 days of receipt of the request
- ✓ A data controller can exclude information that breaches the confidentiality of, or relates to, a third party who has not consented to disclosure
- ✓ Disclosure may be withheld if it would be likely to 'cause serious harm to the physical or mental health or condition of the subject or any other person'

USEFUL WEBSITE

www.dvla.gov.uk – Medical standard of fitness to drive

SUMMARY POINTS FOR CONFIDENTIALITY

- ✓ Confidentiality must always be respected
- ✓ Should only be breached in extreme circumstances
- ✓ Data Protection Act has many implications

Consent

Consent is a fundamental principle of medical law. Most doctors are aware of the importance of obtaining consent from their patients, but many are uncertain about what consent actually means and also fear that their instincts about what is right may not be enough to protect them from a legal challenge.

The case law on consent has evolved significantly over the past decade. There are useful guidelines about English law regarding consent for examination and treatment on the department of health Website (www.doh.gov.uk/consent).

The GMC has issued guidance on seeking patients' consent, which all registered practitioners in the UK should be aware of when counselling patients. For consent to be valid, three conditions must be satisfied. First, the patient must be competent. Second, he or she must have sufficient information to make an informed choice and third, the consent must be given voluntarily.

Doctors must respect the right of their patients to be fully involved in decisions about their care. Wherever possible, they must be satisfied, before providing treatment or investigating a patient's condition, that: the patient has understood what is proposed and why; understands any significant risks or side-effects associated with it; and has given consent.

Any competent adult has the right to give or withhold consent to an examination, investigation or treatment. Consent may be implied, oral or written. Consent should be based on information patients want to know and ought to know about their condition and treatment. This information should include:

- ✓ Details of the diagnosis and prognosis
- ✓ Results of undergoing treatment or refusing treatment
- ✓ Risks of uncertainties of treatment
- ✓ Possible complications of treatment

Patients may change their mind and withdraw their consent at any time. It should also be noted that no person can give consent for another adult; this is often not realised by many healthcare professionals.

What is meant by a 'competent adult'?

A competent adult must be able to:
- ✓ Understand the nature and purpose of treatment
- ✓ Understand the benefits, risks and alternatives
- ✓ Understand the consequences of refusal
- ✓ Retain the information long enough to make an effective decision
- ✓ Make a free choice

Any mentally competent adult can refuse treatment for any reason (rational or irrational) or for no reason at all, even if doing so may result in his or her own death. In addition, a competent pregnant woman may refuse any treatment, even if it would be detrimental to the fetus.

What about consent for incompetent adults?

For an incompetent adult, the doctor should:
- ✓ Act in the patient's best interests
- ✓ Attempt to ascertain the patient's past wishes
- ✓ Review the medical and social knowledge of the patient's background, culture and religion
- ✓ Consult relatives, friends and carers
- ✓ Consider the option which least restricts the patient's future choices

What is the Human Rights Act?

A recent important development is the Human Rights Act 1998 which came into force in October 2000. It is a momentous development in the constitutional history of the UK, and doctors need to take it seriously.

Issues about consent and confidentiality are likely to be affected. Teenagers should have greater autonomy in making decisions about whether to accept or refuse treatment. Parents of children who do not want certain types of treatment on religious or other grounds should have more power to determine what happens to their infant children. In addition, the Act should give patients greater opportunities to obtain information.

Patients will be able to challenge lengthy delays in treatment by the NHS. Elderly people can no longer be subjected to arbitrary 'do not resuscitate' orders in hospital or to degrading treatment in nursing homes. Drug companies too will be vigilant in protecting their rights to property and freedom of speech: bans on direct-to-consumer advertising will almost certainly be challenged. Health professionals will also be able to claim protection under the Act. Junior doctors forced to work long shifts may claim the benefit of Article 4.

Can children give their own consent?

Young people aged 16- and 17-years-old are presumed to have the competence to give consent for themselves. The Fraser (previously Gillick) ruling clarifies the legal position of treating children under the age of 16 years without parental consent – they may now give their consent if they are mature enough to understand the nature, purpose and possible consequences, risks and benefits of their decision and are not making the decision under duress.

Ideally, the child's parents will be involved. If a competent child consents to treatment, a parent cannot override that consent. Legally, a parent can consent if a competent child refuses, but it is likely that taking such a serious step will be rare.

What about consent for children who lack capacity to consent?

Consent can be given on a child's behalf by any one person with parental responsibility or by the court. The Children's Act 1989 describes who may have parental responsibility. These people include:

✓ The child's parents if they are married to each other at the time of conception or birth

✓ The child's mother (but not the father) if they were not so married, unless the father has acquired parental responsibility via a court order or a parental responsibility order or the couple subsequently marry

✓ The child's legally appointed guardian

✓ A person in whose favour the court has made a residence order

✓ A local authority designated in a care order of the child

Failure to obtain a suitable consent may open a doctor to a GMC complaint, a civil claim or even criminal charges.

USEFUL WEBSITES

www.gmc-uk.org – GMC website
www.doh.gov.uk/consent – Reference Guide to Consent for Examination or Treatment, Department of Health

SUMMARY POINTS FOR CONSENT

✓ Valid consent must always be obtained
✓ Competent adults can change their mind about consent
✓ Children are able to give their consent
✓ The Human Rights Act 1998 may affect consent and confidentiality issues

Medical Negligence

It is widely known that the number of medical litigation cases continues to rise. The Medical Defence Union's (MDU's) recent figures indicate an annual increase in litigation of 15%.

To pursue a medical negligence claim a patient has to prove, on the balance of probability (ie meaning more likely than not), three things:

✓ The doctor owed a duty of care
✓ There was a breach of that duty
✓ Harm followed as a result

What is the Bolam standard?

Independent medical doctors use the 'Bolam' standard to assess the doctor's clinical management. This means that the doctor has acted in a way that would be in agreement with a responsible body of doctors practising in the same field, and does not have to be the standard of the majority.

The Bolam test is another tenet of medical law which may be reviewed. This test defines the standard of care that doctors must meet, if they are not to be negligent. Patients' lawyers are keen to argue that it should not be a sufficient defence to a medical accident (especially when life is lost) to say that other responsible professionals would have done the same thing.

However, in cases such as Bolitho and Pearce, the courts have said they will depart from the professional practice approach if they see fit, the ultimate tests being what the court itself thinks was a reasonable amount of information to give the patient. This obviously leaves an element of doubt, as doctors cannot guess what the courts are going to say.

What is the commonest reason for a medical negligence claim?

A recent review of all claims involving GPs by the MDU found that almost half (45.5%) of all settled claims were related to a delay in a patient's diagnosis. However, a delay in diagnosis per se is not necessarily negligent, provided that the clinical management can be shown to be competent and reasonable.

However, the main problems are usually:

✓ Failure to examine properly
✓ Inadequate follow-up arrangements
✓ Lack of appropriate investigations
✓ Reports misfiled in the notes
✓ Poor communication with colleagues and patients
✓ Poor medical record keeping

The increase in litigation in the UK does not reflect changing standards of clinical practice, which remains very high, but rather an increase in patient's expectations and their tendency to resort to litigation. The majority of claims do not go beyond disclosure of medical records, and less than 5% get as far as a court hearing.

 SUMMARY POINTS FOR NEGLIGENCE

✓ Bolam standard often still used
✓ Most claims are due to delayed diagnosis
✓ Harm must result for a negligence claim

Guidelines

Clinical guidelines have increasingly become a familiar part of clinical practice. They have been defined as 'systematically developed statements to assist practitioner and patient decisions about appropriate healthcare for specific clinical circumstances.' The *BMJ* has published a series of four articles on issues in the development and use of clinical guidelines which are still useful to read (*BMJ 1999;318:527–30, 593–6, 661–4, 728–30*). Clinical guidelines are only one option for improving the quality of care. They do, however, have both potential risks and harms.

Guidelines should be practical, realistic and based on valid up-to-date evidence. They should also be easily accessible to practitioners, and should ideally be adapted to suit the local target population. They should always be practical and take into consideration the available resources needed for them to be successfully implemented. A poor example of this is the BTS guidelines for COAD where routine spirometry is recommended.

The successful introduction of guidelines is dependent on many factors, including their clinical context and the methods used for developing, disseminating and implementing them. One survey revealed that although 45% of GPs had seen the National Osteoporosis Guidelines, only 22% had ever used them in their clinical practice (*Osteoporos Rev 1999;7:21–3*). This reflects the major difference between dissemination and implementation of guideline recommendation.

What are NICE guidelines?

The National Institute for Clinical Excellence was introduced in 1999 to appraise new technologies, including drugs, and decide which should be used in the NHS. Its other functions are to produce guidelines and encourage quality improvent. A recent 'Education and Debate' article in the *BMJ* considers what NICE needs to succeed (*BMJ 2002;324:842–5*). This article states that NICE can only fulfil its promise if its guidance is implemented by a health service that supports those changes NICE promotes – which is not the case currently.

No information has been published to date on the implementation by the NHS of NICE's guidance, so it is still not possible to conclude how successful (or unsuccessful) NICE has been in the overall cost-effectiveness and appropriateness of the interventions it discusses.

What are the problems with NICE?

The Consumer's Association has strongly criticised the work of NICE to a House of Commons inquiry. It said they had found 'serious flaws' in all nine of the documents it had reviewed.

The analysis was carried out by the *Drug and Therapeutics Bulletin*, which found the various guidelines, including those for influenza, type 2 diabetes, motor neurone disease and obesity, unreliable. In some cases there were weaknesses in the way evidence about treatments had been collated, interpreted and extrapolated. In others, NICE had looked at treatments in isolation and not at alternative options or previous advice.

The deputy editor of the *Drug and Therapeutics Bulletin* said, 'The NICE guidance issued so far appears to raise as many problems as it seeks to solve'.

Another concern is that because all PCTs are now compelled to implement NICE recommendations, the use of other effective treatments that have not yet been reviewed by the body may be cut, to contain costs. The NHS at a local level will probably have to dent other services' funding in order to fund NICE's recommendations. This will apply both to a specific intervention for which there is no NICE guidance and to whole services for which guidance is never likely (such as those for people with learning disabilities). By focusing on isolated, usually expensive new treatments, NICE is in danger of ignoring the wider picture; for example, in terms of improving quality of life for the elderly, demented patient, is it better to fund expensive medication or to improve the quality of nursing homes?

Another fundamental problem with NICE is that there is denial about one of its main functions, ie rationing.

In the *BMJ* editorial, it was suggested that instead of NICE, we have a body that is directly accountable to the public, more distanced from politics and from pharmaceutical companies (remember the zanamivir fiasco), more open about rationing, uses an ethical framework and looks at the whole picture. However, this is very unlikely to happen and it seems that NICE is here to stay.

What are the benefits of guidelines?

✓ Improve the consistency of care
✓ Empower patients to make more informed choices
✓ Improve the quality of clinical decisions
✓ Can improve efficacy (save money)
✓ Reduce inappropriate practice

What are the problems with guidelines?

✓ Recommendations may be wrong
✓ May be biased
✓ May be inflexible and not relate to individual patients
✓ Evidence used to write the guidelines is not always from appropriate, well-designed studies
✓ Can be time-consuming to use
✓ Need to be updated regularly
✓ Do not address all the uncertainties of clinical practice

What is the role of guidelines in court?

Guidelines could be introduced to a court by an expert witness as evidence of accepted and customary standards of care, but they cannot be introduced as a substitute for expert testimony. Courts are unlikely to adopt standards of care advocated in clinical guidelines as legal 'gold standards' because the mere fact that a guideline exists does not of itself establish that compliance with it is reasonable in the circumstances, or that non-compliance is negligent.

How easy is it to comply with guidelines?

A study published in the *Br J Gen Pract* has highlighted that it is not always easy to comply with guidelines, even if they are well-accepted guidelines. It showed that GPs targeted their actions regarding treatment for their patients with hypertension at a diastolic BP of 100 mmHg rather than at the recommended guideline of 90 mmHg, despite being aware of the guidelines (*Br J Gen Pract 2001;51:9–14*).

Conversely, evaluation of clinical guidelines on the management of infertile couples has demonstrated that guidelines can lead to an improvement in GPs' performance (*BMJ 2001;322:1282–4*).

Difficulties with always adhering to guidelines can be appreciated when considering the following clinical scenario:

A 68-year-old patient with type 2 diabetes presents at the end of a busy Friday afternoon surgery with a sore throat. You notice her blood pressure has not been taken for the past two years. You take it and find her BP to be 146/92 mmHg! There are probably certain questions you might ask yourself when faced with a similar patient:

✓ What shall I tell the patient about their blood pressure?

✓ Is it likely that this patient's BP is consistently raised?

✓ Shall I arrange for her to have blood tests/ECG?

✓ Shall I start medication now with all its potential risks/side-effects?

✓ How will she react to taking another medication when she is already taking other regular medication?

✓ Will this patient realistically respond to advice about weight loss/lifestyle/smoking when she never has before?

✓ What is her compliance with medication really like?

Although you know the BHS guidelines it is not always that easy to stick to them!

Guidelines are essentially written for the management of patient populations rather than for individuals. They will not address all the uncertainties of current clinical practice and should be seen as only one strategy that can help improve the quality of care that patients receive. Although guidelines are meant to tackle variations in practice there is always a risk of standardising practice around the average, which is not necessarily always the best for every clinical situation (*BMJ 1993; 43:146-51*).

SUMMARY POINTS FOR GUIDELINES

✓ Only one option for improving care

✓ Should ideally suit the local target population

✓ Numerous benefits and drawbacks

✓ Do not address all the uncertainties of clinical practice

CHAPTER 15:

ADVANCE DIRECTIVES AND END-OF-LIFE DECISIONS

Chapter 15: Advance Directives and End-of-Life Decisions

Advance Directives

Definition:

An advance directive gives patients the legal right to give or withhold consent to specific medical treatments in advance of becoming incompetent. (*Advance Statements about Medical Treatment – Code of Practice Report of the British Medical Association, April 1995.*)

From October 1999, people in England and Wales have been able to appoint a friend or relative to take healthcare decisions if they lose the ability to make their own decisions.

✓ This is termed a 'Continuing Power of Attorney' and allows the named person, called the 'proxy decision maker' to make decisions regarding the health and welfare of that person.

✓ Competence is best confirmed by having a person's signature witnessed by two people, one of whom should be a doctor capable of attesting to the person's state of mind.

 Advance Statements about Medical Treatment – Code of Practice Report of the British Medical Association, April 1995

Current legal position

✓ In 1997, the Government for England and Wales announced that it believed there to be a clear need for reform of the law to improve and clarify decision-making processes for people unable to make decisions for themselves, or for people who cannot communicate their decisions

✓ It based this view on the extensive work the English Law Commission had undertaken in the preceding six years

✓ The Law Commission had therefore investigated and proposed improvements to the law in this area, including a proposal to introduce legislation to put advance directives on a statutory footing. This was one of the issues on which the Government consulted in 1997

The BMA's Code of Practice is a response to the House of Lords Select Committee on Medical Ethics, which in 1994 called for a Code of Practice on advance directives for health professionals.

✓ Published two years before the Government's consultation, it describes the common law and the BMA's views on advance decisions

✓ Following its consultation, in October 1999 the Government published detailed proposals for law reform

✓ The Lord Chancellor's Department stated its intention to legislate to give statutory recognition to the definitions of capacity and best interests, and to clarify the basis on which decisions may be made on behalf of incapacitated adults

✓ It also proposed to make provision for the appointment of proxies entitled to take medical treatment decisions

✓ Advance directives, however, are not part of the legislative plans. Instead, the Government published clear statements of the present legal position:

'The current law and medical practice is as follows. It is a general principle of law and medical practice that all adults have the right to consent to or refuse medical treatment. Advance statements are a means for patients to exercise that right by anticipating a time when they may lose the capacity to make or communicate a decision.

Adults with capacity have the right to refuse or withdraw their consent to medical treatment. We do not accept that the decision has either to be reasonable or has to be justified to anyone apart from the individual who is making the decision. It follows that the Government respects the right of people with capacity to be able to define, in advance, which medical procedures they will and will not consent to at a time when that individual has become incapable of making or communicating that decision.'

BMA SUMMARY

✓ Although not binding on health professionals, advance statements deserve thorough consideration and respect

✓ Where valid and applicable, the advance directives (refusals) must be followed. Health professionals consulted by people wishing to formulate an advance statement or directive should take all reasonable steps to provide accurate factual information about the various treatment options and their implications

✓ Where an unknown and incapacitated patient presents for treatment, some checks should be made concerning the validity of any directive refusing life-prolonging treatment. In all cases, it is vital to check that the statement or refusal presented is that of the patient being treated and that it has not been withdrawn

✓ If the situation is not identical to the one described in the advance statement or refusal, treatment providers may still be guided by the general spirit of the statement if this is evident. It is advisable to contact any person nominated by the patient as well as the GP to clarify the patient's wishes. If there is doubt as to what the patient intended, the law requires the exercise of a best interests' judgement

✓ If an incapacitated person is known to have held sustained and informed objections to all or some treatment in the past, even though these have not been formally recorded, health professionals may not be justified in proceeding. This applies even in an emergency

✓ If witnessed and made at a time when the patient was competent and informed, such objections may constitute an oral advance directive. Health professionals will need to consider how much evidence is available about the patient's decisions and how convincing it seems. All members of the healthcare team can make a useful contribution to this process

✓ In the absence of any indication of the patient's wishes, there is a common law duty to give appropriate treatment to incapacitated patients when the treatment is clearly in their best interests

BMA CHECKLIST FOR WRITING AN ADVANCE STATEMENT

In drawing up an advance statement you must ensure, as a minimum, that the following information is included:

✓ Full name

✓ Address

✓ Name and address of general practitioner

✓ Whether advice was sought from health professionals

✓ Signature

✓ Date drafted and reviewed

✓ Witness signature

✓ A clear statement of your wishes, either general or specific

✓ Name, address and telephone number of your nominated person, if you have one

Other sources:

Lord Chancellor's Department. 'Making decisions' The Government's proposals for making decisions on behalf of mentally incapacitated adults. London, Stationery Office, October 1999

End-of-Life Decisions

✓ The Dutch have done most of the work in this field
✓ Doctors make end-of-life decisions in about 40% of deaths
✓ 75% involve withdrawal or withholding treatment
✓ Doses of opiates likely to end life given in 25% of cases

Guidelines by BMA 1999 – Withholding and withdrawing life-prolonging treatment

Key principles

✓ Life cannot be preserved at all costs – treatment must be more of a benefit than a burden
✓ Both artificial nutrition and hydration constitute medical treatment
✓ Competent patients have the legal right to refuse treatment
✓ Where patients cannot express their view, doctors must take account of previously expressed wishes, the likelihood of any improvement and the likelihood of the patient experiencing severe pain or suffering
✓ Close cooperation with the other professionals in the team is vital in decision-making
✓ All proposals to withdraw or withhold artificial nutrition and hydration should be formally reviewed by a senior clinician who is not part of the team

General Medical Council. Withholding and withdrawing life-prolonging treatments: good practice in decision-making. London, GMC, 2002

✓ Following the BMA guidelines above, the GMC laid out their directives in 2002
✓ New guidelines on end-of-life decisions
✓ The guidelines were prompted by concerns regarding the withdrawal of treatment from elderly patients and by inappropriate 'do not attempt resuscitation' orders

✓ Sets out the legal and ethical framework for taking decisions
✓ The guidelines remind doctors that patients who are mentally competent have a legal right to refuse treatment even if the outcome is certain death
✓ Patients must not be assumed to lack mental capacity just because their decision might seem irrational or seems to doctors not to be in their best interests
✓ Doctors with a conscientious objection to a decision not to start or to continue with life-prolonging treatment may withdraw from the patient's care, but must hand the care over without delay to another suitably qualified colleague so that patient care does not suffer
✓ Guidance takes account of the differences among the UK jurisdictions of England and Wales, Scotland, and Northern Ireland
✓ In Scotland, proxy decision-makers may be appointed for patients lacking the capacity to decide for themselves
✓ In England and Wales, doctors must take decisions for patients who are mentally incompetent, acting in the patient's best interests and weighing up the benefits and burdens of the proposed treatment
✓ Doctors are reminded that they must not allow factors such as the patient's age, disability or lifestyle to prejudice the choice of treatment

'Doctrine of Double Effect'

States that if measures taken to relieve physical or mental suffering cause the death of a patient, then it is morally and legally acceptable provided the doctor's intent is to relieve distress and not to kill the patient.

In general, the doctor must make a full assessment of the patient's condition, consult with relatives, carers and other healthcare professions involved in the case, and ask for a second medical opinion either from a specialist or from another GP.

Papers

1. *Physician assisted suicide, euthanasia or withdrawal of treatment – Editorial*
(*L. R. Churchill and N. M. King, BMJ 1997;315:137–8*)

The Oregon Death with Dignity Act was passed in 1994. It allows primary care physicians to comply with a request for lethal drugs from a competent patient with less than six months to live.

Holland has become the testing ground for the world, as although assisting with requested euthanasia remains a criminal act, Dutch doctors have not been prosecuted when they follow strict guidelines.

2. *Why active euthanasia and physician assisted suicide should be legalised*
(*L. Doyal and L. Doyal, BMJ 2001;323:1079–80*)

✓ Focused around the Dianne Pretty trial (who suffered from motor neurone disease (MND)); the Court denied her the request of allowing her husband to aid her in ending her life
✓ A professor in ethics at 'Barts' wrote this editorial
✓ Argued that the moral and legal status of not saving a life through failing to treat can be the same as actively taking that life
✓ Provided the circumstances are clinically warranted, doctors should be able to withdraw life-sustaining treatment when they intend to accelerate death as well as to relieve suffering

Editorials in BMJ

Do not resuscitate (DNR) decisions
In 2000, the British Medical Association, the Resuscitation Council (UK) and the Royal College of Nursing jointly said that 'do not resuscitate' orders could be considered only after discussion with the patient or others close to the patient. Age Concern's dossier is evidence that this guideline is being flouted (they have 50 case histories of inappropriate DNR decisions).

Resuscitation after a cardiopulmonary arrest is effective in only one in five patients. Although it may be appropriate to withhold resuscitation when a patient is dying, failure to involve patients in decisions on DNR orders negates their autonomy. It is most unfair for age to be used as a criterion for withholding cardiopulmonary resuscitation. Most patients and their relatives consider that discussions about death and DNR orders are essential aspects of planning their care. It is doctors and nurses who find such discussions painful.

'Do not resuscitate' orders are increasingly used and have greater implications than merely not calling the resuscitation team.

Over two-thirds of patients with 'do not resuscitate' (DNR) orders are not involved in making these decisions. After adjustment for disease severity, prognostic factors, age and other covariates, patients given these orders are more than 30 times more likely to die, suggesting that DNR orders may reduce quality of care.

DNR orders are more commonly used in the United States, for Black people, alcohol misusers, non-English speakers and people infected with HIV, suggesting that doctors have stereotypes of who is not worth saving.

The courts' role in decisions about medical treatment

✓ Circumstances occur in which it is necessary or wise to obtain authority from a court regarding the lawfulness of proposed medical treatments when patients are incapable of consenting or have refused consent to such interventions

✓ For patients in permanent vegetative states, the courts' authority must be obtained before artificial nutrition and hydration is withdrawn

✓ In other cases, the courts can protect doctors from criticism and claims that they have acted unlawfully

✓ In the case of adults, the legal criteria are whether patients lack the capacity to give or refuse consent, and, if so, what is in their best interests; in the case of children, welfare is the paramount consideration

Dealing with children

✓ Those having parental responsibility – usually the parents – can give consent to medical treatment. If the parents refuse to give consent to treatment recommended by the doctors, it will be necessary (and possible) for the consent to be supplied instead through an order of the court

- ✓ There is a starting point that the united view of both parents is correct in identifying where their child's welfare lies
- ✓ This is cancelled out where the court finds on the evidence that their view is contrary to the welfare of the child
- ✓ It is well established that, for example, although Jehovah's Witnesses may in accordance with their religious beliefs withhold consent to blood transfusions for themselves as adults, if their children's lives are endangered the courts will provide the missing consent for the administration of blood
- ✓ When a child is able to express his or her own view, this becomes a factor in the decision about treatment. The courts have described a category of child as 'Gillick Competent' (of sufficient understanding and intelligence to understand fully the specific treatment proposed)
- ✓ A court may use its inherent jurisdiction to override the refusal of consent if satisfied that is what the welfare of the child requires

The special position of 16–18-year-olds
- ✓ Section 8 of the Family Law Reform Act 1969 applies
- ✓ Able to give consent to medical treatment as if they were adult
- ✓ It does not, however, follow that if they refuse to give their consent and are on the face of it capable of making that decision, their refusal will be determinative in the same way as it would be if they were adult
- ✓ No minor of any age has the power by refusing treatment to override a consent given by the court or by a person having parental responsibility. The child's level of competence is relevant in assessing the weight to be given to his or her views, but these views will not determine the issue
- ✓ The paramount consideration is the welfare of the child

CHAPTER 16:

MISCELLANEOUS TOPICS

Chapter 16: Miscellaneous Topics

Refugees

The issues regarding refugees, asylum seekers and immigration have all been raised in the media over the last few years. There is a tendency to blame all of society's ills on asylum-seekers and laws on asylum are getting increasingly tough; for example, the controversial section 55 of the Nationality, Immigration and Asylum (NIA) act of 2002. This came into force on 8 January 2003 and denies asylum seekers National Asylum Support Service (NASS) accomodation and financial benefits if they fail to apply for asylum as soon as reasonably practicable after their arrival in the UK. Potentially, this could mean destitution for many asylum seekers arriving in the UK. Asylum seekers affected by section 55 are still entitled to access primary or secondary healthcare services, and are eligible to apply for help with health costs (eg NHS prescriptions and dental care). In order to apply for help with health costs, an asylum seeker must complete an HCI form, available from One Stop Services or the Health Benefits Division of the NHS.

The issues of refugees are discussed in the summary below:

Refugees and primary care: tackling the inequalities
(D. Jones and P. S. Gill, BMJ 1998;317:1444–6)

This interesting article appeared in the BMJ when a large number of refugees were arriving in England from the troubles in the Balkans. As the twentieth century drew to a close, outbreaks of hatred between human population groups showed no sign of abating and conflicts continued to erupt. Families across the world found themselves forced to leave their homes and seek refuge where it could be found. Globally, there are 18 million refugees, with 230,000 living in the United Kingdom. Almost half of these live in London, where 100,000 people are refugees or awaiting confirmation of refugee status. Many refugees have health problems but experience difficulty having their needs met by the NHS. This article explores the challenges that refugees pose for primary care and suggests alternative strategies to address inequalities in the care of refugees.

- ✓ The refugee population in Britain is highly diverse and is likely to remain large as conflicts continue to occur throughout the world
- ✓ Refugees, unlike other migrants, have had to flee to escape oppression
- ✓ The refugee population is concentrated in the Greater London area, but new legislation resulting in dispersal throughout the UK
- ✓ Refugees may be vulnerable to mental health problems, yet they have difficulty communicating their needs because of language barriers
- ✓ All refugees, including asylum seekers affected by section 55, are entitled to the full range of NHS services free of charge, including registration with a GP. The only exception is that for asylum seekers who have had their application rejected, hospitals have the right to decide on whether to charge, according to the 'individual's complete circumstances'
- ✓ A strategic approach is needed to address the inequalities in primary care

What happens to refugees?

- ✓ Refugee population is not evenly spread
- ✓ Concentrated in areas where local authorities have given refugee housing a higher priority
- ✓ Legislation will result in greater dispersal of refugees, making provision of specialist services more difficult
- ✓ Part 2 of the NIA act outlines the setting up of 'accomodation centres' which should provide full-board accomodation, access to health services, education and training. The refugee council does not envisage that these centres will be established before 2005.
- ✓ 'Cultural bereavement' and coping with 'deeply disruptive change' are widely shared experiences of migration
- ✓ Refugees are distinguished from other migrants by their lack of choice
- ✓ Refugees have had to leave their countries of origin to escape persecution, imprisonment, torture or even death
- ✓ Families may have been physically separated, causing much grief
- ✓ Refugees are often preoccupied by worry about relatives left behind in their country of origin
- ✓ Many refugees, including children, have no other relatives in the UK
- ✓ Poverty and dissatisfaction with housing is widespread

Health problems

✓ A recent UK study of Iraqi refugees found that all had been separated involuntarily from some close family members

✓ 65% had a history of systematic torture during detention

✓ 29% were unable to speak any English

✓ Over 50% had significant psychological morbidity

✓ Evidence that asylum-seekers who have not yet been granted the right to remain are under particular stress

Deficiencies of primary care

✓ All refugees and asylum seekers are entitled to the full range of NHS treatment free of charge

✓ They have the right to register with a GP

✓ There is evidence that some GPs are confused about this

✓ Some patients are asked for their passports when trying to register, in fact GPs do not have the right to demand to see proof of identity

✓ What happens to patients who are unable to produce a valid passport?
  - Are they sent away?
  - Who makes these decisions?

✓ Some practices are, perhaps reluctantly, open for refugees, whereas others are effectively closed, creating neighbouring general practices with very different demographic profiles and unequal needs

✓ When refugees join a GP's list they are often registered on a temporary rather than a permanent basis

✓ This removes financial incentives to undertake immunisation and cervical smear tests

✓ Why do GPs avoid giving refugees permanent registration status?

✓ High mobility of refugees is a myth – 70% of refugees had been living in their current home for more than a year (Home Office Survey 1995)

✓ Language barriers at the reception desk and in the consultation are common

✓ Health authorities lack interpreter services, generally not available outside working hours if they do exist

✓ Telephone interpreting using 'hands free' technology may offer a solution

✓ Lack of adequate professional interpreting services presents a barrier for all non-English-speaking patients, but this barrier is larger for those with psychological and emotional difficulties

Q. If tragic mistakes are made as a result of communication failure, does the moral responsibility rest with the doctor or with a medical system that expects doctors to communicate well but fails to provide adequate resources?

Increasing spending on refugee primary care

✓ Is fully justifiable on clinical and ethical grounds

✓ Requires considerable political courage to prioritise refugees at a time when other groups in the population, such as elderly people and the mentally ill, have been identified as in need of more resources

✓ It is important to remember that many refugees who settle in Britain have made valuable contributions to society

What can be done to improve primary care for refugees?

✓ A strategic approach is required

✓ Provide intensive courses in spoken English

✓ The DoH needs to commission an information pack that includes a certificate of entitlement to NHS treatment and to develop patient-held medical records

✓ The development of a national telephone interpreting service in a range of languages is a priority

✓ A separate capitation payment for refugee patients, together with a new item of service payment linked to the duration of each professionally interpreted consultation, should be introduced

✓ Healthcare facilitators should be recruited from each specific refugee population; they could help to provide patient-held records comprising an accurate and detailed medical history and to support health promotion and screening

Conclusions

✓ The refugee population is likely to remain large

✓ High needs, especially psychological distress, combined with language barriers require a great deal of additional time in consultations

✓ GPs working in inner cities need adequate resources, especially interpreting services, and should be properly rewarded

✓ A truly effective solution requires the political will to develop a comprehensive strategy at national level

Paper

Asylum seekers and health: ABMA and Medical Foundation for the care of the victims of torture dossier

USEFUL WEBSITE

www.bma.org.uk/ap.nsf/Content/Asylum+seekers+and+health

In the joint dossier they state that:

✓ The Government should 'develop a more humane system'

✓ 'The Government's system for the handling of asylum-seekers is not focused on helping but on deterring them. Present procedures are not compassionate but punitive'

✓ 'Health care for asylum seekers in Britain is patchy, belated and often inappropriate'

✓ It contains 22 case histories, reported by doctors, that show how Britain is 'failing' in its obligations to provide healthcare for asylum seekers

✓ The cases document 'the personal cost of this failure, measured in the suffering of refugees'

✓ The Government should 'abolish vouchers and forced dispersal'. They claim that these policies put the health of asylum seekers at risk

✓ The voucher system should be scrapped in favour of cash benefits for asylum seekers

✓ Mothers water down baby milk to make their vouchers go further, and cites cases

Recent Advances in Ethics

Clinical review – Recent advances in medical ethics
(*P. A. Singer, BMJ 2000,321:282*)

This interesting review focused on the continuing evolution of medical ethics through new technology, some of which could be envisaged making good viva material. The goal of medical ethics is to improve the quality of patient care by identifying, analysing and attempting to resolve the ethical problems that arise in practice.

Review advances in five areas:
1. End-of-life care
2. Medical error
3. Priority setting
4. Biotechnology
5. Medical ethics education
+ two future issues: 'eHealth' and 'global bioethics'

1. End-of-life care
See Chapter 15

2. Medical error
The main recent advance is the development of the Tavistock principles, which serve as an ethical foundation for those working to reduce medical error.

All the Tavistock principles are relevant to the problem of medical error, but the most important are:
- ✓ Cooperation with each other and those served is imperative for those working within the healthcare delivery system
- ✓ All individuals and groups involved in healthcare, whether providing access or services, have the continuing responsibility to help improve its quality
- ✓ In developing a culture of safety, clinicians will need to act as role models for their students by applying these principles themselves the next time they encounter a medical error
- ✓ Healthcare leaders will need to 'feel personally responsible for error' and 'declare error reduction to be an explicit organisational goal and [devote] a significant proportion of the board and management agenda... to achieving this goal'

3. Priority setting

Development of an ethics framework – 'Accountability for Reasonableness' – for legitimate and fair decisions on setting priorities.

Priority setting = 'rationing' 20 years ago = 'resource allocation' 10 years ago and will be called 'sustainability' now.

The four conditions of 'Accountability for Reasonableness' are:

1. Publicity – Decisions regarding coverage for new technologies (and other limit-setting decisions) and their rationales must be publicly accessible
2. Relevance – These rationales must rest on evidence, reasons and principles that fair-minded parties (managers, clinicians, patients and consumers in general) can agree are relevant to deciding how to meet the diverse needs of a covered population under necessary resource constraints
3. Appeals – There must be a mechanism for challenge and dispute resolution regarding limit-setting decisions, including the opportunity to revise decisions in the light of further evidence or arguments
4. Enforcement – There must be either voluntary or public regulation of the process to ensure that the first three conditions are met

4. Biotechnology

✓ Emerging consensus on the acceptability of stem-cell research
✓ The UK Nuffield Council on Bioethics have issued a report supporting stem-cell research
✓ Latest in a series of important consensus documents on biotechnology, such as the 'WHO's guiding principles on medical genetics and biotechnology' and the 'Human Genome Organization's' statement on benefit sharing
✓ Stem cells are 'cells with the capacity for unlimited or prolonged self-renewal that can produce at least one type of highly differentiated descendant'
✓ The clinical potential of stem cells is enormous, including neuronal repair, haematological reconstitution and organ transplantation
✓ The problem with embryonic stem cells is that they are derived from human embryos
✓ Opponents of embryonic stem-cell research are concerned with the moral and legal status of the embryo and advocate a moratorium

✓ Proponents, however, focus on the potential benefits to patients

✓ Recent reports suggest that adult stem cells can differentiate into developmentally cell types – this would mitigate the ethical tensions related to embryonic-unrelated stem cells

5. Medical ethics education

✓ The revolution in information technology will dramatically change medical practice

✓ Many ethical issues, including confidentiality of electronic medical records and the relationship of clinical records to research and management of health systems

✓ Dramatic changes in the way doctors learn and access medical literature

Global bioethics

✓ In this era of advanced globalisation the problems of medical ethics can no longer only be viewed from the perspective of wealthy countries

✓ Global bioethics seeks to identify key ethical problems faced by the world's six billion inhabitants, and envisages solutions that transcend national borders and cultures

✓ An International Association of Bioethics has been formed and a discussion board on global bioethics has been launched

'eHealth'

✓ The revolution in information technology will dramatically change medical practice

✓ This raises many ethical issues, including how we can keep electronic medical records confidential and how we use our patient data to research and manage health systems

✓ Doctors will also dramatically change the way they learn and access medical literature

✓ A code of ethics for 'eHealth' has been developed by the Internet Healthcare Coalition, who are an organisation with representatives from industry, academic groups, government, patient and consumer organisations

USEFUL WEBSITE

www.ihealthcoalition.org/ethics/ – contains a draft of the code

CHAPTER 17:

THE CONSULTATION

Chapter 17:
The Consultation

The next group of studies covers many areas of the consultation, at the end of which we will also look at recent studies of non-attendance and telephone consultations.

1. Deprivation, psychological distress, and consultation length in general practice
(A. M. Stirling, et al, Br J Gen Pract 2001;51:456–60)

✓ Up to 40% of patients presenting to GPs are psychologically distressed as measured by screening tools, such as the General Health Questionnaire (GHQ)

✓ Of these distressed patients, doctors correctly identify about half (see previous studies)

✓ Poor mental health is a major predictor of future poor physical health

✓ Failure to diagnose and treat appropriately may promote chronicity, and the inappropriate and unnecessary referral and medical treatment characteristic of somatic fixation

✓ Correct identification of the patient's psychological problem may reduce somatisation

✓ This study aimed to examine factors associated with the presentation and recognition of psychological distress in GPs' surgeries and the interaction of these factors with consultation length

✓ It was a cross-sectional study carried out in the West of Scotland, between November 1997 and May 1998

✓ 1075 consultations of 21 full-time GPs were assessed

✓ The main outcome measures were patient psychological distress (measured by the GHQ), doctors' identification of psychological distress, consultation length and Carstairs Deprivation Category Scores

✓ They showed the mean consultation length was 8.71 minutes and the prevalence of positive GHQ scores was 44.7%. Increasing GHQ (greater psychological distress) and Lower Deprivation Category Scores (greater affluence) were associated with longer consultations

✓ Positive GHQ scoring increased with greater socioeconomic deprivation and also peaked in the 30–39-year age group

✓ Recognition of psychological distress was greater in longer consultations (there was a 50% increase in consultation length associated with a 32% increase in recognition)

✓ They concluded that increasing socioeconomic deprivation is associated with a higher prevalence of psychological distress and shorter consultations

✓ This provides further evidence to support Tudor Harts' 'inverse care law' (the availability of good-quality medical care is inversely proportional to its need) and has implications for the resourcing of primary care in deprived areas

Problems

✓ Because recruitment was by invitation, this group of doctors is not representative

✓ All the practices used were in some way involved in teaching and were therefore potentially more motivated than average

✓ It is likely that these doctors have an interest in psychological medicine

✓ This is borne out in the results, with 59% of distressed patients correctly identified as such by the doctor (which is far higher than previous studies)

✓ Bias may also have resulted from participating GPs knowing that their 'performance' was being observed

2. Preferences of patients for patient centred approach to consultation in primary care: observational study
(*P. Little, et al. BMJ 2001;322:468–72*)

✓ Consecutive patients in the waiting room of three doctors' surgeries took part

✓ One in a deprived area of a large provincial city, the second a training practice serving an urban population of a cathedral city and the third a training practice in a market town serving a mixed urban and rural population; characteristics of the sample were similar to the attending sample from the National Morbidity Survey

✓ 865 patients participated: 95% returned the questionnaire and were similar in demographic characteristic to national samples

✓ Patients were given questionnaires prior to seeing the GP asking them to agree or disagree on questions about what they wanted the doctor to do in the consultation

✓ It focused on communication (agreed with by 88–99% of patients), partnership (77–87%) and health promotion (85–89%)

✓ Fewer wanted an examination (63%), and only one-quarter wanted a prescription

✓ Patients who strongly wanted good communication were more likely to feel unwell, be high attenders and have no paid work

✓ Strongly wanting a partnership was also related to feeling unwell, worrying about the problem, high attendance and no paid work

✓ Those strongly wanting health promotion were high attenders and those worried about their problem

✓ Patients who wanted a prescription were more likely to want good communication, partnership and health promotion

✓ Patients wanting a prescription were more likely to be unmarried, have a partner with no paid work, no education beyond GCSE and be aged over 60

✓ Those wanting an examination were more likely to have no education beyond GCSE and feel worried about their problem

✓ Patients required about 3–5 minutes to complete the questionnaire before seeing the doctor, so those seeing doctors running on time (a small minority) could not be approached

✓ Time limitation meant fewer questions asked

KEY POINTS

✓ They concluded patients in primary care strongly want a patient-centred approach, with communication, partnership and health promotion

✓ Improved communication can improve satisfaction and biomedical outcomes

✓ Involving patients in partnership can have benefits without increasing their anxiety, and with the potential to reduce side-effects of prescribing

✓ Patients with a very strong preference for patient centredness are those who are vulnerable either socioeconomically or because they are feeling particularly unwell or worried

3. Patients unvoiced agendas in general practice consultations: qualitative study

(C. A. Barry, et al, BMJ 2000;320:1246–50)

✓ 20 general practices in SE England and the West Midlands
✓ 35 patients consulting 20 GPs in appointment and emergency surgeries
✓ Patient agendas was confirmed prior to the consultation
✓ The consultation was recorded and the GP interviewed the following day
✓ Patients were interviewed a week later

Results
✓ Average of five points per patient agenda
✓ Voiced agenda items were: most commonly symptoms, requests for diagnoses and prescriptions
✓ Unvoiced agenda items were: worries about possible diagnosis, what the future holds, patients' ideas about what is wrong, side-effects, not wanting a prescription and information relating to social context
✓ 4/35 patients voiced their full agendas
✓ 24 patients voiced all their symptoms, but psychosocial issues were more likely not to be mentioned
✓ Active steps should be taken in daily practice to encourage voicing of patients' agendas

4. Quality at general practice consultations: cross sectional survey

(*J. G. Howie, et al, BMJ 1999;319:738–43*)

- ✓ Questionnaire study
- ✓ 25,000 participants
- ✓ Average length of consultations was 8 minutes
- ✓ Enablement score was linked to small practices, familiarity with GP and length of the consultation
- ✓ Advocated longer consultations to promote continuity of care

5. Evolving general practice consultation in Britain: issues of length and context

(*G. K. Freeman, et al, BMJ 2002;324:880–2*)

Is there any justification for a further increase in mean time allocated per consultation in general practice?
This commissioned, systematic review involving 14 relevant papers attempts to answer the question.
In summary:

- ✓ Longer consultations are associated with a range of better patient outcomes
- ✓ Modern consultations in general practice deal with patients with more serious and chronic conditions
- ✓ Increasing patient participation means more complex interaction, which demands extra time
- ✓ Access difficulties and loss of continuity add to perceived stress and poor performance and lead to further pressure on time
- ✓ Longer consultations should be a professional priority, combined with increased use of technology and more flexible practice management to maximise interpersonal continuity
- ✓ Consistently showed that doctors with longer consultation times prescribe less and offer more advice on lifestyle and other health-promoting activities
- ✓ Longer consultations have been significantly associated with better recognition and handling of psychosocial problems and with better patient enablement

✓ Clinical care for some chronic illnesses is better in practices with longer booked intervals between one appointment and the next

✓ The most effective consultations are those in which doctors most directly acknowledge and perhaps respond to patients' problems and concerns

✓ Research on implementation is needed

6. Observational study of effect of patient centredness and positive approach on outcomes of general practice consultations

(P. Little, et al, BMJ 2001;323:908–11)

✓ This paper attempted to measure patients' perceptions of patient centredness and its relation to outcomes

✓ It was an observational study using questionnaires

✓ Three general practices in SE Hampshire took part

✓ 865 consecutive patients attending the practices were recruited

✓ Participants completed a short questionnaire before their consultation, in which they were asked to agree or disagree on a seven-point Likert scale (very strongly agree to very strongly disagree) with statements about what they wanted the doctor to do. A questionnaire after the consultation asked patients about their perception of the doctor's approach. Both questionnaires were based on the five main domains of the patient-centred model: exploring the disease and illness experience; understanding the whole person; finding common ground; health promotion; and enhancing the doctor–patient relationship.

✓ Patients were followed up after one month and the notes were reviewed after two months for re-attendance, investigation and referral

✓ Main outcome measures were patients' enablement, satisfaction and burden of symptoms

✓ Analysis identified five components:

1. Communication and partnership (a sympathetic doctor interested in a patient's worries and expectations and who discusses and agrees the problem and treatment)

2. Personal relationship (a doctor who knows the patient and their emotional needs)

3. Health promotion

4. Positive approach (being definite about the problem and when it would settle)
5. Interest in effect on patient's life

✓ Satisfaction was related to communication and partnership and a positive approach

✓ Enablement was greater with interest in the effect on life, health promotion and a positive approach

✓ A positive approach was also associated with reduced symptom burden at 1 month

✓ Referrals were fewer if patients felt they had a personal relationship with their doctor

✓ The author concluded that 'if doctors don't provide a positive, patient centred approach patients will be less satisfied, less enabled, and may have greater symptom burden and higher rates of referral.'

7. An exploration of the value of the personal doctor–patient relationship in general practice
(*K. E. Kearley, et al. Br J Gen Pract 2001;51(470):712–18*)

✓ Within the context of general practice, the opportunity exists for a personal relationship to develop between the patient and GP

✓ This has benefits for both patients and GPs:
  • Patient enablement is improved
  • Compliance with medication is increased
  • Clinical decision-making process and disclosure of psychosocial problems are facilitated
  • The doctor–patient interaction itself can be therapeutic, enhanced by feelings of trust and understanding

✓ The aims of this paper were to determine how many patients report having a personal doctor and when this is most valued, to compare the value of a personal doctor–patient relationship with that of convenience and to relate these findings to a range of patient, GP and practice variables

✓ It was a cross-sectional postal questionnaire study

✓ 960 randomly selected adult patients from a stratified random sample of 18 practices and 284 GP principals in Oxfordshire took part

✓ Qualitative interviews with patients and GPs were conducted and used to derive a parallel patient and GP questionnaire

✓ Each patient (100 from each practice) was invited to complete a questionnaire to evaluate his or her experience and views concerning personal care

✓ All GP principals currently practising in Oxfordshire were sent a similar questionnaire, which also included demographic variables

✓ The results showed that 75% of patients reported having at least one personal GP

✓ The number of patients reporting a personal GP in each practice varied from 53% to 92%

✓ Having a personal doctor–patient relationship was highly valued by patients and GPs, in particular for more serious psychological and family issues

✓ 77–88% of patients and 80-98% of GPs valued a personal relationship more than a convenient appointment

✓ For minor illness it had much less value

✓ They concluded that patients and GPs particularly value a personal doctor–patient relationship for more serious or for psychological problems. Whether a patient has a personal GP is associated with their perception of its importance and with factors that create an opportunity for a relationship to evolve

8. Long to short consultation ratio: a proxy measure of quality of care for general practice
(J. G. Howie, et al, Br J Gen Pract 1991;41:48–54)

✓ Howie, in 1991, showed that longer consultations were linked to higher patient satisfaction

✓ This was probably because the longer consultations dealt with more psychological and social issues

9. *Engaging patients in medical decision-making*
(*Editorial BMJ 2001;323:584–5*)

✓ There is a consensus that patients ought to be more involved in their own care

✓ Ethicists generally accept the principle that autonomy (what the competent, informed patient wants) trumps beneficence (what the doctor thinks best for the patient) in all but the most extreme circumstances

✓ Quality in Health Care (Sept. 2001) focused on engaging patients in medical decisions

✓ 12 articles from a MRC conference

✓ The proceedings gave a clear impression that although respecting patients' preferences is a fundamental goal of medicine, these preferences are vulnerable to manipulation and bias

✓ But they are too important to be abandoned by professional frustration

✓ Three questions dominated the debate:

1. Can patients take a leading role in making decisions?
2. Do they want to?
3. What if doctors and public health professionals don't like their choices?

In discussion of these:

✓ Decisions are complicated, and depend on patients' attitudes to risk

✓ Some patients prefer a very bad outcome put off into the future to a moderately bad outcome occurring now

✓ This is one of several reasons why patients' decisions are sometimes at odds with recommendations

✓ Cultural beliefs can have a profound influence on decisions regarding treatment, eg some SE Asian cultures consider that surgery results in perpetual imbalance, causing the person to be physically incomplete in the next incarnation

✓ May go some way to explain why fully informed, shared decision-making is so difficult to conduct in practice

✓ Yet communication with patients can be improved, including evidence-based approaches such as training doctors, coaching patients and using aids to decision-making.

✓ However, not all patients want to make their own decisions. In a study of 1012 women with breast cancer, 22% wanted to select their own treatment, 44% wanted to collaborate with their doctors in the decision and 34% wanted to delegate this responsibility to their doctors (*JAMA 1997; 277:1485–92*)

✓ Yet there is a desire for information that is nearly universal

✓ Concluded, 'Most patients want to see the road map, including alternative routes, even if they don't want to take over the wheel'

Non-Attendance

Non-attendance at general practices and outpatient clinics. Local systems are needed to address local problem
(*D. J. Sharp and W. Hamilton, BMJ 2001;323:1081–2*)

✓ This editorial looked at the problem of non-attendance, the ramifications and thoughts regarding solutions
✓ At times of increasing debate on rationing of resources, this topic tends to be increasingly mentioned in the medical press

In summary

✓ Non-attendance at NHS outpatient clinics and at general practices is more common in deprived populations
✓ The national figure of 12% for non-attendance at outpatient clinics in the United Kingdom hides large variations between specialties and between regions
✓ Studies report figures that range from 5% to 34%
✓ Much less research has been done on non-attendance in general practices, though figures of 3% and 6.5% have been reported
✓ The first figure comes from an unpublished doctor–patient partnership survey in 1998 and an unpublished survey of 500 non-attenders in Exeter. The higher figure is from a study of 221,000 appointments in practices in Sheffield
✓ The main associations with hospital non-attendance are reported as being male sex, youth, the length of waiting time for the appointment and deprivation
✓ Non-attendance in general practices are associated with youth and deprivation, but not sex
✓ Non-attenders are less likely to own a car or a telephone and are more likely to be unemployed

✓ Some non-attendance arises from an inability to cancel the appointment, either because the hospital's system for cancelling or changing appointments is poor or because the patient has no access to a telephone

✓ Non-attendance is not thought to be related to the severity of the patient's condition, except in the case of psychiatric illness where non-attendance may be a marker of severity of illness

✓ The commonest reasons cited for missing an appointment, after forgetting it, are family or work commitments

✓ Patients with lower paid jobs may have difficulty in getting time off work or arranging childcare

✓ These reasons also partly explain the peak age range of 20–30 years in non-attenders, as this is the usual age for raising a family

✓ The key seems to be to allow the patient to select a suitable time and date; indeed, such flexibility may largely explain the lower non-attendance rate in general practices, although evening surgeries and shorter time intervals to the appointment probably also contribute

✓ The strongest predictor of non-attendance is the time interval to the appointment; reducing non-attendance reduces waiting times, which further reduces non-attendance, creating a virtuous circle

✓ Increased consumerism in the NHS means that current systems are stale, at best

✓ No single solution will work across the NHS and in outpatient clinics as well as general practices

✓ Local trusts in primary and secondary care should be able to devise local systems to allow convenient access for their patients

✓ New systems should be the subject of research and development

✓ Non-attendance should fall if some of these measures are adopted, though it will never disappear – we are all human

Telephone Consultations

Paper

Telephone consultations to manage requests for same-day appointments: a randomised controlled trial in two practices

(*B. A. McKinstry, et al, Br J Gen Pract 2002;52:306–10*)

✓ GPs in the UK have recently begun to adopt the use of telephone consultation during daytime surgery as a means of managing demand, particularly requests for same-day appointments

✓ However, it is not known whether the strategy actually reduces GP workload

✓ The aim of the study was to investigate how the use of telephone consultations impacts on the management of requests for same-day appointments, on resource use, indicators of clinical care and patient perceptions of consultations

✓ It was an RCT of all patients (*n* = 388) seeking same-day appointments in each surgery in two urban practices (total population 10,420) over a four-week period

✓ The primary outcome measure was use of doctor time for the index telephone or face-to-face consultation

✓ Secondary outcomes were subsequent use of investigations and of services in the two-week period following consultation, frequency of blood pressure measurement and antibiotic prescriptions and number of problems considered at consultation

✓ Patient perceptions were measured by the Patient Enablement Instrument (PEI) and reported willingness to use telephone consultations in the future

✓ The results showed telephone consultations took less time (8.2 vs 6.7 minutes)

✓ Patients consulting by telephone re-consulted the GP more frequently in the two weeks that followed.

✓ Blood pressure was measured more often in the group of patients managed face-to-face (13.3% vs 6.6%)

✓ There was no significant difference in patient perceptions or other secondary outcomes

✓ They concluded that the use of telephone consultations for same-day appointments was associated with time-saving, and did not result in lower PEI scores

✓ Possibly, however, this short-term saving was offset by a higher re-consultation rate and less use of opportunistic health promotion

Consultation Models

During my registrar year, it seemed a trivial task to learn consultation models in order to pass the exam and show some knowledge when asked. However, I have come to realise that learning these models is one step closer to an increased awareness of how your consultations work, they are of benefit in predicting outcome and as times passes they become second nature.

My argument is that, despite the endless debate of increased paperwork taking time away from patient contact and increased managerial responsibilities, the core of your daily routine remains a one-to-one patient interaction. If this can be achieved more efficiently, with greater satisfaction for the patient and leads to less re-attendance, you would expect there to be an endless line of takers. However, that is not the case. The techniques are often forgotten shortly after the registrar year has ended, and rarely does one look back. As food for thought for those of you who remain free of too much cynicism, these models and their various facets do work in allowing less stressful and more fruitful consultations. They can help you with your stress levels and ultimately keep you going. Use them and experiment during the trainee year, and after if you are so inclined; everybody's style is different and you may find some facets too difficult or unproductive. Obviously you will concentrate on getting your video done, but this still allows tuning of your consultation. For those of you lucky few who were genuinely inspired by your trainer, remember it takes years of practice to make slick consultations look easy, but it is attainable – just enjoy getting there.

For those of you taking the exam, it is advisable to learn the models and some working clinical case models to illustrate certain points. This may be a question in your viva and certainly there is always an odd MCQ or two.

Biomedical Model

The classic medical diagnostic process

Observation:	history and examination
Hypothesis:	provisional diagnosis
Hypothesis testing:	investigations
Deduction:	definitive diagnosis

In essence, this is a hypotheticodeductive model but:

✓ Reductionist: Patient is regarded as a collection of signs, symptoms and diagnosis

✓ Doctor-centred; Patient's ideas, concerns and expectations ignored. Sharing information not important. Emphasis not placed on agreeing management plan.

✓ Agreeing management plan

✓ No progress can be made if no objective physical disorder is unearthed

✓ Omits use of doctor–patient relationship

Other models have been developed that are more holistic:

✓ Not competing, but complementary

✓ Several are often needed to give a broad understanding of something as complex as human interaction

Alternative Models

Byrne and Long Phase I

Phase I	The doctor establishes a relationship with the patient
Phase II	The doctor either attempts to discover or actually discovers the reason for the patient's attendance
Phase III	The doctor conducts a verbal or physical examination, or both
Phase IV	The doctor, or the doctor and the patient, or the patient (in that order of probability) consider the condition
Phase V	The doctor, and occasionally the patient, detail further treatment or further investigation
Phase VI	The consultation is terminated, usually by the doctor

Used the terms 'Doctor-centred' and 'Patient-centred'. This model was produced after analysing more than 2000 tape recordings of consultations.

Pendleton, Schofield, Tate and Havelock
Seven tasks:

1. To define the reason for the patient's attendance, including: the nature and history of the problems; their aetiology; the patients' ideas, concerns and expectations; the effects of the problems
2. To consider other problems: continuing problems and risk factors
3. With the patient, to choose an appropriate action for each problem
4. To achieve a shared understanding of the problems with the patient
5. To involve the patient in the management and encourage him to accept responsibility
6. To use time and resources appropriately: in the consultation and in the long term
7. To establish or maintain a relationship with the patient which helps to achieve the other tasks

Emphasises both the importance of the patient's view and understanding of the problem. Includes the term 'Consultation mapping.'

Stott and Davis

Management of presenting problems	Modification of help-seeking behaviour
Management of continuing problems	Opportunistic health promotion

Neighbour
The inner consultation

Connecting:	needs rapport-building skills
Summarising:	needs listening and eliciting skills to facilitate effective assessment
Hand over:	needs communicating skills to hand over responsibility for management
Safety netting:	needs predicting skills to suggest contingency plan for worst scenario
Housekeeping:	needs self-awareness to clear your mind of the psychological remains of one consultation so that it has no detrimental effect on the next (clearing your head)

Rosenstock, Becker and Maiman
Health beliefs' model
It shows the patient is more likely to accept advice, diagnosis or treatment if the doctor is aware of their ideas, concerns and expectations.

Patient's behaviour is determined by:

✓ Alarming symptoms

✓ Trigger factors such as advice from family and friends, messages from media

✓ Health motivation (interest in health)

✓ Perceived vulnerability to the condition

✓ Perceived seriousness of the condition

✓ Perceived balance of benefits of treatment against costs

✓ Belief that the doctor has/has not understood the patient's concerns

Heron
Six-category intervention model
Doctor can use any of six types of intervention:

1. Prescriptive: instructions; advice
2. Informative: explanations; interpretations; new knowledge
3. Confronting: feedback on behaviour; challenging but caring attitude
4. Cathartic: aiding release of emotions in form of anger, laughter, crying
5. Catalytic: encouraging patient to explore feelings, thoughts and behaviour
6. Supportive: bolstering self-worth

Berne
Transactional analysis ('games people play')

✓ Explores behaviour within relationships

✓ Identifies three 'ego-states':
- Parent: critical or caring
- Adult: logical
- Child: spontaneous or dependent

✓ Examines implications of, and reasons for, the different states

✓ Explores 'games' – useful for analysing why consultations repeatedly go wrong and encouraging doctors to break out of these unproductive cycles of behaviour

Balint

 The doctor, his patient and the illness (1957)
(*Balint. International University Press, Inc. New York 1957*)

The doctor–patient relationship is fundamental. Patients are more than broken machines, and doctors have feelings, which have a function in the consultation.

Proposed:
✓ Psychological problems are often manifested physically and even physical disease has its own psychological consequences which need particular attention
✓ Doctors have feelings and those feelings have a function in the consultation
✓ There needs to be specific training to produce limited but considerable change in the doctor's personality so that he or she can become more sensitive to the patient's thoughts during the consultation

The doctor must:
✓ Discover the patient's beliefs, concerns and expectations about the problem or problems presented
✓ Share his/her own understanding of the problems with the patient in terms that are understood by the patient
✓ Share the decision-making with the patient
✓ Encourage the patient to take appropriate responsibility for his/her own health

KEY CONCEPTS AND PHRASES:

1. The doctor as a drug
2. The child as the presenting complaint:
   Patient may offer another person (eg child) as the problem when there are underlying psychosocial problems
3. Elimination by appropriate physical examination
   May reinforce the patient's belief that neurotic symptoms are in fact due to physical illness
4. Collusion of anonymity:
   - Mistaken beliefs in the origin of symptoms are reinforced by examination
   - Responsibility of uncovering underlying problems becomes increasingly diluted by repeated referral
   - No-one takes responsibility
5. The mutual investment company:
   - Formed and managed by the doctor and the patient
   - 'Clinical illnesses' equal 'Offers' in a long relationship
   - 'Offers' of problems (physical and psychosocial) are presented to the doctor for his 'Acceptance'
6. The flash:
   - When the real reason of the 'Offer' (underlying psychosocial and neurotic illness) is suddenly apparent to both doctor and patient
   - Acts as a central point for change
   - Consultation can now deal with the underlying basic 'Fault'

Note
For the exam, think of clinical scenarios to illustrate each of the above and understand what is meant by each term.

Triaxial model
Address patient's problem in:
1. Physical terms
2. Psychological terms
3. Social terms

Tate's tasks

 From The Doctors' Communication Handbook

Involves the use of concepts featured in other models. Similar to those used to assess tasks in the summative assessment and MRCGP videos.

1. Discover the reasons for attendance:
   ✓ Listen to the patient's description of the symptom
   ✓ Obtain relevant social and occupational information
   ✓ Explore the patient's health understanding
   ✓ Enquire about other problems
   ✓ Obtain additional information about critical symptoms or other details
   ✓ Appropriate physical examination
   ✓ Make a working diagnosis

2. Define the clinical problem(s):
   ✓ Address the patient's problem(s)
   ✓ Assess the severity of the presenting problem
   ✓ Choose an appropriate form of management
   ✓ Involve the patient in the management plan to the appropriate extent

3. Explain the problem(s) to the patient:
   ✓ Share your findings with the patient
   ✓ Tailor the explanation to the needs of the patient
   ✓ Ensure that the explanation is understood and accepted by the patient

4. Make effective use of the consultation:
   ✓ Make efficient use of resources – time, investigations, other professionals, etc
   ✓ Establish an effective relationship with the patient

Glossary

ACE	angiotensin-converting enzyme; also Asthma Control and Expectations
ACEI	angiotensin-converting enzyme inhibitor
AD	Alzheimer's disease
ADAS-cog	Alzheimer's disease assessment scale – cognitive subscale
ADFAM National	National Charity for the Families and Friends of Drug Misusers
ADHD	attention deficit–hyperactive disorder
ADL	activities of daily living
AF	atrial fibrillation
AIDS	acquired immunodeficiency syndrome
AOM	acute otitis media
ARB	angiotensin-II receptor blocker
b	billion (1,000,000,000)
BHS	British Hypertension Society
BM	basal metabolism
BMA	British Medical Association
BMD	bone mineral density
BMI	body mass index
BP	blood pressure
BTS	Blood Transfusion Service
CAMS	Cannabis in Multiple Sclerosis [trial]
CARDS	Collaborative AtoRvastatin Diabetes Study
CARE	Cholesterol and Recurrent Events [study]
CBT	cognitive behaviour therapy
CFC	chlorofluorocarbon
CG	clinical governance
CHARM	Candesartan in Heart Failure Assessment of Reduction in Mortality and Morbidity
CHD	coronary heart disease
CHI	Commission for Health Improvement
CIBIS	Cardiac Insufficiency Bisoprolol Study
COAD	chronic obstructive airways disease
COCP	combined oral contraceptive pill
CONSENSUS	Cooperative North Scandinavian Enalapril Survival Study
COPD	Chronic Obstructive Pulmonary Disease
CPA	care programme approach
CPD	continuous professional development
CPR	cardiopulmonary resuscitation
CSM	Committee on Safety of Medicines
CT	computed tomography

CVA	cardiovascular accident
CVD	cardiovascular disease
DBP	diastolic blood pressure
DCCT	Diabetes Control and Complications Trial
DEXA	dual-energy X-ray absorptiometry
DGH	district general hospital
DNR	do not resuscitate
DoH	Department of Health
DPAS	Drug Prevention Advisory Service
DSPD	dangerous and severely personality-disordered
DTI	Department of Trade and Industry
DVLA	Driver and Vehicle Licencing Agency
DVT	deep vein thrombosis
EBM	evidence-based medicine
ELITE	Evaluation of Losartan in the Elderly [study]
ERA	Estrogen Replacement and Atherosclerosis [trial]
EU	European Union
GHQ	General Health Questionnaire
GMC	General Medical Council
GMS	General Medical Services
GP	general practitioner
GPC	General Practitioners' Committee
GUM	genitourinary medicine
HA	health authority
HDL	high-density lipoprotein
HDP	Hampshire Depression Project
HERS	Heart and Estrogen/Progestin Replacement Study
HIV	human immunodeficiency virus
HMP	Her Majesty's Prisons
HOPE	Healthcare Options Plan Entitlement
HOT	Hypertension Optimal Treatment [trial]
HRT	hormone replacement therapy
IC	independent contractor
IHD	ischaemic heart disease
INR	international normalised ratio
ISDD	Institute for the Study of Drug Dependence
IUCD	intrauterine contraceptive device
LCR	ligase chain reaction
LDL	low-density lipoprotein
LIFE	Lorsartan Intervention For Endpoint [reduction in hypertension]
LIFT	Local Improvement Finance Trust
LIPID	Long-term Intervention with Pravastatin in Ischaemic Disease
LRTI	lower respiratory tract illness
LSP	local strategic partnerships
LVH	left ventricular hypertrophy

m	million
MDU	Medical Defence Union
MERIT-HF	Metoprolol CR/XL Randomised Intervention Trial in Congestive Heart Failure
MI	myocardial infarction
MMR	measles, mumps and rubella
MMSE	Mini-Mental State Examination
MMT	methodone maintenance treatment
MND	motor neurone disease
MS	multiple sclerosis
NA	Narcotics Anonymous
NASS	National Asylum Support Service
NCAA	National Clinical Assessment Authority
NeLH	The National electronic Library for Health
NIA	Nationality, Immigration and Asylum Act
NICE	National Institute for Clinical Excellence
NNT	number needed to treat
NRT	nicotine replacement therapy
NSF	National Service Framework
OA	osteoarthritis
OGTT	oral glucose tolerance test
PALS	Patient Advocacy and Liaison Service
PCG	primary care group
PCT	primary care trust
PD	Parkinson's Disease
PPDPs	Practice and Personal Development Plan
PE	pulmonary embolism
PEI	Patient Enablement Instrument
PFI	Private Financial Initiatives
PHCT	primary healthcare team
PMS	personal medical services
PROGRESS	Peridopril pROtection aGainst REcurrent Stroke Study
ProtecT	Prostate testing for cancer and Treatment
PSA	prostate-specific antigen
PTH	parathyroid hormone
RALES	Randomized Aldactone Evaluation Study
RCGP	Royal College of General Practioners
RCN	Royal College of Nursing
RCOG	Royal College of Obstetricians and Gynaecologists
RCP	Royal College of Physicians
RCPsych	Royal College of Psychiatrists
RCT	randomised controlled trials
RESOLVD	Randomised Evaluation of Strategies for Left Ventricular Dysfunction
SBP	systolic blood pressure
SERMs	selective oestrogen-receptor modulators
SMAC	Standing Medical Advisory Committee

SMAS	Substance Misuse Advisory Service
SPAF	Stroke Prevention in Atrial Fibrillation [trial]
SSRI	selective serotonin-reuptake inhibitors
STD	sexually transmitted disease
STI	sexually transmitted infection
STOP	Swedish Trial in Old Patients
STORM	Sibutramine Trial of Obesity Reduction and Maintenance
TACADE	The Advisory Council on Alcohol and Drug Education
TC	total cholesterol
TCA	tricyclic antidepressant
TIA	transient ischaemic attack
tPA	tissue plasminogen activator
UKPDS	UK Prospective Diabetes Study
ValHeFT	Valsartan Heart Failure Trial
VERT	Vertebral Efficiacy with Risedronate Therapy [trial]
VTE	venous thromboembolism
WHI	Women's Health Initiative [study]
WHO	World Health Organisation
WISDOM	Women's International Study of long Duration Oestrogen after Menopause
WOSCOPS	West of Scotland Coronary Prevention Study

Journals referenced in this book

Am J Cardiol	American Journal of Cardiology
Ann Int Med	Annals of Internal Medicine
Ann Rheum Dis	Annals of Rheumatic Diseases
Arch Dis Child	Archives of Disease in Childhood
Arch Neurol	Archives of Neurology
Asthma	Asthma
BJGP	British Journal of General Practice
BJU Int	BJU (British Journal of Urology) International
BMJ	British Medical Journal
Br J Clin Pharmacol	British Journal of Clinical Pharmacology
Br J Ophthalmol	British Journal of Ophthalmology
Can Med Assoc J	Canadian Medical Association Journal
Circulation	Circulation
Clin Evid	Clinical Evidence
Diabet Med	Diabetes Medicine
Diabetes	Diabetes
Drug Ther Bull	Drug and Therapeutics Bulletin
Eur Heart J	European Heart Journal
Gut	Gut
Heart	Heart
Int J Clin Pract	International Journal of Clinical Practice
J Card Fail	Journal of Cardiac Failure
J Clin Epidemiol	Journal of Clinical Epidemiology
J Consult Clin Psychol	Journal of Consulting and Clinical Psychology
J Fam Pract	Journal of Family Practice
J Hum Hypertens	Journal of Human Hypertension
J Natl Cancer Inst	Journal of the National Cancer Institute
J Public Health Med	Journal of Public Health Medicine
JAMA	Journal of the American Medical Association
Lancet	Lancet
N Engl J Med	New England Journal of Medicine
Osteoporos Rev	Osteoporosis Review
Sex Transm Inf	Sexually Transmitted Infections
Stroke	Stroke
Thorax	Thorax
Tob Control	Tobacco Control
Vaccine	Vaccine

Index